BIRDS OF THE
WEST INDIES

Text and illustrations by Norman Arlott

Collins

I would like to dedicate this book to my
mother Eva and my late father Arthur.

HarperCollins Publishers Ltd
77–85 Fulham Palace Road
Hammersmith
London W6 8JB

The Collins website address is:
www.collins.co.uk

Collins is a registered trademark of
HarperCollins Publishers Ltd

First published 2010

15 14 13 12 11 10

10 9 8 7 6 5 4 3 2 1

A catalogue record for this book is available from the British Library.

ISBN 978-0-00-727718-6

Edited and designed by D & N Publishing, Baydon, Wiltshire

Reproduction by Dot Gradations
Printed and bound by Printing Express, Hong Kong

CONTENTS

Acknowledgements   6
Introduction   6
Area and Species Covered   6
Nomenclature   8
Identification   8
Bird Topography   9

Species Descriptions and Colour Plates
1   Albatross, Fulmar, Petrels and Shearwaters   10
2   Shearwaters and Storm-petrels   12
3   Frigatebirds, Tropicbirds, Boobies and Gannet   14
4   Pelicans, Cormorants and Anhinga   16
5   Bitterns, Green Herons and Night Herons   18
6   Herons and Egrets   20
7   Egrets, Roseate Spoonbill and Flamingo   22
8   Storks, Ibises, Sandhill Crane and Limpkin   24
9   Divers, Grebes and Whistling-ducks   26
10 Tundra Swan and Geese   28
11 Ducks   30
12 Ducks   32
13 Ducks   34
14 Vultures, Bald Eagle, Osprey, Caracara, Swallow-tailed
    Kite and Hen Harrier   36
15 Kites and Hawks   38
16 Hawks and Falcons   40
17 Peafowl, Pheasant, Guineafowl, Junglefowl, Bobwhites
    and Chachalaca   42
18 Rails and Crakes   44
19 Rails, Moorhen, Gallinules and Coots   46
20 Jacana, Pratincole, Thick-knee, Snipe, Turnstone and
    Phalaropes   48
21 Oystercatcher, Stilt, Avocet, Plovers and Sandpipers   50
22 Plovers   52
23 Willet, Shanks, Yellowlegs, and *Tringa* and *Actitis*
    Sandpipers   54
24 Ruff, Upland Sandpiper, Curlews and Whimbrel   56
25 Dowitchers, Godwits, Sanderling and Knot   58
26 *Calidris* Sandpipers   60
27 Skuas   62
28 Gulls   64

29	Gulls	66
30	Terns	68
31	Terns, Noddies, Skimmers and Auks	70
32	Rock Dove, Pigeons and Quail-doves	72
33	Doves and Common Ground-dove	74
34	Parrotlet, Budgerigar and Parakeets	76
35	Parakeets and Parrots	78
36	Parrots	80
37	Smooth-billed Ani and Cuckoos	82
38	Lizard-cuckoos and Cuckoos	84
39	Owls	86
40	Potoo, Nighthawks and Nightjars	88
41	Swifts	90
42	Hummingbirds	92
43	Hummingbirds	94
44	Trogons, Todies and Kingfishers	96
45	Piculet and Woodpeckers	98
46	Sapsucker, Woodpeckers and Flickers	100
47	Tyrant Flycatchers	102
48	Tyrant Flycatchers and Jamaican Becard	104
49	Tyrant Flycatchers	106
50	Tyrant Flycatchers	108
51	Swallows	110
52	Martins and Northern Rough-winged Swallow	112
53	Crows	114
54	Nuthatch, Wrens, Ruby-crowned Kinglet, Gnatcatchers, Wheatear and Bluebird	116
55	Solitaires and Thrushes	118
56	Thrushes	120
57	Catbird, Mockingbirds and Thrashers	122
58	Tremblers, Pipits, Shrike, Waxwing, Palmchat, Starling and Myna	124
59	Vireos	126
60	Vireos	128
61	American Warblers	130
62	American Warblers	132
63	American Warblers	134
64	American Warblers	136
65	American Warblers	138
66	American Warblers	140
67	American Warblers	142
68	Bananaquit, Honeycreeper, Euphonias, Tanagers and Spindalis	144

69 Tanagers, Palm-tanagers and Chat-tanagers 146
70 Cardinal, Saltator, Grosbeaks, Buntings and House Sparrow 148
71 Orangequit, Seedeater, Grassquits and Dickcissel 150
72 Bullfinches, Finches, Zapata Sparrow and Towee 152
73 Dark-eyed Junco and American Sparrows 154
74 American Sparrows, Snow Bunting and Bobolink 156
75 Meadowlark and American Blackbirds 158
76 American Blackbirds, Cowbirds and Grackles 160
77 American Orioles 162
78 American Orioles 164
79 Crossbill, Redpoll, Siskins, American Goldfinch, Canary, Weaver and Bishops 166
80 Waxbills, Whydah and Seedfinch 168

Species Distribution Maps 170
Further Reading 233
Index 234

ACKNOWLEDGEMENTS

Bird books take a relatively short time to paint and write, but the knowledge that enables them to be completed is gained over many, many years. I well remember that my passion started as a very young boy bird nesting (now, quite rightly, frowned upon) with my father. That passion has since been enhanced by being fortunate enough to be in the field with and inspired by some well known and not so well known 'birders'. I must mention the following who have encouraged me and allowed me to pick their brains over the years: the late John G. Williams; the late Eric Hosking; the late Crispin Fisher; Robert Gillmor; the late Basil Parsons; Brian Leflay; and Moss Taylor. This book could not have gone ahead without the help of the staff at the British Museum at Tring, especially Mark Adams and Robert Prŷs-Jones. The maps were prepared by Shane O'Dwyer. David Price-Goodfellow deserves special praise for his skill, and patience, in putting together the various component parts of this book. Without publishers there would not be a book, so it gives me great pleasure to thank everyone at HarperCollins, particularly Myles Archibald and Julia Koppitz. Lastly, but definitely not least, I must thank friends and family who have had to put up with my various mood changes whilst trying to sort out some of the more difficult aspects of putting this book together, my wife Marie probably enduring more than most.

INTRODUCTION

I had long realised that the West Indies needed a 'pocket' book that included all the species of the region, having had a passion for the West Indies and its birds for many years, so much so that my wife and I spent our twenty-fifth wedding anniversary cruising around many of the islands. So when I was approached to produce such a book, I naturally jumped at the chance.

The format of this book follows that of my Palearctic volumes, hence I knew I did not have the space to produce the ultimate field guide, but I could make it a little bit more than just a coloured checklist. My vision was for this book to be a reminder of birds seen as well as a helpful nudge towards what to look for when searching for new birds. Most of the text in this book is based on the type of notes I make before embarking on a field trip to a new area. Hopefully, along with the illustrations, they will help to identify most birds encountered. Obviously the use of more in-depth tomes will be required for some of the trickier species (*see* Further Reading).

Hopefully, within these pages I have been able to add to the pleasure of anticipation or memory, and perhaps even added some extra piece of knowledge about the birds of this beautiful region.

AREA AND SPECIES COVERED

Three major island groupings, the Bahamas, the Greater Antilles and the Lesser Antilles plus San Andrés and Providencia, make up the area covered in this book. I have included the Cayman Islands in the Greater Antilles and the Virgin Islands in the Lesser Antilles, the latter because of their inclusion in the Leeward Islands, one of two groups, the other being the Windward Islands, that historically make up the Lesser Antilles.

Every species recorded in the region, and many of the major subspecies, have been depicted in breeding plumage, and non-breeding plumage when it differs significantly. To keep the

OPPOSITE: Map of the West Indies. The pale sea indicates the area covered by this book.

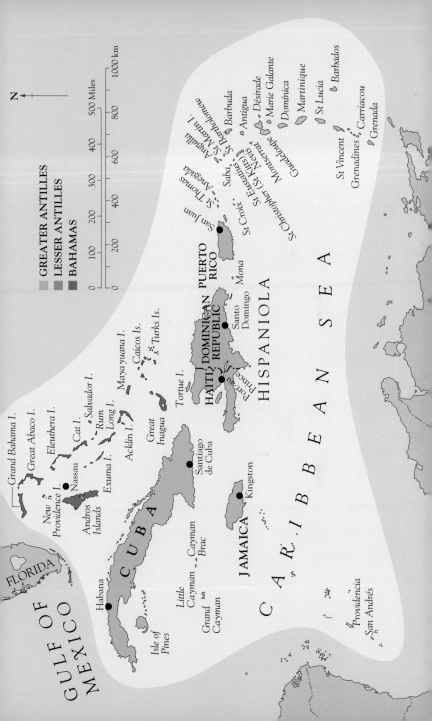

book to a manageable size no juvenile plumages have been illustrated, although, when thought necessary and room permits, a short passage in 'Field Notes' has been included.

I have needed to tweak the established order in some places in order to aid plate composition; hopefully this will not cause too much aggravation.

The abbreviations and symbols used on the plates are as follows:

♂ = Male.
♀ = Female.
br = Breeding.
n-br = Non-breeding.
nom = Nominate race.

NOMENCLATURE

I have headlined the English names that I believe are those used by most birders in the field, which means I have, in many cases, reverted to 'old school' names rather than some of the more modern interpretations (most of these 'new' names, along with other well-used names, are included in parentheses).

IDENTIFICATION

It is hoped that the illustrations will be all that is needed to identify a specific bird, but quite obviously with some of the trickier species more information is needed, hence the need for Field Notes, Voice and Habitat.

FIELD NOTES: Because of the need to keep text to a minimum this section rarely mentions those aspects of a bird that should be obvious from the illustrations, e.g. wing bars, bill shape etc. It is used mainly to point to a bird's habits or to mention facets of identification that are hidden in a standing or perched bird.

VOICE: Probably the first sign of a bird's presence. The descriptions are shown in *italics*. Where space has allowed I have included different interpretations of the same song. Although difficult to produce an accurate reproduction of bird songs or calls in the written word, this section is worth studying in order to get a feel for what is often the most important area of bird identification.

HABITAT: The main habitat preferences mentioned are those in which a species breeds; also included are wintering habitats if appropriate.

DISTRIBUTION: Mainly general, so should be read in conjunction with the maps.

BIRD TOPOGRAPHY

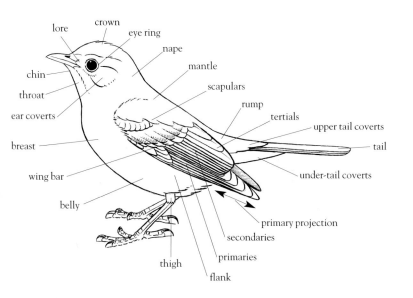

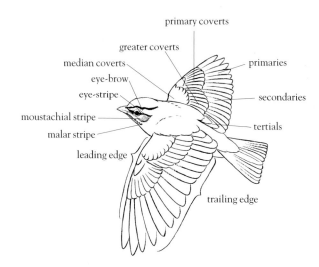

1 ALBATROSS, FULMAR, PETRELS AND SHEARWATERS

1 BLACK-BROWED ALBATROSS (BLACK-BROWED MOLLYMAWK) *Thalassarche melanophus* 80–95cm FIELD NOTES: Juvenile has a grey bill with a dark tip, also a greyish breast band and dark underwing with a hint of a pale central strip. VOICE: Usually silent. HABITAT: Maritime. DISTRIBUTION: Vagrant, recorded from Martinique.

2 FULMAR (NORTHERN FULMAR) *Fulmarus glacialis* 45–50cm FIELD NOTES: Intermediate forms occur. Flies with stiffer, bowed wings than gulls. VOICE: Guttural cackling, varying in speed. HABITAT: Maritime. DISTRIBUTION: Vagrant, recorded from the Virgin Islands, New Providence and the Bahamas.

3 BULWER'S PETREL *Bulweria bulwerii* 26–28cm FIELD NOTES: Usually flies low over water in an erratic buoyant manner. Tail wedge-shaped when fanned. VOICE: Generally silent away from breeding grounds. HABITAT: Maritime. DISTRIBUTION: Vagrant, recorded from Barbados.

4 CORY'S SHEARWATER *Calonectris diomedea* 46–53cm FIELD NOTES: Flight can appear lazy although is actually quite fast. Often follows ships. VOICE: Usually silent away from northern breeding grounds. HABITAT: Maritime. DISTRIBUTION: Migrants occur, at sea, off most islands, mainly in spring.

5 JAMAICAN PETREL *Pterodroma caribbaea* 35–46cm FIELD NOTES: Probably extinct. 'Gadfly' flight typical of the genus – beating wings to gain height followed by long glides and wide banking arcs. VOICE: Probably much as Black-capped Petrel. HABITAT: Bred at high elevations in the Blue Mountains, otherwise maritime. DISTRIBUTION: Jamaican endemic.

6 BLACK-CAPPED PETREL (DIABLOTIN, CAPPED PETREL) *Pterodroma hasitata* 35–46cm FIELD NOTES: Some individuals show a much reduced white collar. Typical 'gadfly' flight, *see* above. Only comes to breeding areas at night. VOICE: At breeding grounds repeatedly utters a drawn out *aaa-aw eek* or *ooow eek*; also a hurt, puppy-like yelp. HABITAT: Mountain cliffs during breeding, post breeding maritime. DISTRIBUTION: From November to May breeds on Haiti and the Dominican Republic, otherwise widely dispersed in deep sea areas.

7 BERMUDA PETREL (CAHOW) *Pterodroma cahow* 38cm FIELD NOTES: Actions typical of the genus. VOICE: At sea generally silent. HABITAT: Maritime. DISTRIBUTION: Vagrant, recorded from the Bahamas.

8 HERALD PETREL (TRINIDADE PETREL) *Pterodroma arminjoniana* 35–39cm FIELD NOTES: Much individual variation in the three main colour morphs. Flight typical 'gadfly', *see* under Jamaican Petrel. Occasionally follows ships. VOICE: Generally silent. HABITAT: Maritime. DISTRIBUTION: Vagrant, recorded from Puerto Rico.

Note: Black-browed Albatross depicted at a smaller scale.

dark

light

2

light

3

1

light

4

5

6

7

8

light

intermediate

8

8

dark

2 SHEARWATERS AND STORM-PETRELS

1 MANX SHEARWATER *Puffinus puffinus* 30–38cm FIELD NOTES: White under-tail coverts. Rapid wing-beats followed by a low, swinging (side to side) glide. Often scavenges around fishing boats. Gregarious. VOICE: Generally silent while at sea. HABITAT: Maritime. DISTRIBUTION: Migrants occur, mainly from November to March, well offshore.

2 AUDUBON'S SHEARWATER *Puffinus lherminieri* 27–33cm FIELD NOTES: Dark under-tail coverts. Fluttering wing-beats followed by short, low glides. Often gregarious. VOICE: At night utters cat-like cries around breeding grounds, from underground burrows gives a distinctive, loud *pimleco*. HABITAT: Breeds in burrows, under rocks, cliff crevices etc., usually from March to July. Post breeding maritime, generally well offshore. DISTRIBUTION: Breeds on the Bahamas and locally on other West Indian islands. Post breeding widely distributed around the Caribbean.

3 NORTH ATLANTIC LITTLE SHEARWATER *Puffinus baroli* 25–30cm FIELD NOTES: Fast, shallow wing-beats followed by a short, low glide, also a fluttering flight close to sea surface. VOICE: Generally silent. HABITAT: Maritime. DISTRIBUTION: Vagrant, recorded from Puerto Rico.

4 GREAT SHEARWATER (GREATER SHEARWATER) *Puffinus gravis* 43–51cm FIELD NOTES: Fast, strong wing-beats followed by long glides on stiff, straight wings. VOICE: Generally silent, although feeding parties often utter a lamb-like bleating. HABITAT: Maritime. DISTRIBUTION: Non-breeding resident mainly from May to July.

5 SOOTY SHEARWATER *Puffinus griseus* 40–46cm FIELD NOTES: Quick wing-beats followed by a long glide. Occasionally occurs in loose flocks. VOICE: Generally silent, although when in a feeding party may utter a high, nasal *aaaa*. HABITAT: Maritime. DISTRIBUTION: Widespread migrant, mainly from May to July.

6 WILSON'S STORM-PETREL *Oceanites oceanicus* 15–19cm FIELD NOTES: Yellow webs between toes, noticeable only at short range. Often dangles feet and 'dances' on sea surface when feeding. Attracted to the wake of boats. VOICE: Occasionally utters a rapid chattering while feeding. HABITAT: Maritime. DISTRIBUTION: Mainly an uncommon non-breeding resident, especially in May and June.

7 LEACH'S STORM-PETREL (LEACH'S PETREL) *Oceanodroma leucorhoa* 19–22cm FIELD NOTES: Feeds erratically with bounding flight then hovering, with shallow wing-beats, often with foot pattering, to seize food from sea surface. Not attracted to boats. VOICE: Generally silent. HABITAT: Maritime. DISTRIBUTION: Uncommon non-breeding resident, mainly from November to June.

8 MADEIRAN STORM-PETREL (HARCOURT'S or BAND-RUMPED STORM-PETREL) *Oceanodroma castro* 19–21cm FIELD NOTES: Methodical search for food, even flight with glides, hovers, usually without foot pattering, to take food from sea surface. VOICE: Usually silent. HABITAT: Maritime. DISTRIBUTION: Recorded off Cuba and Antigua but probably to be found off most West Indian islands.

3 FRIGATEBIRDS, TROPICBIRDS, BOOBIES AND GANNET

1 MAGNIFICENT FRIGATEBIRD *Fregata magnificens* 95–110cm FIELD NOTES: Juvenile all dark with white head and breast. Scavenges around boats and aggressively pursues other seabirds in an effort to steal their fish prey. At breeding sites inflates red gular pouch. VOICE: At breeding grounds rattling and drumming sounds made by vibrating and snapping bill. Generally silent at sea. HABITAT: Breeds colonially, from August to April, usually on small cays and islets, among trees, bushes or rocks. Outside of breeding season spends much time at sea, usually in sight of land, soaring, often at some height. Roosts among mangroves or other trees. DISTRIBUTION: Throughout West Indies.

2 WHITE-TAILED TROPICBIRD *Phaethon lepturus* 70–82cm FIELD NOTES: Juvenile lacks long tail streamers, has yellowish bill and coarse, dark barring on back. Flight pigeon-like, fluttering wing-beats followed by long glides. Feeds by hovering then plunge-diving on half-closed wings. VOICE: A squeaky *chip-chip-chip....* HABITAT: Breeds, mainly March to July, in crevices on steep sea cliffs, otherwise maritime. DISTRIBUTION: Locally common on Bahamas, Cayman Islands and Greater Antilles.

3 RED-BILLED TROPICBIRD *Phaethon aethereus* 90–105cm FIELD NOTES: Juvenile lacks long tail streamers, has yellowish bill, black nape collar and fine dark barring on back. Flight and feeding actions similar to White-tailed Tropicbird. VOICE: A shrill, rasping *kee-arrr*. HABITAT: Breeds, mainly January to June, in crevices on steep sea cliffs, otherwise maritime. DISTRIBUTION: Common on Virgin Islands, local off Puerto Rico and the Lesser Antilles, a vagrant elsewhere.

4 BROWN BOOBY *Sula leucogaster* 64–74cm FIELD NOTES: Juvenile has white parts tinged brown, bill greyish. Feeds by plunge-diving at an angle, not vertical like Gannet. Often gregarious. Attracted to ships. VOICE: At breeding sites male utters high-pitched whistles while female gives grunts and honks. HABITAT: Breeds, usually from March to June, on remote islands or inaccessible sea cliffs, otherwise frequents coastal areas or well out to sea. DISTRIBUTION: Widespread resident.

5 RED-FOOTED BOOBY *Sula sula* 66–77cm FIELD NOTES: Juvenile greyish brown with dull yellow legs. Actions similar to Brown Booby. VOICE: A harsh squawk, also a guttural *ga-ga-ga-ga....* HABITAT: Breeds, mainly from April to June, and roosts on bushes or trees on remote islands, otherwise open sea and less so offshore. DISTRIBUTION: Widespread but local resident.

6 MASKED BOOBY (WHITE or BLUE-FACED BOOBY) *Sula dactylatra* 81–92cm FIELD NOTES: Juvenile very similar to adult Brown Booby but mantle paler with a white collar on hind-neck and brown of head not extending to upper breast. Plunge-dives are usually more vertical than other Boobies. VOICE: Male utters a wheezy or piping whistle, female gives a loud honking or braying. HABITAT: Breeds, mainly from March to May, on flat areas on cliff edges, otherwise well out at sea. DISTRIBUTION: Rare, local resident.

7 GANNET (NORTHERN GANNET) *Morus bassanus* 87–100cm FIELD NOTES: Young birds go through various stages before attaining adult plumage, starting generally brown, sprinkled with white spots, to mainly white with brown blotches on back and wings. Feeds by vertical plunge-diving, often from as high as 30m. VOICE: Generally silent while at sea. HABITAT: Usually maritime. DISTRIBUTION: Vagrant, recorded from the Bahamas and Cuba.

1

2

3

♀

♂

5

5
light
phase

5
brown phase

7

6

7

4

5

6

7

light phase

4 PELICANS, CORMORANTS AND ANHINGA

1 AMERICAN WHITE PELICAN *Pelecanus erythrorhynchos* 125–175cm FIELD NOTES: Does not dive to catch food, feeds by dipping bill into water while swimming. Juvenile has greyish bill and brownish-grey mottled wing coverts. VOICE: Generally silent. HABITAT: Lakes, coastal bays and inlets. DISTRIBUTION: Mainly a vagrant. Rare non-breeding resident on Cuba and Puerto Rico.

2 BROWN PELICAN *Pelecanus occidentalis* 105–150cm FIELD NOTES: Feeds by plunge-diving, when twists with open wings before entering the water; can look quite dramatic. Gregarious, often seen flying in long lines, low over the water. Juvenile brownish-grey above, dingy brown neck and dirty-white underparts. Bill grey. VOICE: Generally silent. HABITAT: Coastal bays, lagoons and occasionally on inland lakes. Breeds, at any time of year, on offshore cays. DISTRIBUTION: Resident in Greater Antilles and southern Bahamas, less common elsewhere.

3 DOUBLE-CRESTED CORMORANT *Phalacrocorax auritus* 74–91cm FIELD NOTES: Compared to Neotropic Cormorant, tail is relatively short, usually more noticeable in flight. Often perches with wings held open to dry waterlogged feathers. Juvenile dark brownish above, dull brown below with paler greyish-white throat, foreneck and upper breast. VOICE: Hoarse grunts and a clear *yaaa yaa ya*. Away from breeding sites usually silent. HABITAT: Sheltered coastal areas also on inland lakes. Breeds colonially, mainly April to June, most often among coastal mangroves. DISTRIBUTION: Resident, breeds on Cuba and parts of the Bahamas, otherwise uncommon in rest of the area.

4 NEOTROPIC CORMORANT (OLIVACEOUS CORMORANT) *Phalacrocorax brasilianus* 63–69cm FIELD NOTES: Longer tailed than Double-crested Cormorant, showing especially in flight. Often perches with wings open to dry waterlogged feathers. Juvenile generally brown, darker above. VOICE: At breeding sites utters grunts and croaks, otherwise usually silent. HABITAT: Inland and coastal waters. Generally found more often on freshwater than Double-crested Cormorant. Breeds colonially, mainly May to June, in trees and bushes near water. DISTRIBUTION: Resident, breeds on Cuba and parts of the Bahamas, mainly a vagrant elsewhere.

5 ANHINGA (AMERICAN DARTER) *Anhinga anhinga* 81–91cm FIELD NOTES: Breeds colonially, often with cormorants, herons and ibises. Often swims with only neck protruding from water. Regularly perches, cormorant-like, with wings open to dry feathers. Juvenile similar to female but browner with less white markings on wing coverts. VOICE: A distinct, rapid, series of clicking notes and guttural grunts. HABITAT: Still, shallow waters including lakes, estuaries and sheltered coastal areas. Breeds, from April to July, in trees or bushes usually above or near water. DISTRIBUTION: Resident on Cuba, a vagrant elsewhere.

5 BITTERNS, GREEN HERONS AND NIGHT HERONS

1 AMERICAN BITTERN (NORTH AMERICAN BITTERN) *Botaurus lentiginosus* 60–85cm FIELD NOTES: Mainly terrestrial. Very secretive. Plumage tone variable, from warm cinnamon-brown to grey-brown. Juvenile lacks black neck patches. VOICE: A deep, far-carrying *oonk-a-loonk*, which is unlikely to be heard in the West Indies. When flushed may utter a rapid, guttural *kok-kok-kok*. HABITAT: Vegetation in and around swamps and marshes. DISTRIBUTION: A non-breeding visitor, mainly October to March, to many parts of the West Indies. Probably under recorded.

2 LEAST BITTERN *Ixobrychus exilis* 28–36cm FIELD NOTES: Skulking, solitary and crepuscular. Often sits motionless. If surprised tends to run through thick vegetation rather than fly; if forced to take flight, rarely does so for more than 25m. Juvenile much as adult female, but duller with dusky streaks on lesser wing-coverts. VOICE: Advertises with a muted, cooing *koo-koo-koo-koo* and at other times utters a chattering *chick-chick-chick-chick*. When alarmed, gives a harsh '*kok*'. HABITAT: Dense vegetation in and around swamps, also among mangroves, breeding, often among dense cattails, from May to August. DISTRIBUTION: Common resident on Cuba, Jamaica, Puerto Rico and the Cayman Islands; less common to rare on other islands of the Greater Antilles and the Bahamas; very rare or a vagrant, recorded from Barbados, in the Lesser Antilles.

3 LITTLE BITTERN *Ixobrychus minutus* 33–38cm FIELD NOTES: Secretive, generally more active at dusk. Actions similar to Least Bittern but probably more often seen in flight, a flight that is quite rapid with clipped wing-beats. Juvenile overall buff-brown with dark streaking above and below. VOICE: When flushed gives a low *quer* or *ker-ak*. The muffled, far-carrying *hoogh*, used when advertising is unlikely to be heard in the West Indies. HABITAT: Dense vegetation of lakes and swamps. DISTRIBUTION: Vagrant, recorded from Barbados.

4 GREEN HERON *Butorides virescens* 40–48cm FIELD NOTES: Often stands, crouched, motionless, watching for prey. Juvenile duller with dark streaks on neck, breast and flanks. White spots on tips of upperwing coverts. On Cuba there is a rare erythristic (reddish) phase. VOICE: When nervous utters a series of knocking *kuk-kuk-kuk…* notes. When flushed delivers a squawking *skyeow*. HABITAT: Waters edge of virtually any wetland area. DISTRIBUTION: Widespread year-round resident.

5 GREEN-BACKED HERON (STRIATED HERON) *Butorides striatus* 40–48cm FIELD NOTES: Actions as Green Heron. Juvenile brownish grey with pale spots on upperwing coverts and dark streaking on neck and underparts. VOICE: When alarmed utters a harsh *kyah*. HABITAT: Similar to Green Heron. DISTRIBUTION: Vagrant recorded from St Vincent.

6 YELLOW-CROWNED NIGHT-HERON *Nyctanassa violacea* 56–70cm FIELD NOTES: Nocturnal, but will venture out at other times. Juvenile generally brown, with pale spotted wings and pale streaks on neck and underparts. VOICE: A squawking *kowk* or *kaow*. HABITAT: Mangrove swamps, mudflats on coast or lakes, sometimes dry areas away from water. Breeds, from March to July, in trees, not necessarily near water. DISTRIBUTION: Common resident on the Bahamas, Greater Antilles and northern Lesser Antilles, less common or rare in rest of the Lesser Antilles.

7 NIGHT HERON (BLACK-CROWNED NIGHT-HERON) *Nycticorax nycticorax* 58–65cm FIELD NOTES: Crepuscular. Juvenile generally brown with heavily spotted wings and pale streaks on neck and underparts. VOICE: A barking *quok* or *quark*. HABITAT: Freshwater swamps, brackish lagoons and salt ponds. Breeds colonially, from January to July, in trees. DISTRIBUTION: Local resident on the Bahamas, Greater Antilles and the northern Lesser Antilles (Virgin Islands), less common or rare in the rest of the Lesser Antilles.

6 HERONS AND EGRETS

1 GREAT BLUE HERON *Ardea herodias* 110–125cm FIELD NOTES: Often stands motionless, or walks stealthily when in search of prey. The white morph (fig1b) is very rare, differs from Great White Egret (Plate 7) by yellowish legs. Flies with head retracted. Juvenile has brownish-black crown, greyish neck, brownish-grey mantle and rufous thighs and wing coverts. VOICE: A croaking *guarr guarr guarr* and in flight, a deep *fraaaahnk*. HABITAT: Freshwater and saltwater areas. Breeds in tall swamp trees, mainly from March to July. DISTRIBUTION: Has bred on Cuba and the Virgin Islands, otherwise a non-breeding resident on the Bahamas, Greater Antilles and northern Lesser Antilles, less common in southern Lesser Antilles.

2 HERON (GREY HERON) *Ardea cinerea* 90–98cm FIELD NOTES: Actions similar to Great Blue Heron. Juvenile has crown dull black, grey mantle and white thighs. VOICE: In flight, gives a harsh *framk*. HABITAT: Freshwater and saltwater areas. DISTRIBUTION: Vagrant, recorded from Montserrat, Martinique and Barbados.

3 LITTLE BLUE HERON *Egretta caerulea* 61–64cm FIELD NOTES: Stealthy foraging action. Flies with head retracted. Juvenile white, very similar to 'white egrets' but usually has dusky tips to primaries and yellowish-green legs and feet. First-winter birds have wings and back blotched with dusky feathers. VOICE: A harsh *gerr*, usually given in flight. HABITAT: Lakes, marshes, estuaries, coastal pools and inlets. DISTRIBUTION: Widespread non-breeding resident.

4 TRICOLOURED HERON (LOUISIANA HERON) *Egretta tricolor* 63–68cm FIELD NOTES: Forages in an active, dashing fashion. Flies with head retracted. Juvenile has rufous neck, with a white foreneck stripe, and a rufous tinge to back and wings. VOICE: A nasal croak, usually given when disturbed. HABITAT: Coastal marshes and mangroves, less common on freshwater lakes and marshes. Breeds in trees, from April to July, often with other heron species. DISTRIBUTION: Common resident in the Bahamas, Greater Antilles and northern Lesser Antilles, otherwise uncommon or rare elsewhere.

5 REDDISH EGRET *Egretta rufescens* 69–81cm FIELD NOTES: Animated foraging actions, often with wings held open. Flies with head retracted. Non-breeding white morph has greyish bill and dark lores. Juvenile of dark morph has neck and back tinged 'chalky', bill plain grey. VOICE: A short grunt or soft groan. HABITAT: Mainly sheltered, shallow coastal waters. DISTRIBUTION: Resident on the Bahamas and Cuba, otherwise local and uncommon on the Greater Antilles and a vagrant in the Lesser Antilles.

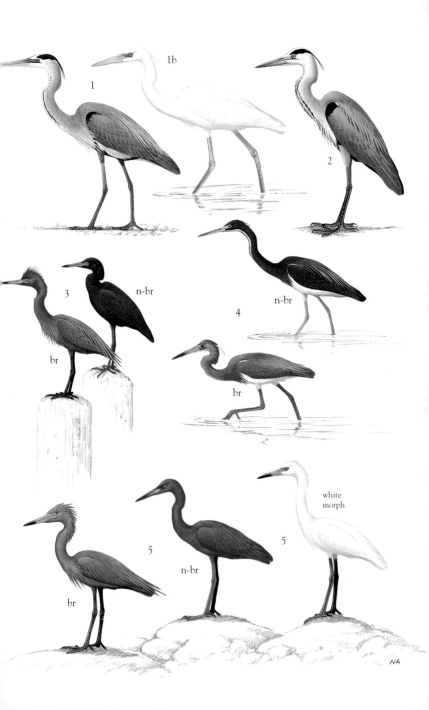

1

1b

2

3

n-br

br

4

n-br

br

5

n-br

5

white
morph

br

NA

7 EGRETS, ROSEATE SPOONBILL AND FLAMINGO

1 GREAT WHITE EGRET (GREAT EGRET) *Ardea alba* 85–102cm FIELD NOTES: Walks stealthily with neck erect when foraging for food. Flies with head retracted. Juvenile and non-breeding adults lack long back plumes. VOICE: A guttural *kroow*, also a grating *karrr*. HABITAT: Saltwater and freshwater swamps and marshes, also rivers and shallow coastal waters. Breeds, mainly April to June, on trees or bushes in wooded swamps, often with other heron species. DISTRIBUTION: Common resident on the Greater Antilles, the Bahamas, Antigua and Guadeloupe, less common elsewhere.

2 LITTLE EGRET *Egretta garzetta* 55–65cm FIELD NOTES: Forages actively, often dashing to and fro, sometimes with wings held open. Flies with head retracted. Juveniles and non-breeding adults lack head and back plumes. Juvenile has bill and feet greenish yellow. There is a dark morph, which is generally dark grey with a whitish chin and dark bill. VOICE: Gives a hoarse *aaah* or *kgarrk* when disturbed. HABITAT: Coastal ponds and lagoons. Breeds in mangroves, often in association with other egrets. DISTRIBUTION: A breeding resident on Barbados, and a non-breeding resident on St Lucia; increasing vagrant elsewhere, recorded from Puerto Rico, Guadeloupe and Martinique.

3 SNOWY EGRET *Egretta thula* 55–65cm FIELD NOTES: Foraging habits much as Little Egret. Flies with neck retracted. Juvenile and non-breeding adults lack head and back plumes. Juvenile has greenish back to legs, blackish on front. VOICE: A rasping *graarr* or a nasal *hraaa*. In flight, may utter a hoarse *charf*. HABITAT: Freshwater swamps, rivers and saltwater lagoons. Breeds among mangroves, mainly from April to July, often in colonies with other herons. DISTRIBUTION: Reasonably widespread in West Indies, common all year on the Bahamas, Greater Antilles, Virgin Islands, Antigua, Guadeloupe and Barbados.

4 WESTERN REEF EGRET (WESTERN REEF HERON) *Egretta gularis* 55–67cm FIELD NOTES: Habits similar to Little Egret. Intermediates, with varying amounts of darkish feathers, also occur. Loses head, back and breast plumes in non-breeding plumage. VOICE: Utters a guttural croak when feeding or alarmed, otherwise generally silent. HABITAT: Rocky and sandy coasts, tidal mudflats, estuaries and coastal lagoons, less so inland. DISTRIBUTION: Rare, but increasing. Records from Barbados, St Lucia and Puerto Rico.

5 CATTLE EGRET *Bubulcus ibis* 48–53cm FIELD NOTES: Gregarious. Regularly flies in loose flocks or lines. In flight, looks stocky. Commonly feeds around grazing livestock. VOICE: At breeding colonies utters coarse croaks, otherwise fairly silent. HABITAT: Pastures, arable fields and marshes. Breeds, mainly from April to July, in mangroves or other wooded areas, roosts in similar areas. DISTRIBUTION: Widespread and common throughout the area.

6 ROSEATE SPOONBILL *Ajaia ajaja* 66–81cm FIELD NOTES: Forages in shallow water, sweeping bill from side to side while moving slowly forward. Flies with neck outstretched. Juvenile mainly white with a pale pink flush on back, wings and underparts. VOICE: On breeding grounds utters a grunting *huh-huh-huh-huh* and a coarse *rrek-ek-ek-ek-ek*, otherwise usually silent. HABITAT: Coastal lagoons, swamps and tidal pools. Breeds colonially, mainly August to December, in mangrove or other coastal trees. DISTRIBUTION: Resident on Cuba, Hispaniola and Great Inagua in the Bahamas. Mainly a vagrant in the rest of the West Indies.

7 GREATER FLAMINGO *Phoenicopterus ruber* 107–122cm FIELD NOTES: In flight, shows black primaries and secondaries, flies with neck and legs outstretched. Juvenile mainly dirty grey-brown. Immature white with a pale pink flush. Often feeds with head submerged while walking steadily forward. VOICE: Feeding flocks utter a constant low, babbling, goose-like chatter. In flight, gives a honking *ka-ha*. HABITAT: Coastal estuaries and lagoons. Breeds colonially, from March to July, on lagoon borders. DISTRIBUTION: Bahamas, especially Great Inagua, Cuba and Hispaniola. Less common on the rest of the Greater Antilles, a vagrant elsewhere.

8 STORKS, IBISES, SANDHILL CRANE AND LIMPKIN

1 WOOD STORK *Mycteria americana* 85–100cm FIELD NOTES: Juvenile has yellowish bill, a dark face and brownish feathered neck. In flight, shows black primaries and secondaries and a black tail. Flies with neck and legs outstretched. VOICE: Generally silent. At breeding grounds utters hissing noises along with bill-clattering. HABITAT: Swamps, coastal mudflats and lagoons, also on inland ponds and lakes. Breeds in mangroves, mainly from November to February. DISTRIBUTION: Rare resident on Cuba and Hispaniola (Dominican Republic), vagrant in other parts of the Greater Antilles, Bahamas and Dominica.

2 WHITE STORK (EUROPEAN WHITE STORK) *Ciconia ciconia* 100–115cm FIELD NOTES: In flight, shows black primaries and secondaries, tail white. Juvenile has reddish bill with extensive dark tip. VOICE: Generally silent. HABITAT: Marshes, damp pastures and arable fields. DISTRIBUTION: Vagrant, recorded from Antigua and Barbuda.

3 JABIRU *Jabiru mycteria* 122–140cm FIELD NOTES: Juvenile has head and neck dusky, upperparts grey with paler feather edges, underparts whitish. VOICE: Generally silent. HABITAT: Shallow marshes, ponds and wet pastures, also occurs on coastal estuaries. DISTRIBUTION: Vagrant, recorded from Grenada.

4 WHITE IBIS (AMERICAN WHITE IBIS) *Eudocimus albus* 56–71cm FIELD NOTES: Gregarious. In flight, shows black tips to the primaries, flies with neck and legs outstretched. Juvenile has brown back and wings, as bird ages becomes increasingly blotched with white, rump white, tail white with black tip, head and neck buff-white finely streaked brown, underparts white, bill orange. VOICE: A harsh nasal, honking *hunk-hunk-hunk* given in flight and when disturbed. Feeding groups render a murmuring *huu-huu-huu*. HABITAT: Wetlands, including saltwater and freshwater areas. Breeds, primarily in mangroves, from April to September. DISTRIBUTION: Resident on Cuba, Hispaniola and Jamaica, non-breeding resident in the Bahamas, a vagrant in other parts of the Greater Antilles.

5 SCARLET IBIS *Eudocimus ruber* 56–61cm FIELD NOTES: Breeding adult has black bill. In flight, shows black tips to the primaries, flies with neck and legs outstretched. Juvenile similar to White Ibis, but rump tinged pink-buff. VOICE: Similar to White Ibis. HABITAT: Coastal mangroves, swamps and lagoons. DISTRIBUTION: Vagrant, recorded from Cuba, Jamaica, Dominica and Grenada.

6 GLOSSY IBIS *Plegadis falcinellus* 55–65cm FIELD NOTES: Gregarious, usually in small groups. Flies with neck and legs outstretched, in loose flocks or undulating lines. Juvenile duller than adult with pale flecks on neck and head. VOICE: Generally silent, although may utter a grunting, sheep-like *grru* or *graa*. HABITAT: Shallow marshes, mudflats and coastal lagoons. Breeds, colonially, in waterside vegetation or small trees, mainly from June to August. DISTRIBUTION: Local resident on Cuba, Hispaniola, Jamaica and Puerto Rico, a non-breeding resident in the Bahamas and a vagrant in the rest of the West Indies.

7 SANDHILL CRANE *Grus canadensis* 100cm FIELD NOTES: Usually in small flocks. Flies with head and neck outstretched. Juvenile lacks red, head and neck brownish, body grey with browner feather edges. VOICE: A repeated, bugle-like *karr-rooo karr-rooo*. HABITAT: Savannahs, marshes and swamp edges. Breeds in grassy areas on savannahs or shallow marsh, from March to July. DISTRIBUTION: Local resident on Cuba.

8 LIMPKIN *Aramus guarauna* 66cm FIELD NOTES: Secretive. Generally crepuscular, best located by call. Flight floppy, with neck and legs outstretched. VOICE: A loud, wailing *kwEEEeeer* or *gua-re-ao*, also a shorter *kwaouk*. HABITAT: Marshes, swamps, lakes and wet wooded areas. Breeds in thick vegetation, generally near water, from June to October. DISTRIBUTION: Resident on Cuba, northern Bahamas (Andros and Eleuthera) and locally on Jamaica, uncommon on other Bahamian islands and Hispaniola.

9 DIVERS, GREBES AND WHISTLING DUCKS

1 GREAT NORTHERN DIVER (COMMON LOON) *Gavia immer* 69–91cm FIELD NOTES: Flies in a hunched-back manner with neck outstretched. Juvenile similar to winter adult but with pale scaly fringes on back. VOICE: Various wailing and manic-laughing sounds, also an even pitched *hahahahahahaha*, which is often given in flight. HABITAT: Mainly coastal. DISTRIBUTION: A migrant recorded mainly off the north coast of Cuba.

2 LEAST GREBE *Podiceps dominicus* 23–26cm FIELD NOTES: Usually stays near thick cover, feeds by diving for aquatic insects, amphibians or small fish. In flight, shows white patch on inner primaries and secondaries. Juvenile similar to non-breeding adult but face pale with dark streaks. VOICE: A nasal *teeen* or *weeek*, also a buzzy, descending *vvvvvvvvvvvv*. HABITAT: Freshwater cattail swamps, ponds with vegetation cover. Breeds among emergent water plants, mainly from April to May and again from September to December. DISTRIBUTION: Resident in the Bahamas, Cuba and Jamaica, a local resident on Hispaniola and Puerto Rico, much rarer or a vagrant elsewhere.

3 PIED-BILLED GREBE *Podylymbus podiceps* 30–38cm FIELD NOTES: Often encountered in family groups, occasionally in large, loose gatherings. When disturbed often swims with body mostly or partially submerged. Feeds by diving for aquatic insects, amphibians, crustaceans and fish. Juvenile as non-breeding adult but with dark streaks on side of head. VOICE: A far-carrying, hollow cackle, starting fast, then slower and ending with a mournful wail. HABITAT: Mainly freshwater areas but also occurs on coastal lagoons. Breeds among emergent water plants, mainly from March to July. DISTRIBUTION: Widespread, though rarer in southern Lesser Antilles.

4 RED-NECKED GREBE *Podiceps grisegena* 40–50cm FIELD NOTES: In flight, upperwing shows large white patches on secondaries and forewing. Feeds by diving for large aquatic insects and fish. VOICE: Wailing, braying and squeaking noises, also a grating *cherk-cherk-cherk*. HABITAT: Lakes with surrounding vegetation; after breeding occurs on more open water, including estuaries and sheltered coastal waters. DISTRIBUTION: Vagrant, recorded from New Providence in the Bahamas.

5 FULVOUS WHISTLING DUCK (FULVOUS TREE DUCK) *Dendrocygna bicolor* 45–53cm FIELD NOTES: In flight, shows a white horseshoe shape on the upper tail coverts. Generally occurs in small groups. Juvenile duller, more greyish. VOICE: A whistling *k-weeoo*, also a harsh *kee*. HABITAT: Freshwater areas with extensive emergent vegetation. Breeds in waterside vegetation, during May and June. DISTRIBUTION: Resident on Cuba, Hispaniola and Puerto Rico. A non-breeding resident on the Bahamas and vagrant elsewhere.

6 WEST INDIAN WHISTLING DUCK (CUBAN or BLACK-BILLED WHISTLING DUCK, WEST INDIAN TREE DUCK) *Dendrocygna arborea* 48–58cm FIELD NOTES: Feeds mainly at night, rests during daylight hours among swamp vegetation or mangroves. Often seen flying, at dusk, from roost areas. Juvenile duller, underpart markings less obvious. VOICE: A shrill, whistled *visisee*. HABITAT: Wooded swamps and coastal mangroves, on royal palm trees, where feeds on the fruits; also grazes on agricultural land. Breeds during any month; usually in a tree cavity but nests have been sited both in bushes and on the ground. DISTRIBUTION: Resident on the Greater Antilles, Bahamas and parts of the northern Lesser Antilles (Virgin Islands, Antigua), a vagrant elsewhere.

7 WHITE-FACED WHISTLING DUCK (WHITE-FACED TREE DUCK) *Dendrocygna viduata* 45–53cm FIELD NOTES: Usually encountered in large flocks. Juvenile duller, head and neck mainly greyish. VOICE: A whistled *tsri-tsri-trseeo*. HABITAT: Mainly freshwater lakes, rivers and marshes. DISTRIBUTION: Vagrant, recorded from Cuba, Dominican Republic and Barbados.

8 BLACK-BELLIED WHISTLING DUCK (BLACK-BELLIED or RED-BILLED TREE DUCK) *Dendrocygna autumnalis* 48–53cm FIELD NOTES: In flight, shows bold white wing-bar on upperwing. Juvenile duller with a grey bill. VOICE: A high-pitched, chattering whistle. HABITAT: Freshwater marsh, shallow lakes and coastal lagoons. DISTRIBUTION: Widespread vagrant. Bred on Puerto Rico and suspected to breed on Cuba.

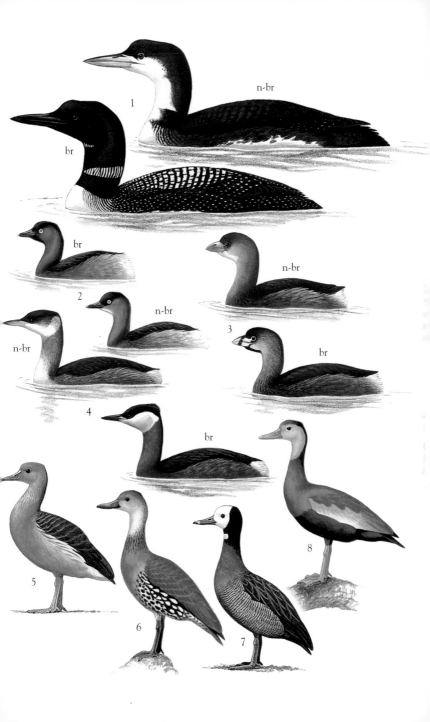

10 TUNDRA SWAN AND GEESE

1 TUNDRA SWAN (WHISTLING SWAN) *Cygnus columbianus* 120–140cm FIELD NOTES: Usually extremely sociable. Juvenile greyish brown, bill pinkish with dark tip. VOICE: A clear, melancholy *kloooo*. In flight, utters a melodious *wow-wow-wow*. HABITAT: Fresh or saltwater marshes. DISTRIBUTION: Vagrant, recorded from Cuba, Puerto Rico, Virgin Islands (St Thomas) and Antigua.

2 SNOW GOOSE (BLUE GOOSE) *Anser caerulescens* 65–84cm FIELD NOTES: Usually highly sociable. White phase shows prominent black primaries in flight. Juvenile white phase has grey crown, hind-neck, back and wings, the latter with feathers edged white. Juvenile blue phase is generally dark slaty-brown. VOICE: In flight, utters a nasal, cackling *la-luk*, said to resemble the barking of a small dog. HABITAT: Wetland borders, especially in coastal areas; also forages on cultivated land. DISTRIBUTION: A rare migrant on Cuba and in the northern Bahamas (Grand Bahama, New Providence and Abaco), a vagrant elsewhere, recorded from the southern Bahamas, Puerto Rico, Barbados and the Virgin Islands (St Croix).

3 WHITE-FRONTED GOOSE (GREATER WHITE-FRONTED GOOSE) *Anser albifrons* 64–78cm FIELD NOTES: In flight, shows white upper tail coverts. Juvenile lacks the white at the base of the bill and has an unmarked belly. Greenland White-fronted Goose *A. a. flavirostris* (fig 3b) has bill more orange and is slightly darker on body and neck. VOICE: In flight, utters a musical *ly-lyok*, otherwise typical goose cackling. HABITAT: Salt marsh, lagoons and grassland. DISTRIBUTION: Vagrant, recorded from Cuba.

4 ORINOCO GOOSE *Neochen jubata* 61–76cm FIELD NOTES: Often perches in trees. Confiding, reluctant to fly. Juvenile a dull version of the adult. VOICE: Male utters a high-pitched whistle, female gives a harsh cackle. HABITAT: Wooded river banks, marshes and wet grassland. DISTRIBUTION: Vagrant, recorded from Barbados and Jamaica.

5 BRENT GOOSE (BRANT) *Branta bernicla* 55–66cm FIELD NOTES: In flight, shows extensive white upper tail coverts. Pale-bellied race *B. b. hrota* and Black Brant *B. b. nigricans* (fig 5b) shown, intermediates could also occur. Usually highly gregarious. Juveniles lack the white neck marks. VOICE: A rolling, gargling *raunk raunk raunk*, given whilst feeding or in flight. HABITAT: Coastal mudflats and grassland. DISTRIBUTION: Vagrant, recorded from Barbados.

6 CANADA GOOSE *Branta canadensis* 90–100cm FIELD NOTES: Usually extremely gregarious. VOICE: A deep, musical honk *ah-hank*, often repeated as birds take flight. HABITAT: Inland and coastal marshes, also agricultural fields. DISTRIBUTION: Vagrant, recorded from the Bahamas and Greater Antilles.

white phase

1

2

blue phase

3b

3

4

5

5b

6

11 DUCKS

1 WOOD DUCK *Aix sponsa* 43–51cm FIELD NOTES: Eclipse male has pink bill otherwise like breeding female. Juvenile resembles dull female, face marks less well defined. VOICE: Male utters a thin, rising *jeeee*. Female has a sharp *cr-r-ek cr-r-ek* and a squealed *oo-eek* when flushed. HABITAT: Usually well wooded freshwater ponds, lakes and rivers. Breeds, from July to October, in a tree cavity, generally near water. DISTRIBUTION: Resident on Cuba, non-breeding resident on northern Bahamas; a vagrant to the rest of the Greater Antilles and northern Lesser Antilles.

2 GREEN-WINGED TEAL *Anas carolinensis* 34–38cm FIELD NOTES: Flight rapid with much twisting and turning. VOICE: Males utter a soft, high-pitched *preep-preep*. Females may give a nasal *quack* when alarmed. HABITAT: Freshwater and saltwater marshes, lakes and lagoons. DISTRIBUTION: Non-breeding resident in northern Bahamas; mainly a vagrant elsewhere.

3 AMERICAN BLACK DUCK *Anas rubripes* 53–62cm FIELD NOTES: In flight, shows a striking white underwing. VOICE: Males have a rasping *kreeep*. Females utter the classic *quack quack quack*. HABITAT: Virtually any type of water body. DISTRIBUTION: Vagrant, recorded from the Bahamas and Puerto Rico.

4 MALLARD *Anas platyrhynchos* 50–65cm FIELD NOTES: Probably one of the most familiar birds in the world. Eclipse males similar to females but bill dull yellowish and breast with a russet flush. VOICE: Similar to American Black Duck. HABITAT: Virtually any type of water body. DISTRIBUTION: Rare non-breeding resident in northern Bahamas and Cuba, a vagrant elsewhere.

5 WHITE-CHEEKED PINTAIL (BAHAMA PINTAIL or DUCK) *Anas bahamensis* 41–51cm FIELD NOTES: Usually seen singly, in pairs or in small groups. VOICE: Males utter a low whistle. Females have a descending series of quacks. HABITAT: Freshwater or saltwater pools and lagoons, mangrove swamps, creeks and estuaries. DISTRIBUTION: Resident in the Bahamas and most of the Greater Antilles; a vagrant on Jamaica, Grand Cayman and in parts of the Lesser Antilles.

6 PINTAIL (NORTHERN PINTAIL) *Anas acuta* 51–56cm (breeding male 61–65cm) FIELD NOTES: Long neck and tail make for an elongated look in flight. Usually forms large flocks post breeding. VOICE: Male utters a mellow *proop proop*. Female has a series of weak quacks and a low croak when flushed. HABITAT: Spends non-breeding season on lakes and estuary mudflats. Marshes and coastal lagoons. DISTRIBUTION: An uncommon or rare non-breeding resident on the Bahamas and most of the Greater Antilles; a vagrant on Jamaica, the Cayman Islands and the Lesser Antilles.

7 BLUE-WINGED TEAL *Anas discors* 37–41cm FIELD NOTES: The commonest non-breeding duck. In flight, both sexes show a bright pale blue forewing and lack a white trailing edge to secondaries. VOICE: Males utter a thin *tsee-tsee*. Female has a high-pitched quack. HABITAT: Shallow areas of swamps, lakes and coastal lagoons. DISTRIBUTION: Widespread from October to April.

8 CINNAMON TEAL *Anas cyanoptera* 38–48cm FIELD NOTES: Wing pattern of both sexes similar to Blue-Winged Teal. VOICE: Similar to Blue-winged Teal. HABITAT: Shallow freshwater lakes and marshes. DISTRIBUTION: Vagrant, recorded from the Bahamas, Cuba, Jamaica, Puerto Rico, the Virgin Islands, Antigua and Barbados.

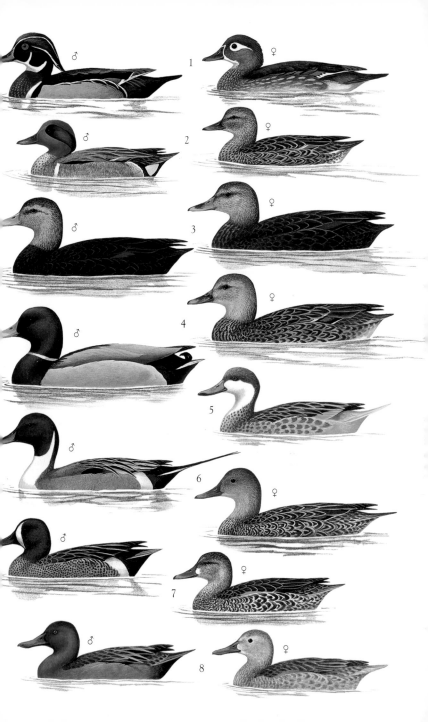

1

2

3

4

5

6

7

8

12 DUCKS

1 GARGANEY *Anas querquedula* 37–41cm FIELD NOTES: In flight, upperwing of male shows a pale grey forewing, green secondaries with a wide white trailing edge, at a distance can appear white winged; female upperwing darker, with white trailing edge to secondaries. VOICE: Male utters a rattling *kherek*. Female has a high, nasal quack. HABITAT: Freshwater lakes usually with fringing vegetation, also found on sheltered coastal waters. DISTRIBUTION: Vagrant, recorded from Barbados and Puerto Rico.

2 SHOVELER (NORTHERN or EUROPEAN SHOVELER) *Anas clypeata* 44–52cm FIELD NOTES: Upperwing of male shows a pale blue forewing separated from green secondaries by a white wing bar, female wing duller with thinner white wing bar. In flight, large bill makes birds look 'front heavy'. VOICE: Generally silent. Female utters a quacking *gak-gak-gak-ga-ga*. HABITAT: Mainly freshwater lakes and marshes with surrounding and emergent vegetation. DISTRIBUTION: Found throughout the area, mainly from October to May; some birds stay all year as non-breeders.

3 GADWALL *Anas strepera* 46–55cm FIELD NOTES: In flight, upperwing of both males and females show a white patch on the inner secondaries. VOICE: Usually fairly silent. Male utters a sharp *ahrk* and a low whistle. Female has a mechanical, Mallard-like quack. HABITAT: Mainly freshwater areas with fringing vegetation. DISTRIBUTION: Rare non-breeding resident to the Bahamas, also recorded from Cuba, Jamaica, Hispaniola, Guadeloupe and St Lucia.

4 WIGEON (EURASIAN WIGEON) *Anas penelope* 45–50cm FIELD NOTES: In flight, upperwing of male shows large white forewing patch, underwing grey. VOICE: Male utters a clear, whistling *wheeooo* and the female a growling *krrr*. HABITAT: Estuaries and nearby grassland, coastal bays and freshwater lakes and ponds. DISTRIBUTION: Vagrant, October to April, recorded from Hispaniola, Puerto Rico, Barbados and Barbuda.

5 AMERICAN WIGEON (BALDPATE) *Anas americana* 45–50cm FIELD NOTES: In flight, upperwing of male shows large white forewing patch, underwing has a white central area. VOICE: Similar to Wigeon but weaker and throatier. HABITAT: Mainly freshwater ponds, lakes and marshes. DISTRIBUTION: Throughout the area as a migrant or non-breeding visitor, mainly from October to April.

6 CANVASBACK *Aythya valisineria* 48–61cm FIELD NOTES: Diagnostic sloping forehead. In flight, appears elongated, upperwing uniform pale grey, almost white toward body. VOICE: Generally silent away from breeding grounds. Male utters a soft, squeaky cooing and the female a harsh *krrr krrr*. HABITAT: Lakes, coastal lagoons, sheltered bays and estuaries. DISTRIBUTION: Occurs from October to March, rare on Cuba and a vagrant on the Bahamas, Jamaica, Hispaniola, Puerto Rico and St Lucia.

7 REDHEAD *Aythya americana* 45–56cm FIELD NOTES: Steep forehead. In flight, upperwing of both sexes show pale grey primaries and secondaries, which contrast with darker grey forewing. VOICE: Generally silent. Female utters a low *grehp*, also a harsh *squak*. HABITAT: Saltwater or freshwater lakes and marshes. DISTRIBUTION: Occurs from November to March, very rare on the Bahamas, Cuba and Barbados, with vagrant records from Hispaniola and Jamaica.

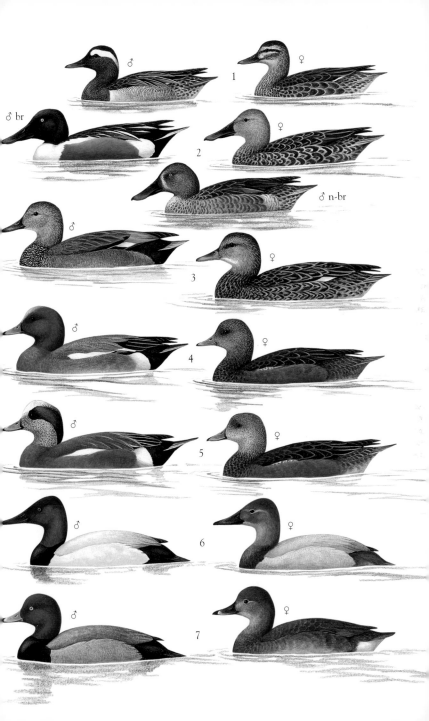

13 DUCKS

1 RING-NECKED DUCK *Aythya collaris* 37–46cm FIELD NOTES: In flight, upperwing of both sexes shows grey primaries and pale grey secondaries that contrast with dark forewing. Underwing grey with slightly paler grey central area. VOICE: Generally silent, female may utter a rough, growling *trrr trrr*. HABITAT: Open freshwater lakes. DISTRIBUTION: Non-breeding visitor, from October to March, common on Cuba and New Providence and Eleuthera in the Bahamas, less common on the rest of the Bahamas, Hispaniola, Jamaica, Puerto Rico and the Virgin Islands. A vagrant elsewhere in the area.

2 SCAUP (GREATER SCAUP) *Aythya marila* 40–51cm FIELD NOTES: In flight, upperwing of both sexes shows a distinct wide white bar on inner primaries and secondaries, forewing medium grey. VOICE: Generally silent away from breeding grounds. HABITAT: Mainly maritime. DISTRIBUTION: A rare migrant, recorded from the Bahamas, St Croix in the Virgin Islands and Barbados, chiefly from September to February. Recorded as a vagrant on Jamaica.

3 LESSER SCAUP *Aythya affinis* 38–46cm FIELD NOTES: In flight, upperwing of both sexes has pale grey inner primaries and a wide white bar on secondaries, forewing dark grey. VOICE: Generally silent away from breeding grounds. HABITAT: Sheltered coastal waters, estuaries and inland lakes. DISTRIBUTION: Locally common non-breeding visitor, from November to March, to the Bahamas and Cuba, much less common elsewhere, rare in the Lesser Antilles.

4 BUFFLEHEAD *Bucephala albeola* 33–38cm FIELD NOTES: In flight, male upperwing has large white patch covering secondaries and forewing coverts, female has patch mainly confined to secondaries. VOICE: Generally silent apart from an occasional growl given by male or a series of guttural notes uttered by the female. HABITAT: Lakes, rivers and coastal waters. DISTRIBUTION: Occurs from October to March, rare on Cuba and a vagrant, recorded from Eleuthera in the Bahamas, Jamaica and Puerto Rico.

5 GOLDENEYE (COMMON GOLDENEYE) *Bucephala clangula* 42–50cm FIELD NOTES: In flight, male upperwing has a large white patch covering secondaries and forewing coverts; female patch is split by two thin black bars on coverts. VOICE: Generally silent. HABITAT: Lakes and coastal waters. DISTRIBUTION: Vagrant, recorded from Eleuthera in the Bahamas.

6 HOODED MERGANSER *Lophodytes cucullatus* 42–50cm FIELD NOTES: Eclipse male similar to female but eye pale. In flight, upperwing of both sexes generally dark with a small white bar on greater coverts. VOICE: Generally silent. HABITAT: Lakes and coastal lagoons. DISTRIBUTION: Rare, occurs from November to February, in the Bahamas, Cuba, Hispaniola, Puerto Rico, the Virgin Islands, Martinique and Barbados.

7 RED-BREASTED MERGANSER *Mergus serrator* 52–58cm FIELD NOTES: In flight, upperwing of male has large white patch covering secondaries and forewing coverts split by two thin black bars. Female similar except forewing lesser coverts dark grey. VOICE: Generally silent away from breeding sites. HABITAT: Coastal waters and inland lakes. DISTRIBUTION: Rare visitor to the Bahamas and most of the Greater Antilles, from November to March.

8 MASKED DUCK *Nomonyx dominicus* 30–36cm FIELD NOTES: Tends to remain hidden among aquatic vegetation. In flight, upperwing of both sexes show a large white patch. VOICE: Male utters a loud *kuri-kuroo*. Female gives low hisses and clucks. HABITAT: Freshwater pools and marshes with extensive vegetation. DISTRIBUTION: Resident on the Greater Antilles (most common on Cuba); rare on Guadeloupe, Martinique and Barbados; elsewhere a rare vagrant.

9 RUDDY DUCK *Oxyura jamaicensis* 35–43cm FIELD NOTES: Sociable. West Indian race (fig 9b) has variable black markings on white face patch. VOICE: Generally silent. During display most sounds produced by tapping bill against inflated chest. HABITAT: Lakes with fringe vegetation, brackish lagoons and sheltered coastal bays. DISTRIBUTION: Locally common in the Bahamas and Greater Antilles, local populations augmented by North American birds from October to March.

14 VULTURES, BALD EAGLE, OSPREY, CARACARA, SWALLOW-TAILED KITE AND HEN HARRIER

1 BLACK VULTURE (AMERICAN BLACK VULTURE) *Coragyps atratus* 58–68cm
FIELD NOTES: Juvenile duller, head has less 'folds' and is lightly feathered dark grey. VOICE: Generally silent but may utter a soft hissing or barking. HABITAT: Open country and around human habitations, where they scavenge on rubbish dumps. DISTRIBUTION: A vagrant, recorded from the Bahamas, Cuba, Jamaica and Grenada.

2 TURKEY VULTURE *Cathartes aura* 64–81cm FIELD NOTES: Juvenile browner, bare skin on head dark grey. VOICE: At breeding sites utters various hissing and clucking sounds, otherwise generally silent. HABITAT: Open areas and around human habitations, where often found around rubbish dumps. Breeds, from February to April, in crevices, on cliff ledges and on the ground under thick vegetation. DISTRIBUTION: Resident in parts of the Bahamas (Grand Bahama, Abaco and Andros) and the Greater Antilles, except the Cayman Islands, where it is only a rare wanderer. Also recorded as a vagrant in the Virgin Islands.

3 BALD EAGLE *Haliaeetus leucocephalus* 79–84cm FIELD NOTES: Juvenile generally dark brown, becoming blotched with white on belly, back and head before adult plumage is gained in fourth year. VOICE: A loud, cackling *kweek-kik-ik-ik-ik-ik* and a lower *kak-kak-kak-kak*. HABITAT: Freshwater lakes, rivers and coastal lagoons. DISTRIBUTION: A vagrant recorded from Puerto Rico and the Virgin Islands (St John).

4 OSPREY *Pandion haliaetus* 55–58cm FIELD NOTES: Feeds on fish, soaring over water before plunging feet first onto prey. Juvenile similar to adult but feathers of mantle and upperwing fringed pale. VOICE: A series of mournful whistles, also a shrill, whistled *teeeeaa*. When alarmed utters a hoarse, sharp *kew-kew-kew-kew*. HABITAT: Freshwater lakes, coastal lagoons and estuaries. Breeds from April to June, with nest placed on exposed tree or cliff. DISTRIBUTION: Resident race *P. h. ridgwayi* (fig 4b) breeds in southern Bahamas and Cuba (northern offshore cays and in the Zapata Swamp). North American birds widespread in West Indies from September to April.

5 CRESTED CARACARA *Caracara cheriway* 50–63cm FIELD NOTES: Juvenile browner with dark streaking on breast and upper back. VOICE: A harsh, cackling *ca-ca-ca-ca*. HABITAT: Palm savannahs, open country and pastures. Breeds, from February to December, mainly in palm trees. DISTRIBUTION: Local resident on Cuba. Vagrant on Jamaica.

6 SWALLOW-TAILED KITE (AMERICAN SWALLOW-TAILED KITE) *Elanoides forficatus* 51–66cm FIELD NOTES: Agile, graceful flyer. Juvenile very similar to adult but streaked buff on head and breast. VOICE: A whistled *ke-wee-wee hewee-we* or *peat-peat-peat klee-klee-klee*. HABITAT: Coastal swamps and marsh, estuaries and savannahs. DISTRIBUTION: A rare migrant or vagrant, mainly on Cuba and northern Bahamas, from August to October and from February to June.

7 HEN HARRIER (NORTHERN HARRIER) *Circus cyaneus* 44–52cm FIELD NOTES: Juvenile similar to adult female but with plain rufous-tinged underparts and underwing-coverts. VOICE: A piercing *eeeya*, also a rapid *chek-ek-ek-ek-ek*. HABITAT: Marshlands, both fresh and brackish, also open country. DISTRIBUTION: Local non-breeding resident on the Bahamas, Cuba, Hispaniola and Puerto Rico. A rare migrant or vagrant elsewhere in the West Indies.

15 KITES AND HAWKS

1 HOOK-BILLED KITE *Chondrohierax uncinatus* 38–43cm FIELD NOTES: Endangered. A dark phase occurs that is all dark with a pale band on tail. Juvenile brown above with a white nuchal collar, creamy white below barred light rust; tail has 4 or 5 bands. VOICE: A shrill scream and a 2- or 3-note whistle. HABITAT: Dry scrubland and mountain forests. Breeds from March to July. DISTRIBUTION: Grenada.

2 CUBAN KITE *Chondrohierax wilsonii* 38–43cm FIELD NOTES: Endangered. Juvenile dark above with a white nuchal collar, creamy white below with rust-coloured barring. VOICE: A rattling *kekekekekekekeke*. HABITAT: Riverside forests. DISTRIBUTION: Oriente Province in north-eastern Cuba.

3 SNAIL KITE *Rostrhamus sociabilis* 43–48cm FIELD NOTES: Flight slow and buoyant. Juvenile much like dull adult female, mottled brown above, buff below streaked brown. Legs yellow to orange. VOICE: A cackling *ka-ka-ka-ka-ka*, a grating *krrkrrkrrkrr* and a harsh *kerwuck*. HABITAT: Marshes and swamps. Breeds in patches of vegetation or on dead tree stumps above water, from March to July. DISTRIBUTION: Cuba.

4 COMMON BLACK HAWK (CRAB HAWK) *Buteogallus anthracinus* 51–58cm FIELD NOTES: Juvenile dark above, pale below with heavy dark streaking on breast and dark barring on thighs and under-tail coverts, tail pale with 4 or 5 dark bars. VOICE: A series of sharp whistles or screams and a harsh *haaaah*. HABITAT: St Vincent race occurs in montane forest, Cuban race found around coastal forests, swamps and beaches. Breeds from April to June. DISTRIBUTION: Resident on St Vincent and Cuba, more common on the latter. A vagrant on Puerto Rico, St Lucia, Grenada and the Grenadines. The Cuban Black-hawk *B. (a.) gundlachii* (fig 4b) treated here as a race, has recently been given full species status.

5 RIDGWAY'S HAWK *Buteo ridgwayi* 36–41cm FIELD NOTES: Endangered. Juvenile lacks rufous wing coverts, underparts buff-white with grey and brown streaks. VOICE: Various squealing notes. HABITAT: Occurs in undisturbed forests where it breeds from January to March. DISTRIBUTION: Now virtually confined to a small area in the north-east of the Dominican Republic.

6 BROAD-WINGED HAWK *Buteo platypterus* 35–41cm FIELD NOTES: Juvenile has brown upperparts and pale below streaked with brown, similar to the adult of the Cuban race *B. p. cubanensis* (fig 6b). VOICE: A piercing high-pitched whistle. HABITAT: Deciduous and mixed woodlands, migrating birds also frequent more open areas. Breeds from January to June. DISTRIBUTION: Cuba, Puerto Rico (rare), St Christopher (uncommon), Antigua and the southern Lesser Antilles from Dominica to Grenada. Recorded as a vagrant on Jamaica and Barbados.

7 SWAINSON'S HAWK *Buteo swainsoni* 48–56cm FIELD NOTES: There is a dark phase, mostly dark brown with a paler, dark-barred ventral region. Juvenile has dark upperparts, fringed buff, underparts pale heavily blotched dark brown. VOICE: A long, high scream, also a whistled *pi-tip pi-tip pi-tip*. HABITAT: Variable, including woodland and open country. DISTRIBUTION: Vagrant, recorded from Hispaniola.

8 RED-TAILED HAWK *Buteo jamaicensis* 48–64cm FIELD NOTES: Regularly seen soaring. Juvenile underparts heavily streaked, tail pale grey with darker bars. VOICE: A rasping scream, said to sound like a rusty hinge. HABITAT: Mountains, woodland, open country and around human habitations. DISTRIBUTION: Resident on northern Bahamas, Greater Antilles and a few islands in the northern Lesser Antilles (Virgin Islands, St Bartholomew, Saba, St Christopher, Nevis and St Eustatius), a vagrant elsewhere.

9 WHITE-TAILED HAWK *Buteo albicaudatus* 51–61cm FIELD NOTES: Juvenile very dark above, blotched and barred blackish below, breast white, tail pale grey lightly barred darker. VOICE: A high-pitched *ke ke ke ke*; also harsh *kareeeev*. HABITAT: Semiarid open country and coastal grassland. DISTRIBUTION: Vagrant recorded from St Vincent.

16 HAWKS AND FALCONS

1 SHARP–SHINNED HAWK *Accipiter striatus* 25–35cm FIELD NOTES: Typical *Accipiter* flight, dashing and agile when tracking down prey, also soaring (note square end to tail) and gliding with occasional flaps when exploring territories. Juvenile brown above, buff-white below with tawny streaking. Puerto Rican race *A. s. venator* has more distinct tail bands. Cuban race *A. s. fringilloides* has side of head clearer rufous. VOICE: A high-pitched *kew kew kew kew*. HABITAT: Mountain and hill forests; migrant birds in Cuba said to occur in coastal forests. Breeds from March to June. DISTRIBUTION: Greater Antilles, migrants also occur in the Bahamas, Jamaica and the Virgin Islands (St John).

2 GUNDLACH'S HAWK *Accipiter gundlachi* 43–51cm FIELD NOTES: In soaring flight note rounded end to tail. Actions similar to Sharp-shinned Hawk. Juvenile brown above, pale buff below streaked brown. VOICE: A cackling *kek-kek-kek-kek...* and a wailing squeal. HABITAT: Mountain and lowland forests, swamps and coastal woodland. Breeds mainly from March to June. DISTRIBUTION: Cuba.

3 AMERICAN KESTREL *Falco sparverius* 23–30cm FIELD NOTES: Watches for prey from high exposed perch or by hovering. Apart from the migrant nominate birds, 3 other races occur in the area: Cuban race *F. s. sparveroides* (figs 3b and 3c), Hispaniolan race *F. s. dominicensis* (both adults lack rufous crown and have little spotting on underparts) and Puerto Rican race *F. s. caribearum* (male has darker spotting on underparts and black shaft streaks on tail). VOICE: A shrill *killi-killi-killi-killi*. HABITAT: Cosmopolitan, including forest edge, open areas, villages, towns and cities. Breeds from January to August, nests placed in tree, rock or building cavity or on building or cliff ledges. DISTRIBUTION: Widespread in the area.

4 KESTREL (COMMON or EURASIAN KESTREL) *Falco tinnunculus* 31–37cm FIELD NOTES: Frequently hovers or uses prominent perches when seeking prey. VOICE: A shrill *kee-kee-kee-kee* and a trilling *vriii*. HABITAT: Almost any type of open country with adequate perches, cliffs, villages, towns and cities. DISTRIBUTION: Vagrant recorded from Martinique.

5 PEREGRINE FALCON *Falco peregrinus* 36–50cm FIELD NOTES: Prey usually captured and killed in mid-air following a high-speed pursuit and stoop. Juvenile brown above, pale below with dark streaking, head pattern as adult but browner. VOICE: A loud *ka-yak ka-yak ka-yak*; also a shrill *kek-kek-kek* when alarmed. HABITAT: Primarily rocky coastal areas, may occur inland, even in large towns. DISTRIBUTION: Widespread, but rare throughout the region from October to April.

6 MERLIN *Falco columbarius* 25–34cm FIELD NOTES: When pursuing prey, flight is often dashing and slightly undulating with twists and turns. VOICE: A rapidly repeated, high-pitched *ki-ki-ki-ki-kee*; female has a similar series but lower pitched. HABITAT: Coastal lagoons, woodlands and forest edge. DISTRIBUTION: A migrant and scarce resident, mainly from October to March, throughout the region.

7 BAT FALCON *Falco rufigularis* 24–29cm FIELD NOTES: Hunts predominantly around dusk and dawn, prey (mainly bats, birds and large insects) usually taken in flight. Juvenile as male, except throat more buff and under-tail coverts with black bars or spots. VOICE: A shrill *ke-ke-ke* or *kiu-kiu-kiu-kiu*. HABITAT: Mainly forested areas. DISTRIBUTION: Vagrant recorded from Grenada.

nom

3

3c

dark
phase

♂

light
phase

3b

♂

♀

4

♂

5

6

♂

♀

7

HA

1

2

3 ♀

♂

4 ♀

♂

5

6 ♀

♂

7

17 PEAFOWL, PHEASANT, GUINEAFOWL, JUNGLEFOWL, BOBWHITES AND CHACHALACA

1 COMMON PEAFOWL (PEACOCK) *Pavo cristatus* Male 180–230cm, Female 90–100cm FIELD NOTES: Unmistakable. Normally roosts in trees. VOICE: A far-carrying, wail *may-awe-may-awe-may-awe* or *kee-ow-kee-ow-kee-ow*; also some donkey-like braying. HABITAT: Forest edge, nest usually under thick bushes, also feeds in various open areas. DISTRIBUTION: Bahamas (Little Exuma), introduced in the 1950s.

2 PHEASANT (COMMON or RINGED-NECKED PHEASANT) *Phasianus colchicus* Male 66–90cm, Female 53–63cm FIELD NOTES: Generally 2 forms, ring-necked and green-necked; introduced birds can be very variable compared with birds in their native range. Females can also be very variable, some being much darker. VOICE: A harsh *korkk korrk KO KO korkk-kok*, often followed by a noisy 'wing-whirring'. When alarmed gives a rapid *kut-UK kut-UK kut-UK*. HABITAT: Very varied, including open woodland, woodland edge and open country. DISTRIBUTION: Introduced to the Bahamas (Eleuthera) and Cuba (Isle of Youth).

3 HELMETED GUINEAFOWL *Numida meleagris* 60–65cm FIELD NOTES: Usually in small groups; forages on the ground, roosts in trees. Some races have bare skin of head more blue. VOICE: A loud, raucous *kek-ke-kek-ke-kek-kek-kek*. Females utter a far-carrying *ka-bak*. Foraging flocks give a *chenk-chenk-chenk* contact call and a plaintive *GHER-cheeng CHER-cheeng*. HABITAT: Dry scrubland. DISTRIBUTION: Introduced. Locally common in the Dominican Republic and rare on Cuba, Puerto Rico, the Virgin Islands (St Croix), St Martin and Barbuda.

4 RED JUNGLEFOWL *Gallus gallus* Male 65–78cm, Female 41–46cm FIELD NOTES: The ancestor of domestic chickens. Male unmistakable, female superficially like female pheasant but never has long tail feathers. VOICE: Males utter the very familiar *cock-a-doodle-do*, generally given at dawn or dusk. HABITAT: Forests and forest edge. DISTRIBUTION: Introduced. Very local in the Dominican Republic, Puerto Rico and the Grenadines.

5 NORTHERN BOBWHITE (COMMON BOBWHITE) *Colinus virginianus* 24–28cm FIELD NOTES: Shy, usually found in small groups foraging in cover. Cuban race endemic; paler races (such as fig 5b) introduced on other islands. VOICE: Male utters a rising *bob-WHITE* or *bob-bob-WHITE*. Flocks keep contact with a thin, anxious *a-loie-a-hee*. Various other sounds noted, including a raucous squealing and a whistled *hoy*. HABITAT: Scrub and fields with extensive cover. Breeds from May to July. DISTRIBUTION: Resident on Cuba. Introduced to the Bahamas, Hispaniola and Puerto Rico.

6 CRESTED BOBWHITE *Colinus cristatus* 18–23cm FIELD NOTES: Generally shy, pairs or small groups usually keeping to cover. VOICE: A *coo-kwee* or *pwit pwit PWEET*; also a wheezy, repeated *WHEEchee*. Flocks keep contact with various chirping and cheeping notes. HABITAT: Agricultural land, scrub and hedgerows. DISTRIBUTION: Grenadines (Mustique).

7 RUFOUS-VENTED CHACHALACA *Ortalis ruficauda* 55cm FIELD NOTES: Forages, usually in small groups, both on the ground and in trees, feeding on fruits, shoots, tender leaves and flowers. VOICE: A raucous *chachalaca chachalaca chachalaca...* or *cocrico cocrico cocrico....* Utters a low chuckling while feeding. HABITAT: Open woodland, shrubby trees and palms. Breeds from March to July, usually in a small tree. DISTRIBUTION: Resident in the Grenadines (Union Island).

18 RAILS AND CRAKES

1 KING RAIL *Rallus elegans* 38–48cm FIELD NOTES: Shy and secretive, feeding mostly at dawn and dusk. More often heard than seen. Juvenile darker above, buff below with dark speckling. VOICE: A repeated *ket ket ket ket ket…*. HABITAT: Tall, dense vegetation in swamps, canals and flooded areas. Breeds from June to September. DISTRIBUTION: Resident on Cuba, vagrant on Jamaica.

2 CLAPPER RAIL *Rallus longirostris* 31–40cm FIELD NOTES: Mainly crepuscular, more often heard than seen. Juvenile similar to King Rail; underparts, especially breast area, dirty buff-white. VOICE: Very similar to King Rail, a series of 'clapping' notes *kek kek kek kek* accelerating and then slowing. HABITAT: Mangroves and salt marshes. Nests among mangrove roots during April and May. DISTRIBUTION: Resident in the Bahamas and Greater Antilles, although local on Jamaica and Hispaniola; also local in the Lesser Antilles (Virgin Islands, Barbuda, St Christopher, Guadeloupe and Martinique).

3 VIRGINIA RAIL *Rallus limicola* 20–25cm FIELD NOTES: Mainly crepuscular, shy and secretive. Juvenile like a very dull adult above; below breast and flanks have dark, ill-defined barring. VOICE: A series of rapid *kid kid kidic kidic* notes; also a pig-like grunting *wep wep wep wepwepwepwepwepppprrr*, which usually descends and accelerates. HABITAT: Freshwater or brackish and saltwater water bodies with dense vegetation. DISTRIBUTION: Resident on Grand Bahama and Cuba (rare), from September to April; also a vagrant recorded from the Bahamas and Puerto Rico.

4 SORA *Porzana carolina* 20–23cm FIELD NOTES: Secretive, but will feed in the open if undisturbed. Non-breeding adults have black of throat obscured by pale feather edgings. Grey of adults replaced with brownish buff on juveniles. VOICE: A plaintive *ker-wee* and a high-pitched descending whinny. When alarmed gives a loud, sharp *keek*. HABITAT: Thickly vegetated freshwater and saltwater swamps, including rice fields and mangroves. DISTRIBUTION: Occurs from October to April throughout the region.

5 SPOTTED CRAKE *Porzana porzana* 22–24cm FIELD NOTES: Secretive, but will feed in the open if undisturbed. When disturbed tends to slip quietly into thick cover. VOICE: A high-pitched whiplash-like *whitt*; also a ticking *tik-tak* and a croaking *qwe-qwe-qwe*. HABITAT: Marshes, bogs, wet grassland and rice fields. DISTRIBUTION: Vagrant recorded from St Martin.

6 YELLOW-BREASTED CRAKE *Porzana flaviventer* 14cm FIELD NOTES: Feeds mainly at dawn and dusk; will feed in the open on floating vegetation or by wading in shallow water at swamp edges. Juvenile like adult but with indistinct barring on neck and breast. VOICE: A harsh, rolling *k'kluk kurr-kurr* and a single or repeated *kreer* or *krreh*. HABITAT: Freshwater swamps with fringing and floating vegetation. Breeds from March to June, nest placed among or on aquatic plants. DISTRIBUTION: Uncommon resident in Greater Antilles.

7 ZAPATA RAIL *Cyanolimnas cerverai* 29cm FIELD NOTES: Critically endangered. It appears to be almost flightless. Virtually unknown, juvenile undescribed. VOICE: A low *cutucutu-cutucutu-cutucutu*, said to sound like a bouncing ball; also a loud *kwowk* or *kuck-kuck* resembling call of Limpkin (Plate 8). HABITAT: Swamp with dense, tangled bush, low trees, sawgrass and cattails. Breeds September/October and possibly December/January. DISTRIBUTION: Zapata Swamp, Cuba.

19 RAILS, MOORHEN, GALLINULES AND COOTS

1 BLACK RAIL *Laterallus jamaicensis* 14cm FIELD NOTES: Shy and secretive, tends to stay well hidden in marsh plants; more often heard than seen. VOICE: Two high-pitched notes followed by a lower note, *kic-kic-kerr*, given mainly at night. When alarmed utters a growling *krr-krr-krr*. HABITAT: Wet meadows, freshwater and saline marshes. DISTRIBUTION: Resident on Hispaniola; non-breeding visitor, from October to March, on Cuba, Jamaica and Puerto Rico. Vagrant recorded from the Bahamas (Eleuthera) and Antigua.

2 YELLOW RAIL *Coturnicops noveboracensis* 16–19cm FIELD NOTES: Very secretive. In flight, has distinctive white secondaries. VOICE: A *tick-tick tickticktick tick-tick tickticktick*, said to sound like tapping two pebbles together. HABITAT: Grassy marshes, damp grassland, salt marshes and rice fields. DISTRIBUTION: Vagrant recorded from Grand Bahama.

3 SPOTTED RAIL *Pardirallus maculatus* 28cm FIELD NOTES: Very secretive, more often heard than seen. Juvenile browner with less spotting, bill and legs duller. VOICE: A grunt followed by a rasping screech, also an accelerating *tuk-tuk-tuk-tuk*, similar to call of Zapata Rail. HABITAT: Freshwater swamps with emergent plant life, also rice fields. DISTRIBUTION: Resident on Cuba (mainly Zapata Swamp), Hispaniola (north-east Dominican Republic) and Jamaica (very rare, recorded from the Black River Morass).

4 PURPLE GALLINULE *Porphyrio martinica* 30–36cm FIELD NOTES: Feeds readily in the open, although typically stays close to cover. Walks on floating vegetation and clambers among reeds and bushes. Juvenile head, neck and flanks ochre-brown, rest of underparts white, mantle browner, wings brownish blue. VOICE: A high-pitched *kyik*; also a wailing *ka-ka-ka* and a nasal, honking *pep-pep-pep pePA pePA*. HABITAT: Well-vegetated lakes, pools, marshes and rice fields. Breeds from July to September in cattails or rice grass. DISTRIBUTION: Resident on Greater Antilles (uncommon on Jamaica, Grand Cayman and Puerto Rico). Mainly a migrant to the Bahamas and a vagrant to the Lesser Antilles, although a rare resident on St Bartholomew, Montserrat and Barbados.

5 MOORHEN (COMMON MOORHEN or GALLINULE) *Gallinula chloropus* 22–23cm FIELD NOTES: Often relatively tame. Regularly swims with a jerky action. Juvenile has dark brown upperparts and dull grey underparts with diagnostic white flank stripe. VOICE: A bubbling *krrrruk* or *kurr-ik*; also a cackling *kik-kik-kik-kik*. HABITAT: Swamps, mangroves, lake edges, ponds, rivers and ditches, all with fringing vegetation. Breeds at any time (peaks from May to September). DISTRIBUTION: Common throughout the region.

6 CARIBBEAN COOT *Fulica caribbaea* 38–40cm FIELD NOTES: Usually occurs in flocks. Juvenile dull grey above, paler grey below. VOICE: Various cackling and clucking notes. HABITAT: Mainly open freshwater lakes and ponds. Breeds at any time with peaks from April to June and September to November. DISTRIBUTION: Resident on Hispaniola, Puerto Rico, Jamaica and Virgin Islands; a rare wanderer elsewhere in the Lesser Antilles.

7 AMERICAN COOT *Fulica americana* 38–40cm FIELD NOTES: Habits and actions very similar to Caribbean Coot. Juvenile virtually indistinguishable from Caribbean Coot. VOICE: Similar to Caribbean Coot. HABITAT: Similar to Caribbean Coot. DISTRIBUTION: Resident, although not common, in the Bahamas, Cuba, Hispaniola, Cayman Islands and Jamaica. Numbers boosted from September to April by migrants from North America, making it a common non-breeding resident in the Bahamas and the Greater Antilles; mainly a vagrant elsewhere.

20 JACANA, PRATINCOLE, THICK-KNEE, SNIPE, TURNSTONE AND PHALAROPES

1 NORTHERN JACANA *Jacana spinosa* 19–23cm FIELD NOTES: Forages principally by walking on floating vegetation. In flight, shows bright yellow primaries and secondaries. VOICE: A noisy cackling, usually given in flight. HABITAT: Mainly freshwater ponds, swamps and rivers with floating vegetation. Breeds, among waterside plants, from April to September. DISTRIBUTION: Resident on Cuba, Jamaica and Hispaniola; vagrant on Puerto Rico.

2 COLLARED PRATINCOLE (COMMON or RED-WINGED PRATINCOLE) *Glareola pratincola* 23–26cm FIELD NOTES: In flight, shows a white trailing edge to secondaries, upperwing has dark primaries that contrast with paler coverts and mantle. Underwing has reddish-chestnut coverts. Tail deeply forked. VOICE: A harsh *kik* or *kirrik* and a rolling *kikki-kirrik-irrik*. HABITAT: Flat open areas, fields and sand-flats, usually near water. DISTRIBUTION: Vagrant recorded from Barbados.

3 DOUBLE-STRIPED THICK-KNEE *Burhinus bistriatus* 38–43cm FIELD NOTES: Mainly crepuscular or nocturnal. In flight, from above, shows white patch on inner primaries. VOICE: A chattering, strident *ca-ca-ca-ca-ca-ca-ca...*, descending in pitch, often given at dusk, dawn or night. HABITAT: Semiarid open grasslands and agricultural country. Breeds in April and May. DISTRIBUTION: Hispaniola.

4 JACK SNIPE *Lymnocryptes minimus* 17–19cm FIELD NOTES: Secretive, tends to wait until nearly trodden on before being flushed; flies away with less erratic movements than Snipe. VOICE: Generally silent, although may utter a weak *gah* when flushed. HABITAT: Wet grassy places surrounding lakes, pools and rivers etc. DISTRIBUTION: Vagrant on Barbados.

5 SNIPE (COMMON or WILSON'S SNIPE) *Gallinago gallinago* 25–27cm FIELD NOTES: When flushed flies off in an erratic, zigzag manner. In flight, underwing looks dark, actually tightly barred black and white. VOICE: When flushed gives a harsh *scaaap* or *scresh*. HABITAT: Grassy fringes of lakes, rivers; also flooded grassy areas. DISTRIBUTION: Widespread in the region, most common on Cuba, Hispaniola and the Bahamas, from October to April.

6 TURNSTONE (RUDDY TURNSTONE) *Arenaria interpres* 21–26cm FIELD NOTES: In flight, upperwing shows prominent white bar and white patch on inner wing coverts. Centre of back and lower rump white, split by dark band on upper rump. VOICE: A rapid, staccato *trik-tuk-tuk-tuk-tuk, tuk-e-tuk*. When alarmed, utters a sharp *chick-it*, *kuu* or *teu*. HABITAT: Mudflats, lake edges and sandy or rocky shores. DISTRIBUTION: Widespread in the region in most months, although less common during June and July.

7 WILSON'S PHALAROPE *Phalaropus tricolor* 22–24cm FIELD NOTES: In flight, shows white patch on lower rump. Tends to swim less than other phalaropes and when feeding on land walks quickly with a feverish pecking action. VOICE: Generally silent, but sometimes utters a soft, grunting *aangh*, *wennf* or *vimp* in flight. HABITAT: Shallow water bodies. DISTRIBUTION: Mainly a rare migrant on Barbados, Jamaica, Puerto Rico, the Virgin and Cayman Islands, a vagrant elsewhere; recorded from August to May.

8 GREY PHALAROPE (RED PHALAROPE) *Phalaropus fulicaria* 20–22cm FIELD NOTES: In flight, upperwing shows a wide white wing-bar. Regularly swims, spinning on the water to stir up food particles. VOICE: In flight, utters a sharp *pik*. HABITAT: Mainly pelagic, sometimes occurs on coastal pools and lagoons. DISTRIBUTION: Vagrant (October to January) recorded from Cuba, the Virgin Islands and Antigua.

9 RED-NECKED PHALAROPE (NORTHERN PHALAROPE) *Phalaropus lobatus* 18–19cm FIELD NOTES: In flight, upperwing shows a white wing-bar. Feeding actions much as Grey Phalarope. VOICE: In flight, utters a harsh *twick*. HABITAT: Mainly at sea, sometimes on coastal marshes and lagoons. DISTRIBUTION: Rare migrant to the Bahamas, Cuba and Hispaniola, primarily from October to January; also a vagrant with records from Jamaica and Puerto Rico.

21 OYSTERCATCHER, STILT, AVOCET, PLOVERS AND SANDPIPERS

1 AMERICAN OYSTERCATCHER *Haematopus palliatus* 40–44cm FIELD NOTES: In flight, from above, shows large white wing-bar and white lower rump. VOICE: A shrill, piping *kleep kleep kleep*.... HABITAT: Rocky shores and headlands. Breeds on remote beaches from May to July. DISTRIBUTION: Widespread, generally more common on the central Bahamas, Puerto Rico, the Virgin Islands and Guadeloupe.

2 BLACK-NECKED STILT *Himantopus mexicanus* 34–39cm FIELD NOTES: Unmistakable. In flight, shows black wings with a white tail and rump that extends as a V on the back. Juvenile browner, hind-neck greyish. VOICE: A loud, repeated *kik kik kik kik*.... HABITAT: Various water bodies including mudflats, coastal salt-marshes and freshwater pools. Breeds from primarily April to August. DISTRIBUTION: Widespread throughout the region.

3 AMERICAN AVOCET *Recurvirostra americana* 40–50cm FIELD NOTES: Unmistakable. Readily swims, upending to feed, much like a dabbling duck. VOICE: A high-pitched *kleet* or *kluit*. HABITAT: Shallows of lakes, lagoons and tidal mudflats. DISTRIBUTION: Rare on the Bahamas and Cuba from July to January, elsewhere a vagrant with records from Jamaica, Puerto Rico, the Virgin and Cayman Islands.

4 LAPWING (NORTHERN LAPWING, GREEN PLOVER, PEEWIT) *Vanellus vanellus* 28–31cm FIELD NOTES: In flight, looks black and white, from above shows mainly white tail, black at tip, and white wing-tips. VOICE: A plaintive *wee-ip* or *pee-wit*. HABITAT: Grasslands, less often on estuaries and coastal marshes. DISTRIBUTION: Vagrant, recorded from the Bahamas (Paradise Island), Puerto Rico, Martinique and Barbados.

5 GREY PLOVER (BLACK-BELLIED PLOVER) *Pluvialis squatarola* 27–30cm FIELD NOTES: In flight, shows white rump and upperwing bar, underwing is white with black axillary patch. VOICE: A mournful *tlee-oo-ee*. HABITAT: Coastal mudflats and beaches. DISTRIBUTION: Generally common throughout region, mainly August to May.

6 AMERICAN GOLDEN PLOVER (LESSER GOLDEN PLOVER) *Pluvialis dominica* 24–28cm FIELD NOTES: Wing-tips project beyond tail, shorter tertials than on Pacific Golden Plover. Slightly shorter-legged than Pacific Golden Plover. VOICE: A sharp *klu-eet*, *kleep* or *klu-ee-uh*. In flight, utters a mournful, level-pitched *queedle*. HABITAT: Grasslands, fallow fields and coastal mudflats. DISTRIBUTION: Widespread, but rare, throughout the region, primarily from August to November and from March to April.

7 PACIFIC GOLDEN PLOVER (ASIAN or EASTERN GOLDEN PLOVER) *Pluvialis fulva* 23–26cm FIELD NOTES: Wing-tips project beyond tail, tertials long. Slightly longer-legged than American Golden Plover. Non-breeding adults generally yellower in tone than American Golden Plover. VOICE: In flight, utters a rising *quit*, *chu-wit* or *kowidl*, lower pitched than American Golden Plover. HABITAT: Coastal mudflats and beaches, sometimes on inland grassland. DISTRIBUTION: Vagrant, recorded from Barbados.

8 BUFF-BREASTED SANDPIPER *Tryngites subruficollis* 18–20cm FIELD NOTES: Can be very approachable. In flight, shows white underwing with dark grey tips to flight feathers and primary coverts, the latter forming a distinct dark crescent. VOICE: Generally silent; occasionally utters a short *prrreet* when flushed. HABITAT: Short-grass areas, also mud surrounds of lakes and rivers. DISTRIBUTION: Rare in the Lesser Antilles from September to November. A vagrant elsewhere, recorded from the Greater Antilles and the Bahamas.

1

2

n-br
3
br

4
n-br br

5
n-br

6
br n-br br

7
br n-br

8

22 PLOVERS

1 PIPING PLOVER *Charadrius melodus* 17–19cm FIELD NOTES: In flight, from above, shows white upper tail coverts, black-tipped tail and a wide white wing-bar. Typical plover feeding action, quick runs with frequent stops to pick up food. VOICE: A whistled *peep*, *peep-lo* or *peep peep peep-lo*. When alarmed, gives a series of soft whistles. HABITAT: Coastal and lake shores. DISTRIBUTION: Occurs, from August to March, in the Bahamas, Greater Antilles and Lesser Antilles (St Croix in the Virgin Islands; a vagrant to the rest of the Lesser Antilles).

2 SNOWY PLOVER (KENTISH PLOVER) *Charadrius alexandrinus* 14–15cm FIELD NOTES: Forages by running with short stops to pick up food, generally a quicker action than Piping, Semipalmated and Ringed Plovers. In flight, from above, shows white wing-bar and white sides to tail. VOICE: A low *ku-wheet*, a hard *quip* and a low *krut*. HABITAT: Sandy beaches, salt flats, lake and lagoon edges. Breeds, primarily on sandy beaches, from January to August. DISTRIBUTION: Southern Bahamas and Greater Antilles (rare on Cuba, vagrant to Jamaica and the Cayman Islands); in the Lesser Antilles, resident on the Virgin Islands (Anegada), St Martin and St Bartholomew, a vagrant elsewhere.

3 COLLARED PLOVER *Charadrius collaris* 14–15cm FIELD NOTES: In flight, upperwing shows a very narrow white wing-bar and white sides to tail. Juvenile lacks black frontal crown and black breast band, the latter replaced by dark pectoral smudge. VOICE: A sharp *peek*; also a short *kip* or *chit*. HABITAT: Coastal mudflats, beaches, coastal lagoons and river banks. Breeds on mudflats, from January to September. DISTRIBUTION: Resident on Grenada, also recorded from Barbados, St Martin, St Christopher and St Lucia.

4 RINGED PLOVER (GREAT or COMMON RINGED PLOVER) *Charadrius hiaticula* 18–20cm FIELD NOTES: Very similar to Semipalmated Plover, best distinguished by voice. VOICE: A mellow, rising *too-lee* and a soft *too-weep* or *wip* when alarmed. HABITAT: Primarily coastal beaches and mudflats. DISTRIBUTION: Vagrant, recorded from Barbados.

5 SEMIPALMATED PLOVER *Charadrius semipalmatus* 17–19cm FIELD NOTES: Typical plover feeding actions, quick runs with frequent stops to pick up food. In flight, upperwing shows white wing-bar and white sides to tail. VOICE: A clear, whistled *chee-wee* or *chuwit*. When alarmed, gives a sharp *chip-chip* or *tup-tup*. HABITAT: Coastal mudflats. DISTRIBUTION: Common throughout the region from August to May.

6 KILLDEER *Charadrius vociferus* 23–26cm FIELD NOTES: Fairly typical plover foraging actions, short runs, then standing to 'look' before picking up food. Prominent white bar on upperwing, and chestnut-orange rump. VOICE: A shrill *kill-dee*, *kill-deeah* or variations such as *twill-wee-wee-wee*. HABITAT: Wet grasslands, edges of lakes, pools and estuaries. Breeds from May to July. DISTRIBUTION: Resident in the Bahamas, Greater Antilles (uncommon in the Cayman Islands) and the northern Lesser Antilles (Virgin Islands south to St Bartholomew), much rarer in the rest of the Lesser Antilles.

7 WILSON'S PLOVER (THICK-BILLED PLOVER) *Charadrius wilsonia* 18–20cm FIELD NOTES: In flight, upperwing shows a white wing-bar, edges of outer upper tail coverts white, forming a patch. Crown colour variable, West Indies breeding birds show more rufous. VOICE: A musical, whistled *quit*, *whit* or *queet*. When alarmed, utters a sharp *dik* or *dik-ik*. HABITAT: Coastal beaches, salt ponds and mudflats. Breeds from March to July. DISTRIBUTION: Resident throughout the region, although less common or rare on the Cayman Islands and in the southern Lesser Antilles.

23 WILLET, SHANKS, YELLOWLEGS, AND *TRINGA* AND *ACTITIS* SANDPIPERS

1 GREENSHANK (COMMON or GREATER GREENSHANK) *Tringa nebularia* 30–35cm FIELD NOTES: In flight, shows white rump and back. Actions and habits very similar to Greater Yellowlegs. VOICE: A ringing *chew-chew-chew*. HABITAT: Various wetland areas, both coastal and inland, usually confined to the shallows. DISTRIBUTION: Vagrant, recorded from Puerto Rico and Barbados.

2 WILLET *Tringa semipalmatus* 33–41cm FIELD NOTES: Generally nervous, often the first bird from mixed groups to fly off in alarm. In flight, underwing distinctly black and white, white wing-bar contrasting with black primary tips and underwing coverts; upperwing similar but coverts grey-brown. VOICE: When alarmed gives a loud *wik wik wik wik*. At breeding grounds utters a rolling *pill-will-willet*. HABITAT: Salt marsh, lake shores, sandy beaches and tidal mudflats. Breeds from April to July. DISTRIBUTION: Resident in the Bahamas, Greater Antilles and northern Lesser Antilles (Virgin Islands, Antigua); mainly a non-breeding resident in the rest of the Lesser Antilles.

3 GREATER YELLOWLEGS *Tringa melanoleuca* 29–33cm FIELD NOTES: Forages by walking on shore or wading in shallow water, picking ground or water surface in search of food; often dashes around chasing after small fish. In flight, shows white rump. VOICE: A slightly descending *teu-teu-teu*. HABITAT: Shores and shallows of various freshwater or saltwater bodies. DISTRIBUTION: Widespread throughout the region, primarily from August to October, although occurs in most months apart from June and July.

4 LESSER YELLOWLEGS *Tringa flavipes* 23–25cm FIELD NOTES: Foraging actions much as Greater Yellowlegs; tends to be more delicate and rarely dashes around. In flight, looks like a smaller version of Greater Yellowlegs. VOICE: A flat *tew-tew* or single *tew*. HABITAT: Shores and shallows of various freshwater and saltwater bodies. DISTRIBUTION: Widespread throughout the region, mainly from August to October and from March to May.

5 SPOTTED REDSHANK (DUSKY REDSHANK) *Tringa erythropus* 29–32cm FIELD NOTES: Often wades up to belly. Moulting birds have non-breeding plumage blotched with black. In flight, shows white oval stretching from rump to centre of back. VOICE: A distinctive *chu-it* or a short *chip* given in alarm. HABITAT: Estuaries, lagoons and marshes. DISTRIBUTION: Vagrant, recorded from Barbados.

6 WOOD SANDPIPER *Tringa glareola* 19–21cm FIELD NOTES: In flight, shows white rump and narrow barring on tail. VOICE: A high-pitched *chiff-iff-iff*; also a *chip* or *chip-chip-chip* given in alarm. HABITAT: Lake and pond shores, flooded grassland and marshes. DISTRIBUTION: Vagrant, recorded from Barbados.

7 SOLITARY SANDPIPER *Tringa solitaria* 18–21cm FIELD NOTES: Walks slowly and deliberately, picking food delicately off the surface of water or ground. In flight, shows dark rump, outer tail feathers white with broad dark bars. VOICE: An excited *peet, peet-weet-weet* or *tewit-weet*. HABITAT: Shores of freshwater lakes, pools, rivers etc. DISTRIBUTION: Throughout the region, although nowhere common, from November to May; most numerous during September and October.

8 SPOTTED SANDPIPER *Actitis macularia* 18–20cm FIELD NOTES: Walks steadily with bobbing rear end; has fluttering or flicking wing-beats during low flight. Upperwing shows a short white bar. VOICE: A double *peet-weet* or a short, whistled *peet*. HABITAT: Edges of lakes, rivers and ponds, mangroves and also coastal shores and rice fields. DISTRIBUTION: Throughout the region, mainly from August to May.

24 RUFF, UPLAND SANDPIPER, CURLEWS AND WHIMBREL

1 RUFF (REEVE: female) *Philomachus pugnax* 26–32cm FIELD NOTES: Breeding males are unmistakable but very variable; moulting males resemble breeding females but have breast and flanks splattered with dark blotches. In flight, shows narrow white bar on upperwing and prominent white sides to long upper tail coverts. Forages with a steady gait, regularly pecking food from ground or water surface; recorded swimming, feeding phalarope-like. VOICE: Generally silent; in flight, may utter a muffled *prrreet*. HABITAT: Lake, pond and river margins, wet grasslands and marshes. DISTRIBUTION: A migrant on Barbados and a vagrant elsewhere, recorded from August to May although more often during September and October.

2 UPLAND SANDPIPER *Bartramia longicauda* 28–32cm FIELD NOTES: Forages plover-like, runs swiftly with sudden stops. Regularly perches on fence posts or telegraph poles. Flight stiff and fluttering, upperwing showing dark primaries; tail long. VOICE: A piping *quip-ip-ip-ip* or *qui-di-di-du*, the last syllable lower-pitched than the rest. HABITAT: Grasslands. DISTRIBUTION: A rare migrant or vagrant throughout the region, occurring mainly from August to October and again during April and May.

3 ESKIMO CURLEW *Numenius borealis* 29–34cm FIELD NOTES: Critically endangered, possibly extinct. Underwing coverts cinnamon, closely barred dark brown. VOICE: Not well documented: a rippling *tr-tr-tr* and a soft, whistled *bee-bee*; other calls said to recall those of Upland Sandpiper. HABITAT: Coastal grassland, fields and occasionally mudflats. DISTRIBUTION: Vagrant, recorded from Puerto Rico, Guadeloupe, Barbados, the Grenadines and Grenada.

4 WHIMBREL *Numenius phaeopus* 40–46cm FIELD NOTES: Note pale mid-crown stripe. Underwing coverts pale brown, barred dark brown. Vagrant European race (fig 4b) has white rump, lower back and underwing coverts. Feeds both by probing and surface picking. VOICE: A rapid, liquid *qui qui qui qui qui*. HABITAT: Coastal areas, marshes and swamps. DISTRIBUTION: Throughout the region, recorded in most months, but generally rare or uncommon.

5 CURLEW (EURASIAN or COMMON CURLEW) *Numenius arquata* 50–60cm FIELD NOTES: In flight, shows white rump, lower back and underwing coverts. Feeds mainly by deep probing, but also picks food, such as crabs, from land surface. VOICE: A far-carrying *cour-lee* and, when disturbed, a stammering *tutututu*. HABITAT: Coastal mudflats, marshes and inland grassland. DISTRIBUTION: Vagrant recorded from Eleuthera in the Bahamas.

6 LONG-BILLED CURLEW *Numenius americanus* 51–66 cm FIELD NOTES: In flight, upperwing shows much cinnamon on inner primaries and secondaries; primary coverts and outer three primaries blackish; underwing coverts distinctly cinnamon. Feeds by deep probing and surface picking. VOICE: A loud, rising *cur-lee* or *coooLI*. HABITAT: Coastal mudflats, marshes, lagoons and occasionally grassland. DISTRIBUTION: Vagrant, recorded from Cuba, Jamaica, Puerto Rico, the Virgin Islands (St Croix) and Antigua.

♀ br 1

♂ n-br

2

1

♂ br
varieties

♂ br

3

4b

4

5

6

25 DOWITCHERS, GODWITS, SANDERLING AND KNOT

1 SHORT-BILLED DOWITCHER (COMMON DOWITCHER) *Limnodromus griseus* 25–29cm FIELD NOTES: Difficult to separate from Long-billed Dowitcher, especially in non-breeding plumage. Central North American race *L. g. hendersoni* (fig 1b), which may turn up in the West Indies, has breeding plumage very similar to that of Long-billed Dowitcher. In flight, shows white oval from upper rump to mid back. White bars on tail usually wider than black bars. VOICE: In flight, utters a mellow, rapid *tututu* or *chu-du-du*. HABITAT: Mainly coastal mudflats. DISTRIBUTION: Resident throughout the region from August to April, more frequent in the Bahamas, Greater Antilles and Barbados.

2 LONG-BILLED DOWITCHER *Limnodromus scolopaceus* 27–30cm FIELD NOTES: Very difficult to separate from Short-billed Dowitcher in non-breeding plumage, although breast tends to be slightly darker grey, ending abruptly on lower breast. In flight, shows white oval from upper rump to mid back. White bars on tail usually much narrower than black bars, making tail appear dark. VOICE: In flight, utters a thin, high *keek* or *kik-kik-kik-kik*. HABITAT: Prefers shallow fresh or brackish water bodies, but also frequents coastal mudflats. DISTRIBUTION: Rare migrant, recorded from Cuba, Jamaica, Hispaniola, the Cayman Islands, the Virgin Islands, St Christopher and Barbados.

3 BLACK-TAILED GODWIT *Limosa limosa* 40–44cm FIELD NOTES: In flight, from above, appears black and white due to bold white bar on upperwing, white rump and black tail. Underwing mainly white. VOICE: In flight, gives a yelping *kip* or *kip-kip-kip*. Feeding birds utter a low *kett*, *tuk* or *chuk*. HABITAT: Estuaries, mudflats, lakeshores and grassland. DISTRIBUTION: Vagrant, recorded from St Christopher.

4 MARBLED GODWIT *Limosa fedoa* 40–51cm FIELD NOTES: In flight, superficially resembles Long-billed Curlew, but bill shorter and straight. VOICE: In flight, utters a harsh *cor-ack* or *kaaWEK*. HABITAT: Costal mudflats and marshes. DISTRIBUTION: A rare migrant or vagrant, recorded in the Greater and Lesser Antilles, from August to April.

5 HUDSONIAN GODWIT *Limosa haemastica* 36–42cm FIELD NOTES: In flight, from above, similar to Black-tailed Godwit, although white wing-bar narrower and confined to primaries and outer secondaries. Underwing grey flight feathers and black coverts. VOICE: A soft *chow-chow*, a nasal *toe-wit*, *wit* or *kweh-weh*, and other variations. HABITAT: Lake and pond shores, coastal mudflats, flooded grasslands and rice fields. DISTRIBUTION: Uncommon or rare throughout most of the West Indies; mainly during September and October.

6 BAR-TAILED GODWIT *Limosa lapponica* 37–41cm FIELD NOTES: European race has white rump, back and underwing, Siberian race *L. l. baureri* has white rump closely barred grey and white, underwing barred and mottled dark grey-brown. VOICE: A high-pitched *kik*, *kiv-ik* or *kak-kak-kak-kak*, and variations of these. HABITAT: Muddy or sandy coastal shores. DISTRIBUTION: Vagrant, recorded from St Croix in the Virgin Islands.

7 SANDERLING *Calidris alba* 20–21cm FIELD NOTES: Feeds along water's edge, typically with rapid runs interspersed with quick dips to pick up prey. In flight, upperwing shows a broad white bar and a dark leading edge, this most noticeable in non-breeding plumage. VOICE: In flight, gives a hard *twick* or *kip*; when repeated forms a quick trill. HABITAT: Mainly sandy or muddy coastal shores. DISTRIBUTION: Generally common throughout the region, mainly from September to April.

8 KNOT (RED or LESSER KNOT) *Calidris canutus* 23–25cm FIELD NOTES: In flight, shows narrow white bar on upperwing; lower rump is white, sparsely marked with black. VOICE: A soft, nasal *knut*, *wutt* or *whet*. HABITAT: Muddy or sandy coastal shores. DISTRIBUTION: Throughout the region but generally rare; a vagrant in the Lesser Antilles, apart from Barbados, where it occurs regularly.

26 *CALIDRIS* SANDPIPERS

1 SEMIPALMATED SANDPIPER *Calidris pusilla* 13–15cm FIELD NOTES: Usually very gregarious. Forages by running head down with frequent stops to pick and probe for food. VOICE: A harsh *chrup* or *kreet*. HABITAT: Coastal, lake and pool shores. DISTRIBUTION: Generally common throughout the region; most frequent between August and May.

2 WESTERN SANDPIPER *Calidris mauri* 14–17cm FIELD NOTES: Compared to Semipalmated Sandpiper, bill is slightly more down-turned, longer and thicker based; also tends to forage more often in water. VOICE: A thin, high-pitched *jeet* or *cheet*. HABITAT: Mainly coastal shores. DISTRIBUTION: Generally common throughout the region, mainly from September to March.

3 LITTLE STINT *Calidris minuta* 12–14cm FIELD NOTES: Faster feeding action than Semipalmated Sandpiper. Fine-tipped straight bill. VOICE: A short *stit* and a weak *tee tee tee tee* given when alarmed. HABITAT: Coastal mudflats and the shores of lakes, pools and rivers. DISTRIBUTION: Vagrant, recorded from Antigua and Barbados.

4 LEAST SANDPIPER *Calidris minutilla* 13–15cm FIELD NOTES: Gregarious, often feeding alongside Semipalmated Sandpiper. Tends to adopt a crouched attitude when feeding. VOICE: A shrill, rising *trreee*, *prrrep* or *kreeep*; also a low, vibrant *prrrt*. HABITAT: Coastal mudflats, marshes, lakes and pond fringes. DISTRIBUTION: Widespread common migrant from August to October and during April and May; also occurs as an uncommon non-breeding resident from November to March.

5 WHITE-RUMPED SANDPIPER *Calidris fuscicollis* 15–18cm FIELD NOTES: In flight, shows white rump; at rest, wings project beyond tail. VOICE: A high-pitched *jeeet* or *eeet*; also a short *tit* or *teet*. HABITAT: Inland and coastal wetland areas. DISTRIBUTION: Uncommon migrant throughout the region, mainly from August to October and during March and April.

6 BAIRD'S SANDPIPER *Calidris bairdii* 14–17cm FIELD NOTES: At rest, wings project beyond tail. Usually occurs singly or in small groups. VOICE: A low *preeet*; also a grating *krrt* and a sharp *tsick*. HABITAT: Mainly on the fringes of lakes and pools that are bordered by grassland. DISTRIBUTION: Rare migrant, recorded from Dominica, St Lucia, Barbados, the Grenadines (Mustique), the Cayman Islands (Grand Cayman) and the Virgin Islands (St Croix), during September and October.

7 PECTORAL SANDPIPER *Calidris melanotos* 19–23cm FIELD NOTES: In flight, upperwing shows fine white wing-bar, also white rump with a broad black central stripe. VOICE: A reedy *churk* or *trrit*. HABITAT: Coastal and inland wetlands, wet meadows and grassy areas. DISTRIBUTION: Widespread but uncommon migrant, from August to November and also during March and April.

8 DUNLIN (RED-BACKED SANDPIPER) *Calidris alpina* 16–22cm FIELD NOTES: In flight, has prominent white bar on upperwing and white sides to rump and upper tail coverts. VOICE: A rasping *kreeep* and a low *beep*. HABITAT: Salt marsh, lake borders and coastal mudflats. DISTRIBUTION: Rare resident, from August to April, in the Bahamas, Cuba, Jamaica, Puerto Rico and the Virgin Islands. Vagrant on the Cayman Islands, St Christopher, Dominica and Barbados.

9 CURLEW SANDPIPER *Calidris ferruginea* 18–23cm FIELD NOTES: In flight, has a white bar on upperwing and a prominent white rump. Regularly wades up to belly. VOICE: A rippling *chirrup*. HABITAT: Coastal mudflats, lagoons and marshes. DISTRIBUTION: Vagrant, recorded from Barbados (regular), Puerto Rico, the Virgin Islands (Virgin Gorda), Antigua, Dominica, Grenada and the Grenadines (Carriacou) from April to June and during September and October.

10 STILT SANDPIPER *Calidris himantopus* 18–23cm FIELD NOTES: In flight, shows white rump, upperwing appears plain and feet protrude beyond tail. Often wades up to belly. VOICE: A soft *kirrr* or *drrr*; also a hoarse *djew*. HABITAT: Inland and coastal wetlands. DISTRIBUTION: Locally common on Hispaniola, Puerto Rico and the Virgin Islands; elsewhere generally uncommon, most frequent from August to November.

27 SKUAS

1 POMARINE SKUA (POMARINE JAEGER) *Stercorarius pomarinus* 46–51cm FIELD
NOTES: The bulkiest of all the 'smaller' skuas. Pursues other seabirds in a bid to steal food, has
been known to go as far as killing the victim of these chases. Juveniles lack the elongated
central feathers and have variable coloured upperparts, from mid to dark brown, barred paler
with paler underparts, barred dark. Head uniform in colour, from grey-brown to dark brown; in
flight, shows distinct white flash at base of primaries. VOICE: Away from breeding grounds
generally silent, although occasionally utters barking sounds. HABITAT: Primarily pelagic.
DISTRIBUTION: Widespread, but uncommon, from October to May.

2 ARCTIC SKUA (PARASITIC JAEGER) *Stercorarius parasiticus* 41–46cm FIELD NOTES:
Aerobatic as it chases and harries seabirds in an attempt to make them disgorge food. Juveniles
lack elongated central feathers, colour very variable, many similar to juvenile Pomarine
Skuas, especially dark individuals, pale forms usually show buff or grey-buff head; in flight,
shows distinct white flash at base of primaries. VOICE: Away from breeding grounds generally
silent. HABITAT: Primarily pelagic. DISTRIBUTION: Widespread, but uncommon, from August to
May.

3 LONG-TAILED SKUA (LONG-TAILED JAEGER) *Stercorarius longicaudus* 48–53cm
FIELD NOTES: In flight, often gives the impression of being heavy-chested. Less piratical than
other skuas, usually chooses terns if indulging in pursuits. The 'dark' morph shown is very rare
and said to be only found breeding on Greenland, some 'experts' seem to doubt the validity of
this 'form'. Juveniles lack the long central tail feathers, although they do have a slight
extension, and are very variable in colour, generally dark above, barred pale, paler below
barred dark; there is a very dark morph that appears almost totally black; all forms show less
white on the primaries than other 'small' skuas. VOICE: Generally silent. HABITAT: Primarily
pelagic. DISTRIBUTION: Widespread, but rare migrant, from August to October and from March
to May.

4 GREAT SKUA (BONXIE) *Stercorarius skua* 53–58cm FIELD NOTES: Very aggressive to
other seabirds, recorded killing victims when attempting to rob them of food. Juveniles have
rufous underparts, grey-brown head and upperparts, the latter with pale rufous feather edges.
VOICE: Generally silent. HABITAT: Primarily pelagic. DISTRIBUTION: Probably widespread, from
November to May.

5 SOUTH POLAR SKUA (MacCORMICK'S SKUA) *Stercorarius maccormicki* 50–55cm
FIELD NOTES: Various intermediate morphs between the two depicted, all tend to lack any rufous
in plumage. Juveniles of pale and dark forms are similar to respective adults, but with some
pale feather edges on upperparts and a black-tipped blue bill. VOICE: Generally silent. HABITAT:
Primarily pelagic. DISTRIBUTION: Probably widespread, but rare, from May to October.

dark morph

pale morph

1

dark morph

pale morph

1

pale morph

dark morph

2

dark morph

pale morph

2

pale morph

dark morph

3

intermediate morph

3

pale morph

dark morph

4

4

dark morph

5

pale morph

5

28 GULLS

Due to the complex plumages of young gulls (often a 4-year process to get from the brown of juveniles to the grey of adults) it is difficult to cover all of these adequately within such a limited text. It would therefore be advisable for the reader to refer to books that cover this area more fully (*see* Further Reading).

1 BLACK-HEADED GULL (COMMON BLACK-HEADED GULL) *Chroicocephalus ridibundus* 37–43cm FIELD NOTES: First winter (sub-adult) birds much as non-breeding adult with the addition of a black tip to tail, legs and bill more yellow or pinkish-orange, the latter with a dark tip, and upperwing with brownish centres to feathers of tertials, lesser, median and inner greater coverts. VOICE: A high-pitched *karr*, *kreeay* or *krreearr*, also a sharp *kek-kek*. HABITAT: Coastal areas, including harbours, lakes and inland grasslands. DISTRIBUTION: Rare, from November to June, on Puerto Rico (locally regular), the Virgin Islands, Guadeloupe and Barbados. Recorded as a vagrant from the Bahamas, Cuba, Antigua, St Lucia and Grenada.

2 SLENDER-BILLED GULL *Chroicocephalus genei* 42–44cm FIELD NOTES: Usually looks longer-necked. First winter (sub-adult) plumage very similar to that of first-winter Black-headed Gull, although head pattern much weaker. Often in small parties. VOICE: A harsh, rolling *krerrr*; other notes similar to those of Black-headed Gull but lower pitched. HABITAT: Lagoons, estuaries and sheltered coastal bays. DISTRIBUTION: Vagrant, recorded from Antigua.

3 BONAPARTE'S GULL *Chroicocephalus philadelphia* 28–30cm FIELD NOTES: Note pale underwing. First winter (sub-adult) plumage very similar to that of Black-headed Gull, although slightly greyer hind-neck, blackish bill and pink legs. VOICE: A grating, tern-like *gerrr* or *reeek*. HABITAT: Coastal areas, including harbours. DISTRIBUTION: Uncommon or rare on Cuba, the Bahamas and Barbuda, from August to April; also recorded as a vagrant on Hispaniola, Puerto Rico, Antigua and Martinique.

4 LITTLE GULL *Hydrocoloeus minutus* 25–30cm FIELD NOTES: Note dark underwing and buoyant tern-like flight. Upperwings of first-winter birds show a distinct W formed by a dark diagonal across wing coverts and dark outer primaries; tail with a dark tip. VOICE: A tern-like *kik-kik* or *keck-keck-keck*. HABITAT: Coasts or nearby lakes and lagoons. DISTRIBUTION: Vagrant, recorded from Puerto Rico.

5 SABINE'S GULL *Xema sabini* 27–33cm FIELD NOTES: Graceful, tern-like flight. Juvenile has black tip to tail, and black bill, a similar wing pattern to adult but with greys replaced with ochre-brown; mantle, hind-neck, ear coverts and crown also ochre-brown. VOICE: A grating *kerr* or *kyeer kyeer*. HABITAT: Mainly pelagic. DISTRIBUTION: Vagrant, recorded from Cuba.

6 KITTIWAKE (BLACK-LEGGED KITTIWAKE) *Rissa tridactyla* 38–40cm FIELD NOTES: Flight buoyant and agile with long glides. Juvenile has pattern on upperwings similar to that of adult Sabine's Gull but with the addition of a black diagonal bar that forms a distinct W; also has a black collar on hind-neck, black smudge on ear coverts, black-tipped tail and black bill. VOICE: Generally silent away from breeding sites. HABITAT: Primarily pelagic. DISTRIBUTION: Rare, from December to March, in the Bahamas, also recorded as a vagrant off Cuba, Hispaniola, Jamaica, the Virgin Islands, Guadeloupe and St Lucia.

29 GULLS

See note on Plate 28 referring to young gulls.

1 RING-BILLED GULL *Larus delawarensis* 43–47cm FIELD NOTES: Sociable, often associating with other gulls. First-winter birds have a black-tipped tail, pink bill with black tip; secondaries, lesser and median wing coverts have brown centres, secondary coverts mostly plain grey, outer primaries black, inner primaries pale grey. VOICE: A mellow *kowk*, although generally silent away from breeding grounds. HABITAT: Coastal areas including harbours, inland on grasslands and around urban locations. DISTRIBUTION: Common in the northern Bahamas and on Hispaniola, widespread but less common or rare elsewhere, mainly from December to March.

2 AMERICAN HERRING GULL *Larus (argentatus) smithsonianus* 55–67cm FIELD NOTES: Second-winter birds have mantle, lesser and median coverts dark centred, secondary wing-coverts with dark barring, outer primaries dark, inner primaries pale grey, tail mainly dark. Bill pinkish with a dark tip. Third-winter similar to non-breeding adult, but head more marked and brownish markings on secondaries. VOICE: A load, laughing *keeah-keeah-keeah-keah-kau-kau…*, also a short *keeah*, *keeow* or *kyow*. When alarmed utters a *gag-ag-ag*. HABITAT: Mainly coastal areas, including harbours. DISTRIBUTION: Widespread, but nowhere common although numbers are increasing, mainly from October to March.

3 LESSER BLACK-BACKED GULL *Larus fuscus* 51–61cm FIELD NOTES: Adult mantle variable, dark in nominate, dark grey in *L. f. graellsii* (fig 3b). Gregarious, often associates with other gull species. Second-winter birds have a broad black band on end of tail, wing feathers and mantle look mottled due to brownish feather centres, primaries and primary coverts dark brown-black, bill black with pale base to lower mandible. VOICE: Similar to American Herring Gull, although lower in pitched and more nasal. HABITAT: Coastal areas. DISTRIBUTION: Very rare, but increasing, throughout the region.

4 GREAT BLACK-BACKED GULL *Larus marinus* 64–78cm FIELD NOTES: Can be aggressive and predatory. Flight heavy and powerful. Second-winter birds very similar to American Herring Gull, although mantle shows darker feather centres and inner secondaries contrast less with outer primaries. VOICE: A hoarse *oow oow oow*, also a deep *owk*. HABITAT: Mainly coastal. DISTRIBUTION: Recorded on Puerto Rico from October to March, otherwise a vagrant recorded from Cuba, Hispaniola, St Bartholomew, Barbados and the Bahamas.

5 LAUGHING GULL *Larus atricilla* 36–41cm FIELD NOTES: The common gull of the region. Flight graceful, with long-winged appearance. First-winter birds have upperwing coverts mottled light brown, underwing mottled with dark brown; tail has wide black terminal band; mantle and hind-neck grey, merging with darker grey ear coverts. VOICE: A high-pitched, laughing *ka-ka-ka-ka-ka-kaa-kaa-kaaa-kaaa*; also a shorter *kiiwa* or *kahwi*. HABITAT: Mainly coastal areas. DISTRIBUTION: Widespread throughout the region, recorded in all months although most numerous from April to September.

6 FRANKLIN'S GULL *Larus pipixcan* 32–38cm FIELD NOTES: First-winter birds have tail mainly white with narrow black tip that does not reach to the outer feathers, wings more uniform grey, underwing clean white, hind-neck white and head pattern similar to non-breeding adult. VOICE: Common calls are a short, soft *kruk*, *queel* or *kowii*. HABITAT: Estuaries, sandbanks and coastal lagoons. DISTRIBUTION: Vagrant, recorded mainly from August to January, on Hispaniola, Puerto Rico, St Bartholomew and Guadeloupe.

30 TERNS

1 CASPIAN TERN *Hydroprogne caspia* 47–54cm FIELD NOTES: Feeds mainly by hovering then plunge-diving. Upperwing shows grey outer primaries with darker tips, outer primaries on underwing dark grey. Tail forked. VOICE: A loud, croaking *krah, krah-krah* or *kree-ank*. HABITAT: Coastal areas, including harbours. DISTRIBUTION: Rare non-breeding resident, occurring at any month, to the southern Bahamas, Cuba, Jamaica, Hispaniola and Barbados, a vagrant elsewhere.

2 ROYAL TERN *Sterna maxima* 45–50cm FIELD NOTES: Feeds mainly by plunge-diving. Upperwing similar to Caspian Tern, underwing pale with a dark trailing edge to outer primaries. Tail deeply forked. VOICE: A low-pitched, grating *kerriup, krree-it* or *kirruck*. HABITAT: Coastal beaches, harbours and lagoons. Breeds in colonies on small cays, from April to July. DISTRIBUTION: Generally common throughout the region; numbers are boosted by migrants from October to April.

3 ARCTIC TERN *Sterna paradisaea* 33–38cm FIELD NOTES: Main feeding method is a short hover followed by a plunge-dive. From below, all primaries appear translucent. Tail deeply forked, with long streamers. VOICE: A piping *pee-pee-pee*, a rattling *kt-kt-kt-krr-kt* and, when alarmed, a high *kree-ah* or *kree-err*. HABITAT: Primarily pelagic but also noted resting among Roseate Tern colonies. DISTRIBUTION: Migrant on Puerto Rico, from June to October, vagrants recorded from Cuba and the Virgin Islands (St Croix and St John); probably under-recorded.

4 FORSTER'S TERN *Sterna forsteri* 33–36cm FIELD NOTES: Feeding actions similar to Arctic Tern. Usually looks bulkier than Common and Arctic Tern. Tail deeply forked, grey centred with long streamers. VOICE: A rolling, nasal *kyarr, kwarr* or *kreerr*; also a rapid *kek-ke-kek….* HABITAT: Coastal areas. DISTRIBUTION: Mainly a rare migrant, from November to April, to the Bahamas, Cuba, the Cayman Islands, Hispaniola, Puerto Rico and the Virgin Islands. Vagrants have been recorded from Jamaica, Antigua, Montserrat and St Vincent.

5 COMMON TERN *Sterna hirundo* 32–39cm FIELD NOTES: Feeding actions similar to Arctic Tern. From below, inner primaries appear translucent. Tail deeply forked, with long streamers. VOICE: A rapid *kye-kye-kye-kye…*; also a *kirri-kirri-kirri*, or similar. When alarmed, gives a screeching *kreeeearh* or *kreee-eer* and a sharp *kik*. HABITAT: Mainly coastal areas. Breeds from May to July, usually on sandy beaches bounded by vegetation, stones or rocks. DISTRIBUTION: Rare resident on Cuba and the Bahamas. Migrants occur, from May to October, throughout the region.

6 ROSEATE TERN *Sterna dougallii* 33–41cm FIELD NOTES: Feeding actions similar to Arctic Tern, although tends to hover less and 'fly into the water' often from a higher level than Common Tern. Tail deeply forked with very long tail streamers. VOICE: A short, soft *cher-vik* and a rasping *kraak* or *zraaach*. HABITAT: Coastal areas. Breeds in colonies, from May to July. DISTRIBUTION: Widespread, although mostly uncommon or rare, from April to September.

7 SANDWICH TERN *Sterna sandvicensis* 36–41cm FIELD NOTES: Often plunge-dives from a considerable height. Tail deeply forked. Cayenne Tern *S. s. eurygnatha* (fig 7b) occurs among Sandwich Terns in colonies off Puerto Rico and the Virgin Islands. VOICE: A grating *kirruck* or *kerRICK*; also a short *krik* or *krik-krik*. HABITAT: Coastal areas. Breeds, from May to July, in colonies on seashores. DISTRIBUTION: Resident on the Bahamas, Cuba, Puerto Rico and the Virgin Islands, otherwise a non-breeding resident in rest of the region from October to March.

8 LARGE-BILLED TERN *Phaetusa simplex* 38cm FIELD NOTES: Feeds mainly by plunge-diving. From above, shows distinctive wing pattern, primaries black, primary coverts, secondaries and outer secondary coverts white, the rest of the wing coverts grey, contiguous with mantle. Superficially like Sabine's Gull. Tail deeply forked. VOICE: A raucous *sqe-ee* and a nasal *ink-oink*. HABITAT: Inland water bodies, mangroves, beaches and estuaries. DISTRIBUTION: Vagrant, recorded from Cuba.

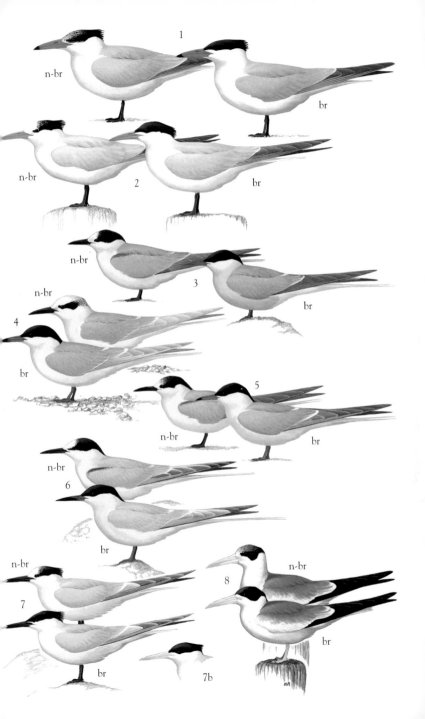

31 TERNS, NODDIES, SKIMMERS AND AUKS

1 LEAST TERN (AMERICAN LITTLE TERN) *Sterna antillarum* 22–25cm FIELD NOTES: Feeds by plunge-diving, with much hovering. Tail and rump pale grey, tail deeply forked. VOICE: A rapid *kid-ick kid-ick kid-ick* and a rasping *zr-e-e-e-p*. HABITAT: Coasts, inland lakes and lagoons. Breeds from April to July. DISTRIBUTION: Throughout the region.

2 GULL-BILLED TERN *Gelochelidon nilotica* 33–43cm FIELD NOTES: Feeds by hawking or dipping to pick prey from water or ground. Shallow forked tail. VOICE: A nasal *kayWEK kay-WEK*; also a rattling *aach* given when alarmed. HABITAT: Coastal shores and lagoons, inland lakes and grasslands. Breeds from May to July. DISTRIBUTION: Resident from the southern Bahamas to the Virgin Islands and off Anguilla, from April to August. Post breeding, found more widely.

3 BLACK TERN *Chlidonias niger* 22–24cm FIELD NOTES: Buoyant flight, regularly dipping to pick insects from water. Non-breeding birds have grey rump and tail, the latter shallowly forked. VOICE: A weak *kik* or *kik-kik*; also a shrill, nasal *kyeh* or *kreek* when alarmed. HABITAT: Lakes, marshes and estuaries. DISTRIBUTION: Common migrant on Jamaica and Puerto Rico from April to November, less common or rare elsewhere in the region.

4 WHITE-WINGED TERN (WHITE-WINGED BLACK TERN) *Chlidonias leucopterus* 23–27cm FIELD NOTES: Actions similar to Black Tern. Non-breeding birds have a white rump and pale grey tail; the latter shallowly forked, often appearing square. VOICE: A short *kek* and a rasping *kesch*. HABITAT: Lakes, marshes and estuaries. DISTRIBUTION: Vagrant, recorded from the Bahamas, the Virgin Islands and Barbados.

5 WHISKERED TERN *Chlidonias hybridus* 23–29cm FIELD NOTES: Actions similar to Black Tern. Non-breeding birds have rump and tail pale grey, the latter shallowly forked. VOICE: A short *kek* or *kek kek*. HABITAT: Lakes, marshes and sheltered coastal areas. DISTRIBUTION: Vagrant, recorded from Barbados.

6 BRIDLED TERN *Onychoprion anaethetus* 34–36cm FIELD NOTES: Feeds by plunge-diving and by dipping to pick prey from water. Tail deeply forked. VOICE: A yapping *wep-wep* or *wup-wup*. HABITAT: Generally pelagic; when breeding, April to July, found on remote islets. DISTRIBUTION: Generally common throughout the region.

7 SOOTY TERN *Onychoprion fuscata* 36–45cm FIELD NOTES: Feeds mainly by dipping to pick prey from water, occasionally plunge-dives. Tail deeply forked. VOICE: A distinctive *ker-wacki-wah*, or *wide-a-wake*. HABITAT: Generally pelagic; when breeding, April to August, found on remote islets. DISTRIBUTION: Resident throughout the region.

8 BROWN NODDY (COMMON NODDY) *Anous stolidus* 38–45cm FIELD NOTES: Feeds mainly by hovering and dipping to pick prey from water. VOICE: A crow-like *kwok-kwok*, *karruuk* or *krao*. HABITAT: Usually pelagic; when breeding, April to August, found on offshore cays. DISTRIBUTION: Widespread resident.

9 BLACK NODDY (WHITE-CAPPED NODDY) *Anous minutus* 35–39cm FIELD NOTES: Feeding actions similar to Brown Noddy. Best distinguished by voice. VOICE: A distinctive *tik-tikoree* and a staccato rattle. HABITAT: Usually pelagic. DISTRIBUTION: Vagrant, recorded from Puerto Rico, the Virgin Islands, Anguilla and Barbados. May be overlooked as a breeding bird.

10 BLACK SKIMMER *Rynchops niger* 40–51cm FIELD NOTES: Unmistakable. Feeds by 'ploughing' water with lower mandible whilst in skimming flight. Often nocturnal. VOICE: A soft, nasal *yep* or *yip*. HABITAT: Sheltered coastal waters and lagoons. DISTRIBUTION: Rare migrant on Cuba, Hispaniola, Puerto Rico, the Virgin Islands and the Bahamas, also a vagrant to Jamaica, the Cayman Islands and Grenada.

11 LITTLE AUK (DOVEKIE) *Alle alle* 17–19cm FIELD NOTES: Rapid whirring flight. VOICE: Generally silent. HABITAT: Primarily pelagic, blown inland during storms. DISTRIBUTION: Vagrant, recorded from Cuba and the Bahamas.

32 ROCK DOVE, PIGEONS AND QUAIL-DOVES

1 ROCK DOVE *Columba livia* 31–34cm FIELD NOTES: Known throughout the world, these very variable 'town pigeons' all originate from the true Rock Dove of Europe. VOICE: A moaning *oh-oo-oor*. HABITAT: Cities, towns and villages. DISTRIBUTION: Virtually throughout the region.

2 SCALY-NAPED PIGEON (RED-NECKED PIGEON) *Patagioenas squamosa* 36–40cm FIELD NOTES: Mainly arboreal, feeding alone or in small groups. Often seen flying over forests. VOICE: A strongly accentuated *who who hoo-oo-hoo*, the last three syllables sounding like 'who-are-you'. HABITAT: Mainly mountain forests, but on St Christopher and Barbados it occurs in towns and villages. Breeds mainly from March to June. DISTRIBUTION: Greater and Lesser Antilles.

3 WHITE-CROWNED PIGEON *Patagioenas leucocephala* 33–36cm FIELD NOTES: Gregarious, often in very large roosts and breeding colonies. Mainly arboreal. VOICE: A loud, clear *Cruu cru cu-cruuu*, sounding like 'Who-took-two'. HABITAT: Principally coastal woodlands and inland forests when food available. DISTRIBUTION: Throughout, although rare in most of the Lesser Antilles.

4 PLAIN PIGEON (BLUE PIGEON) *Patagioenas inornata* 38–40cm FIELD NOTES: Gregarious, mainly arboreal. Jamaican race *P. i. exigua* darker, with white eye surrounded by red orbital skin. VOICE: A low *whoo wo-oo* or similar. HABITAT: Lowland forests, mountain forests, mangroves and coastal scrub. DISTRIBUTION: Greater Antilles.

5 RING-TAILED PIGEON (JAMAICAN RING-TAILED PIGEON) *Patagioenas caribaea* 38–48cm FIELD NOTES: Gregarious, usually in small flocks, arboreal. VOICE: A deep *croo-croo-croooo*. HABITAT: Mountain and hill forests. Breeds from February to August. DISTRIBUTION: Jamaica.

6 BRIDLED QUAIL-DOVE *Geotrygon mystacea* 24–30cm FIELD NOTES: Secretive, forages on the ground, usually in deep cover. More often heard than seen. VOICE: A mournful *who-whooo*. HABITAT: Dark undergrowth in dense forest and wooded ravines. Breeds from May to July. DISTRIBUTION: Resident on Puerto Rico and the Lesser Antilles, although absent from Anguilla, St Martin, Barbados, St Vincent, Grenada and the Grenadines.

7 KEY WEST QUAIL-DOVE *Geotrygon chrysia* 27–31cm FIELD NOTES: Ground feeder, usually under the cover of bushes and trees. VOICE: A low, slightly descending *ooooo*; also an *ooooowoo*, with the second syllable accentuated and slightly higher. HABITAT: Dense woodland and thickets. Breeds from February to August. DISTRIBUTION: Resident on the Bahamas, Cuba, Hispaniola and locally on Puerto Rico.

8 GREY-HEADED QUAIL-DOVE (HISPANIOLAN QUAIL-DOVE) *Geotrygon caniceps* 26–30cm FIELD NOTES: Forages on the ground, often along tracks. Regularly calls from elevated perch. Hispaniolan race, *G. c. leucometopsis*, has purer white forehead and is generally darker. VOICE: A low *hoot hoot hoot hoot*; call of Hispaniolan race similar but with a sudden change to *coo-o-o*. HABITAT: Mainly mountain forest and coffee plantations in Dominican Republic and tropical lowland forest, bordering swamps, in Cuba. DISTRIBUTION: Resident on Cuba and Hispaniola.

9 RUDDY QUAIL-DOVE *Geotrygon montana* 21–28cm FIELD NOTES: Forages on the ground, usually under cover. VOICE: A low, fading *cooo*. HABITAT: Mainly dense forests and coffee plantations on hills and mountains, also locally in coastal forests. Breeds from February to August. DISTRIBUTION: Resident on the Greater and Lesser Antilles.

10 CRESTED QUAIL-DOVE (JAMAICAN QUAIL-DOVE) *Geotrygon versicolor* 27–31cm FIELD NOTES: Forages on the ground, generally in deep shade although will venture onto tracks. VOICE: A low *woof-woo-wooo*. HABITAT: Mountain forests. Breeds from March to June. DISTRIBUTION: Endemic resident on Jamaica.

11 BLUE-HEADED QUAIL-DOVE *Starnoenas cyanocehala* 29–34cm FIELD NOTES: Endangered. Forages on the ground, usually in pairs. VOICE: A hollow *huuup-up huuup-up*. HABITAT: Forests with a thick overhead cover and an open floor with a quantity of leaf litter. Breeds from April to July. DISTRIBUTION: Resident on Cuba.

33 DOVES AND COMMON GROUND-DOVE

1 COLLARED DOVE (EURASIAN or EUROPEAN COLLARED DOVE) *Streptopelia decaocto* 31–33cm FIELD NOTES: Feeds mainly on the ground. Buff-grey under-tail coverts. The widely domesticated African Collared Dove *S. roseogrisea* (fig 1b) has white under-tail coverts and can often be paler. Juveniles of both species lack black and white neck collar. VOICE: A loud *kook-koooo-kook* or similar; also a harsh *kreair* or *whaaa*, usually given on landing. HABITAT: Urban areas. Breeds primarily from March to June. DISTRIBUTION: Northern Bahamas, western Cuba, Cayman Islands, and a few islands in the Lesser Antilles; it is expected to colonise the whole region.

2 SPOTTED DOVE (NECKLACE DOVE) *Streptopelia chinensis* 30cm FIELD NOTES: Feeds on the ground. In flight, shows broad white terminal patch on outer tail feathers. Juvenile lacks neck spotting, this area replaced with grey. VOICE: A melodious *coo croo-coo-oo* or *coocoo croor-croor*. HABITAT: Cultivated areas and around human habitations. Breeds from April to July. DISTRIBUTION: Virgin Islands (St Croix).

3 WHITE-WINGED DOVE *Zenaida asiatica* 28–30cm FIELD NOTES: In flight, upperwings show a large white central patch. Feeds in trees and on the ground, usually gregarious. VOICE: A rhythmic *who hoo who hoo-oo* or *who hoo who hoo hoo-ah hoo-hoo-ah who oo*. HABITAT: Open woodland, arid scrub, mangroves and gardens. Breeds, colonially, primarily from April to June. DISTRIBUTION: The Bahamas, Greater Antilles and the Virgin Islands.

4 ZENAIDA DOVE *Zenaida aurita* 25–28cm FIELD NOTES: Primarily a ground feeder, although will feed in fruiting trees. In flight, secondaries have a white trailing edge and the outer tail feathers have greyish-white tips. VOICE: A mournful *coo-oo coo coo coo*, very similar to Mourning Dove. HABITAT: Open coastal areas, urban gardens, open woodland, pine woods and scrub thickets. Breeds from February to June in wet areas, from April to June in arid areas and all year round in urban areas. DISTRIBUTION: Resident throughout the region.

5 MOURNING DOVE (AMERICAN MOURNING DOVE) *Zenaida macroura* 30–31cm FIELD NOTES: Feeds mainly on the ground. Female paler with less iridescence on neck and less grey on the head. VOICE: A mournful *oo-woo woo woo woo*, similar to Zenaida Dove. HABITAT: Lowland open country, agricultural areas and dry coastal forests, frequently near fresh water. Breeds from March to August. DISTRIBUTION: The Bahamas and Greater Antilles.

6 EARED DOVE (VIOLET-EARED DOVE) *Zenaida auriculata* 22–25cm FIELD NOTES: Feeds primarily on the ground, usually in pairs or small groups but occasionally in large flocks; often roosts communally. VOICE: A gentle *oooa-oo* or *u-ooa-oo*. HABITAT: Lowland semiarid brush. Breeds from December to September. DISTRIBUTION: Lesser Antilles (St Vincent, the Grenadines, Grenada, Barbados, Martinique and St Lucia).

7 COMMON GROUND-DOVE *Columbina passerina* 15–18cm FIELD NOTES: Common. Mainly a ground feeder, usually in pairs or small groups. VOICE: A repetitive *coo coo coo coo coo...*, *co-coo co-coo co-coo...* or *hoooip hoooip hoooip...*. HABITAT: Variety of open areas such as cultural land, woodland, savannah and urban gardens. Breeds in any month, but mainly during May and June. DISTRIBUTION: Widespread resident throughout the region.

8 CARIBBEAN DOVE *Leptotila jamaicensis* 29–33cm FIELD NOTES: Forages on the ground, often under the cover of bushes. VOICE: A high-pitched *cu-cu-cu-oooo*. HABITAT: Open areas, gardens and thick secondary forests in lowland and foothills. Breeds from March to May. DISTRIBUTION: Jamaica, Cayman Islands, San Andrés and the Bahamas (New Providence).

9 GRENADA DOVE *Leptotila wellsi* 28–31cm FIELD NOTES: Critically endangered. Feeds on the ground. VOICE: A descending *oooo*. HABITAT: Scrubby woods on hillsides and lowlands. Breeds from December to February and in July, may vary according to rainfall. DISTRIBUTION: Grenada.

34 PARROTLET, BUDGERIGAR AND PARAKEETS

1 GREEN-RUMPED PARROTLET (GUIANA or COMMON PARROTLET) *Forpus passerinus* 12–13cm FIELD NOTES: Gregarious, usually in flocks of from 5 to 50. Flight swift with many twists and turns. VOICE: A shrill *chee chee chee*; also a *tsup-tsup*. Feeding flocks keep up a constant twittering. HABITAT: Open country in dry lowlands and hills, frequents any elevation in Jamaica. Breeds from April to July. DISTRIBUTION: Jamaica and Barbados.

2 BUDGERIGAR *Melopsittacus undulatus* 18cm FIELD NOTES: Popular cagebird that occurs in a variety of colours. In flight, shows a yellow wing-bar. VOICE: A subdued screech and a pleasant warble that is commonly uttered in flight. Feeding groups regularly utter quiet chattering. HABITAT: Grassland. DISTRIBUTION: Escapes recorded from Puerto Rico, Grand Cayman, Jamaica, Guadeloupe and Dominican Republic.

3 MONK PARAKEET *Myiopsitta monachus* 28–29cm FIELD NOTES: Gregarious and noisy. Flight swift with rapid wing-beats. VOICE: A loud, staccato, shriek and a high-pitched chattering. HABITAT: Palm groves, urban gardens and parks. DISTRIBUTION: Introduced to Puerto Rico and Grand Cayman.

4 BLACK-HEADED PARAKEET (NANDAY PARAKEET or CONURE) *Nandayus nenday* 36cm FIELD NOTES: Flight is swift and direct with rapid wing-beats. Gregarious, usually in small flocks. VOICE: A screeching *kree-ah kree-ah*, generally given in flight; perched birds often utter a shrill chatter. HABITAT: Scrubby woodland, palm groves and meadows with nearby thickets. DISTRIBUTION: Introduced on Puerto Rico.

5 CANARY-WINGED PARAKEET *Brotogeris versicolurus* 23cm FIELD NOTES: Gregarious, usually in flock of 10 to 50, occasionally recorded in very large flocks. Upperwing shows white inner primaries and secondaries with yellow secondary coverts. Underwing also has white inner primaries and secondaries. VOICE: A high, scratchy *krere-krere*; feeding flocks utter a high-pitched chattering. HABITAT: Coastal woodlands, hills and foothills of mountains, also urban areas. DISTRIBUTION: Introduced to Puerto Rico.

6 OLIVE-THROATED PARAKEET (OLIVE-THROATED CONURE) *Aratinga nana* 22–26cm FIELD NOTES: Gregarious, generally in small flocks. Flight is rapid and erratic. VOICE: High-pitched screeches. HABITAT: Forests, scrubby woodland, crop fields and urban areas. Breeds from March to June. DISTRIBUTION: Resident on Jamaica.

7 ORANGE-FRONTED PARAKEET (ORANGE-FRONTED CONURE) *Aratinga canicularis* 23–25cm FIELD NOTES: Gregarious, usually in small flocks. Flight is swift and direct with rapid wing-beats interspersed with brief glides. VOICE: A raucous *can-can-can*, a shrill screech and, whilst feeding, a quiet chattering. HABITAT: Wooded pastures and among ornamental trees in urban areas. DISTRIBUTION: Introduced on Puerto Rico.

8 BROWN-THROATED PARAKEET (BROWN-THROATED CONURE) *Aratinga pertinax* 23–28cm FIELD NOTES: Usually encountered in pairs or small flocks. Flight is swift and erratic with sudden changes of direction. Juveniles have brownish ear coverts, throat and upper breast tinged greenish, forehead tinged with green and brown. Upper mandible pale horn. VOICE: Harsh squawks; in flight, utters a shrill *crik crik ...crak crak*, which is repeated rapidly. HABITAT: High scrub, with seasonal descents to feed in fruiting trees. Breeds from March to July. DISTRIBUTION: Primarily on St Thomas; also recorded from Saba, Dominica, Guadeloupe and Martinique.

9 MITRED PARAKEET (MITRED CONURE) *Aratinga mitrata* 31–38cm FIELD NOTES: Race *A. m. alticola* has red restricted to forehead. Flight swift and direct. VOICE: Harsh cries and a rising *kreeep*. HABITAT: Usually the edges of mountain forests and mountain scrub. DISTRIBUTION: Escape? Recorded from Puerto Rico.

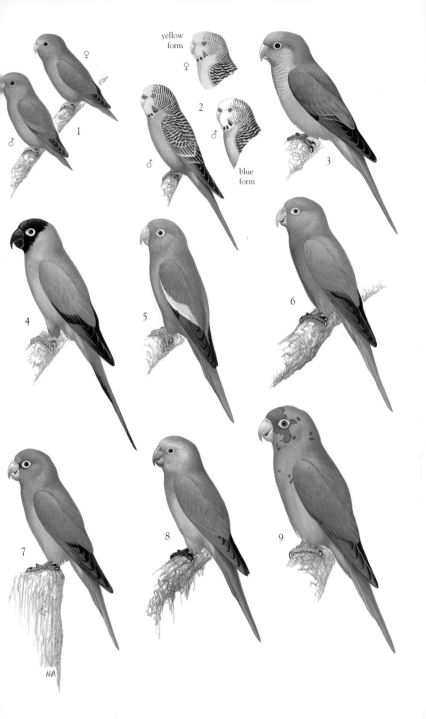

yellow
form

♀

♂

2

♂

blue
form

NA

35 PARAKEETS AND PARROTS

1 HISPANIOLAN PARAKEET (HISPANIOLAN CONURE) *Aratinga chloroptera*
30–33cm FIELD NOTES: Gregarious, usually in small groups. In flight, which is swift and direct, shows red underwing-coverts. VOICE: A shrill screech, given when perched or in flight. HABITAT: Mainly mountain forests but also in arid lowlands, often attracted to crops. Breeds from February to June. DISTRIBUTION: Hispaniola, where endemic, also introduced to Puerto Rico and Guadeloupe.

2 CUBAN PARAKEET (CUBAN CONURE) *Aratinga euops* 24–27cm FIELD NOTES: Gregarious, generally occurs in small groups. In flight, which is swift and direct, shows red underwing-coverts. VOICE: A loud, repeated *crick-crick-crick*, usually uttered in flight. When feeding or at rest gives a low chattering. HABITAT: Savannahs with cabbage palms, forest edge and also cultivated areas. Breeds from March to April. DISTRIBUTION: Cuban endemic.

3 ROSE-THROATED PARROT (ROSE-THROATED AMAZON) *Amazona leucocephala* 28–33cm FIELD NOTES: Usually occurs in small, noisy groups. Each of the islands inhabited by this parrot has a distinct race, *A. l. leucocephala* (Cuban Parrot), *A. l. caymanensis* (Cayman Islands Parrot) (fig 3b) and *A. l. bahamensis* (Bahama Parrot) (fig 3c). VOICE: In flight, utters a harsh *squawk-squawk*; also a variety of harsh screeches and shrill shrieks when perched. HABITAT: Primarily forests, at all elevations. Breeds from March to July. DISTRIBUTION: Cuba, Bahamas and the Cayman Islands.

4 YELLOW-BILLED PARROT (YELLOW-BILLED AMAZON) *Amazona collaria* 28–31cm FIELD NOTES: Generally occurs in small flocks feeding among the top-most branches, sometimes mixing with Black-billed Parrot. Usually somewhat wary. Flies with rapid, shallow wing-beats. VOICE: In flight, gives a bugling *tuk-tuk-tuk-taaah*, and a high-pitched *tah-tah-eeeeep* when perched. HABITAT: Forests on hills and mountains, mainly at mid-elevations; after breeding, may spread to more open areas, including gardens and cultivations. Breeds chiefly from March to July. DISTRIBUTION: Jamaica, mainly in Cockpit Country, Mount Diablo and the John Crow Mountains.

5 HISPANIOLAN PARROT (HISPANIOLAN AMAZON) *Amazona ventralis* 28–31cm FIELD NOTES: Usually encountered in pairs, family groups or even quite large flocks, easily located as they fly over the forest canopy, screeching constantly. VOICE: In flight, utters an almost continual loud screech; at rest, or while feeding, groups often emit a low growl or chatter. HABITAT: Forests, woodlands, palm savannah and scrub. Breeds from February to June. DISTRIBUTION: Endemic on Hispaniola, introduced on Puerto Rico.

6 PUERTO RICAN PARROT (PUERTO RICAN AMAZON) *Amazona vittata* 29–30cm FIELD NOTES: Critically endangered, numbers less than 300 wild birds. Some birds may show a slight red tinge to the belly. VOICE: In flight, gives a loud, far-carrying *kar kar*; when feeding, often utters a low chuckling. HABITAT: Mid-elevation wet forests. Breeds from February to June. DISTRIBUTION: Eastern Puerto Rico.

7 BLACK-BILLED PARROT (BLACK-BILLED AMAZON) *Amazona agilis* 25–26cm FIELD NOTES: Usually forages amid treetops in flocks of 5 to 30 or so. Best located as they fly over the forest canopy emitting their screeching calls. Sometimes associates with Yellow-billed Parrot. VOICE: In flight, gives a bugling *tuh-tuh* and sharp screech; when perched, or feeding, often gives a low growl. HABITAT: Wet mid-level forests on mountains and hills. Breeds from March to June. DISTRIBUTION: Jamaica.

36 PARROTS

1 RED-CROWNED PARROT (RED-CROWNED or GREEN-CHEEKED AMAZON)
Amazona viridigenalis 30–33cm FIELD NOTES: In flight, shows distinctive red patch on secondaries. Usually seen in flocks, often noisy as they fly from tree to tree. VOICE: A harsh *kee-craw craw craw* or *keet kau-kau-kau-kau*. HABITAT: Lowland wet forests and scrub. Breeds from March to June. DISTRIBUTION: Introduced on Puerto Rico.

2 ORANGE-WINGED PARROT (ORANGE-WINGED AMAZON) *Amazona amazonica* 31–32cm FIELD NOTES: In flight, shows orange-red patch on secondaries. Usually seen in pairs, although flocks also occur, especially at roosts. VOICE: A shrill *kee-ik kee-ik kee-ik* or *kweet kweet kweet kweet*; also a variety of screeches and whistles. HABITAT: Lowland second-growth forests. DISTRIBUTION: Introduced to Puerto Rico and Martinique.

3 YELLOW-HEADED PARROT (YELLOW-HEADED AMAZON) *Amazona oratrix* 36cm FIELD NOTES: In flight, shows red patch on secondaries. Generally encountered in pairs. VOICE: A screeching *kurr-owk* and other raucous squawks. HABITAT: Lowland second-growth forests on Puerto Rico's northern coast. DISTRIBUTION: Introduced to Puerto Rico.

4 RED-NECKED PARROT (RED-NECKED AMAZON) *Amazona arausiaca* 40cm FIELD NOTES: Endangered. In flight, shows red patch on secondaries. Usually occurs in pairs or family groups, forming larger flocks in the non-breeding season. Forages mainly in the forest canopy, sometimes associating with the Imperial Parrot. VOICE: Utters a drawn out *rrr-eee*. HABITAT: Rainforest, usually at mid-elevations. Breeds primarily from March to May. DISTRIBUTION: Endemic to Dominica.

5 ST VINCENT PARROT (ST VINCENT AMAZON) *Amazona guildingii* 41–46cm FIELD NOTES: Endangered. Very variable, 2 main colour morphs, one basically golden brown the other greenish. Usually occurs in small groups foraging in the forest canopy. Flight is rapid and direct with jerky wing-beats. VOICE: In flight, gives a *gua gua gua* or *quaw quaw quaw*. While feeding, utters squeaks and squabbling noises. HABITAT: Primarily mature moist mountain forest. Breeds mainly from March to June. DISTRIBUTION: Endemic to St Vincent.

6 ST LUCIA PARROT (ST LUCIA AMAZON) *Amazona versicolor* 42–46cm FIELD NOTES: Endangered. Forages in the forest canopy, generally in pairs or small parties, difficult to locate; may give presence away when feeding, with the utterance of low sounds or by dropping discarded pieces of fruit. In flight, shows red patch on secondaries. VOICE: In flight, gives a raucous screeching. HABITAT: Mainly tropical moist forest. Breeds from February to May. DISTRIBUTION: Endemic to St Lucia.

7 IMPERIAL PARROT (IMPERIAL AMAZON) *Amazona imperialis* 46–51cm FIELD NOTES: Endangered. Usually occurs in pairs or small groups foraging in the tops of trees or flying over the forest canopy, sometimes in the company of Red-necked Parrots. In flight, shows a red patch on the secondaries. VOICE: In flight, gives a metallic, trumpeting *eeeee-er*; while perched, utters various shrieks, squawks, whistles and bubbly trills. HABITAT: Moist, mid- to high-elevation forest. Breeds from February to July. DISTRIBUTION: Endemic to Dominica.

brown
morph

green
morph

1

2

3

4

5

6

7

37 SMOOTH-BILLED ANI AND CUCKOOS

1 SMOOTH-BILLED ANI *Crotophaga ani* 30–33cm FIELD NOTES: Usually occurs in small noisy flocks, walking on the ground, on branches and clambering through vegetation in search of insects. Flight is direct, with quick choppy wing-beats interspersed with short glides. Juvenile browner with smaller bill. VOICE: An ascending whistled *queee-ik* or *a-leep*; also a thin, descending *teeew*. HABITAT: Various open lowland areas, with scattered trees or bushes. Breeds at any month, occupying a bulky nest that is occasionally used by several females. DISTRIBUTION: Common on the Bahamas, Greater Antilles and the following islands in the Lesser Antilles: the Virgin Islands, Dominica, St Vincent and Grenada; it is less common on Martinique and Guadeloupe. Rare on San Andrés.

2 CUCKOO (COMMON or EURASIAN CUCKOO) *Cuculus canorus* 32–34cm FIELD NOTES: Female as male but with a brownish tinge to breast. There is a rufous morph where head, breast, mantle, wings and tail are rufous barred dark brown. Often perches horizontally with tail cocked and wings drooped. VOICE: A far-carrying *cu-coo* or similar variant, also a harsh *gowk gowk* when excited. Female utters a bubbling *puhuhuhuhuhuhuhu*. HABITAT: Wide ranging including woodland, forest edge, open country with scattered bushes and trees. DISTRIBUTION: A vagrant, recorded from Barbados.

3 BLACK-BILLED CUCKOO *Coccyzus erythropthalmus* 27–31cm FIELD NOTES: Skulking. In flight, upperwing shows dull rufous brown on base of primaries. Undertail of adult is grey, each feather with a narrow white tip and a narrow black subterminal bar; juvenile tail has smaller white tips and no black. VOICE: A hollow *cu-cu-cu* or *cu-cu-cu-cu*; also a descending *k-k-k-k or kru-dru*. HABITAT: Thickets, forest and woodland edge and mangroves. DISTRIBUTION: A migrant on the northern Bahamas (New Providence, Andros and Grand Bahama), Cuba and Hispaniola, also a vagrant, recorded from Jamaica, the Cayman Islands, Puerto Rico, Antigua, Dominica, St Lucia and Barbados.

4 YELLOW-BILLED CUCKOO *Coccyzus americanus* 28–32cm FIELD NOTES: Skulking. In flight, upperwing shows distinct rufous bases to primaries. Undertail of adults blackish with wide white tips, juvenile similar but tips a little smaller and less well defined. Juvenile eye ring greyish. VOICE: A hollow, wooden *ka-ka-ka-ka-ka-ka...kow-kow-kowlp-kowlp-kowlp*; also a dove-like *cloom...cloom.....cloom* and a descending *too too too too too to to to*. HABITAT: Dry forests and lowland scrub. Breeds from April to July. DISTRIBUTION: A migrant throughout the region. A breeding resident, from May to August, on Cuba, Hispaniola, Puerto Rico and, rarely, on Jamaica, St Martin and in the Virgin Islands, may breed in the Bahamas.

5 DARK-BILLED CUCKOO *Coccyzus melacoryphus* 27cm FIELD NOTES: Skulking and secretive, keeping mostly to the low branches of mangroves. In flight, upperwing is uniform brown. Undertail black with wide white tips. VOICE: A low *cu-cu-cu-cu-cu* or *cu-cu-cu-cu-cu-klop klop kulop*; also utters a dry rattle. HABITAT: Primarily mangrove swamps or nearby countryside. DISTRIBUTION: A vagrant, recorded from Grenada.

6 MANGROVE CUCKOO *Coccyzus minor* 28–30cm FIELD NOTES: A shy, skulking bird, with a light and dark morph, usually located by call. In flight, upperwing is uniform brown. Undertail black with wide white tips. VOICE: A low *gawk gawk gawk gawk gawk gawk*; also a single *whit*. HABITAT: Forests, dry scrub, mangroves, plantations and thickets. Breeds from February to June. DISTRIBUTION: Reasonably common resident throughout the region.

light morph

dark morph

38 LIZARD-CUCKOOS AND CUCKOOS

1 GREAT LIZARD-CUCKOO (CUBAN LIZARD-CUCKOO) *Coccyzus merlini*
44–54cm FIELD NOTES: Forages in the middle storey and canopy, often descending to the ground where it runs with its tail out straight, making it appear mongoose-like. Birds on the Bahamas (*C. m. bahamensis*) (fig 1b) are more secretive than those on Cuba, which can be very tame. Underside of tail feathers grey with black subterminal bar and white tip. VOICE: A guttural *ka-ka-ka-ka-ka-ka-kau-kau-ko-ko* and *tuc-wuh-h*. HABITAT: Thickets with dense vegetation and vines, tropical lowland evergreen forest, abandoned coffee plantations and overgrown pastures. Breeds, in dense vegetation, from April to October. DISTRIBUTION: Cuba and the Bahamas (New Providence, Andros and Eleuthera).

2 PUERTO RICAN LIZARD-CUCKOO *Coccyzus vieilloti* 40–48cm FIELD NOTES:
Retiring, habitually sits quietly among dense vegetation, more often heard than seen; forages mainly in the middle storey and canopy. Juvenile breast has a cinnamon wash, rather than the grey of the adult. Underside of tail feathers grey with black subterminal bar and broad white tip. VOICE: An emphatic *ka-ka-ka-ka-ka-ka-ka-ka-ka...*, which accelerates and increases in loudness. Also a soft *caw*. HABITAT: Tropical deciduous forest, tropical lowland evergreen forest, woodland, dry coastal forest and coffee plantations. Probably breeds in all months of the year. DISTRIBUTION: Endemic to Puerto Rico.

3 HISPANIOLAN LIZARD-CUCKOO *Coccyzus longirostris* 41–46cm FIELD NOTES:
Forages by striding or creeping and crawling along branches, often in thick vegetation, from the canopy to near the ground. Regularly sits quietly for several minutes. Birds from Gonâve Island *C. l. petersi* (fig 3b) have greyish-white throat. Underside of tail feathers black with broad white tips. VOICE: Similar to Great Lizard-cuckoo; also a harsh *tchk* and a *tick cwuh-h h*. HABITAT: Tropical forests, woodlands, thickets and coffee plantations. Breeds from March to June. DISTRIBUTION: Endemic to Hispaniola, including Saona, Tortue and Gonâve Islands.

4 JAMAICAN LIZARD-CUCKOO *Coccyzus vetula* 38–40cm FIELD NOTES: Forages from the understorey to the canopy, moving slowly along branches and among vegetation. More often heard than seen. Underside of tail feathers black with broad white tips. VOICE: A rapid, low *cak-cak-cak-ka-ka-k-k*. HABITAT: Tropical forests, woodlands and wooded ravines, semiarid country with trees and shrubs. Breeds from March to August. DISTRIBUTION: Endemic to Jamaica.

5 CHESTNUT-BELLIED CUCKOO *Coccyzus pluvialis* 48–56cm FIELD NOTES: Often seen running along forest branches or gliding from tree to tree; generally forages in the middle storey or the canopy. More often heard than seen. Underside of tail feathers black with broad white tips. VOICE: A guttural, accelerating *quawk-quawk-ak-ak-ak-ak-ak-ak*. HABITAT: Mid-elevation open wet forests, secondary forest, open woodland, thickets and gardens. Breeds from March to June. DISTRIBUTION: Endemic to Jamaica.

6 BAY-BREASTED CUCKOO (RUFOUS-BREASTED CUCKOO) *Coccyzus rufigularis*
43–51cm FIELD NOTES: Shy and secretive. Forages in the middle storey and canopy, may be seen as it leaps from branch to branch. Underside of tail feathers black with broad white tips. VOICE: A loud *cua...u-ak-u-ak-ak-ak-ak-ak-ak-ak*; also a lamb-like bleating. HABITAT: Mainly dry deciduous forests, also found locally in mountain rainforest and arid lowlands. Breeds from March to June. DISTRIBUTION: Endemic to Hispaniola.

39 OWLS

1 BARN OWL *Tyto alba* 32–38cm FIELD NOTES: Nocturnal, although often hunts by day; quarters with a slow and buoyant flight. Depicted are *T. a. furcata* (fig 1a) from Cuba, Jamaica and the Cayman Islands and *T. a. pratincola* (fig 1b) from the Bahamas and Hispaniola. VOICE: A shrill *shrrreeeee* and loud clicks. HABITAT: Open areas, open woodland and around urban dwellings. Breeds mainly from August to April. DISTRIBUTION: Resident on the Bahamas, Cuba, Hispaniola, Jamaica and the Cayman Islands. Vagrant on Puerto Rico.

2 ASHY-FACED OWL *Tyto glaucops* 26–35cm FIELD NOTES: Nocturnal. Foraging actions similar to Barn Owl. Race with rufous face, *T. g. insularis* (fig 2b) occurs on islands in Lesser Antilles; the similar, but darker race *T. g. nigrescens*, occurs on Dominica. VOICE: A screeching *criiissssh* and clicks, followed by a hissing cry. Birds on Dominica are said to have a piercing scream and a loud click. HABITAT: Open woodland, forest, scrub, caves, agricultural land and urban areas. Breeds from January to June. DISTRIBUTION: Hispaniola, Dominica, St Vincent, Bequia, Union, Carriacou and Grenada.

3 BARE-LEGGED OWL (CUBAN SCREECH-OWL) *Gymnoglaux lawrencii* 20–23cm FIELD NOTES: Nocturnal, spends the day hidden in holes of trees or caves. VOICE: A low, repeated *cu-cu-cu-cucucu*. Females utter a harsh scream. HABITAT: Wooded areas. Breeds from January to June. DISTRIBUTION: Cuba.

4 PUERTO RICAN SCREECH-OWL *Otus nudipes* 23–25cm FIELD NOTES: Nocturnal, spends the day hidden in dense vegetation or in a hole in a tree. VOICE: A short trill or chatter, also a whoop or a maniacal laugh. HABITAT: All types of forest and woodland. Breeds from April to June. DISTRIBUTION: Puerto Rico and the Virgin Islands (St John, St Thomas, St Croix, Virgin Gorda, Tortola and Guana).

5 CUBAN PYGMY OWL *Glaucidium siju* 16–17cm FIELD NOTES: Feeds by day or night. Travelling flight undulating, but swift and agile when in pursuit of prey. VOICE: A low, repeated *uh uh uh*; during breeding season gives a *hui-hui-chiii-chiii-chi-chi-chi...*, which increases in strength. HABITAT: Woods and plantations. Breeds from December to April. DISTRIBUTION: Endemic to Cuba.

6 BURROWING OWL *Athene cunicularia* 23cm FIELD NOTES: Nocturnal, but feeds diurnally during the breeding season, often by walking or hopping after prey on the ground. VOICE: A soft, high-pitched *coo-coooo*; utters a clucking chatter when alarmed. HABITAT: Open scrubby areas, pastureland, sandy pine savannahs and limestone ravines. Breeds from December to July. DISTRIBUTION: The Bahamas, Cuba and Hispaniola.

7 STYGIAN OWL *Asio stygius* 41–46cm FIELD NOTES: Nocturnal. Large size and dark plumage make it unmistakable. VOICE: A loud *uh*. During the breeding season male gives a low-pitched, repeated *fool*, the female answers with a high-pitched *niek*. HABITAT: Dense deciduous and pine forests. Breeds from November to May. DISTRIBUTION: Cuba and Hispaniola.

8 SHORT-EARED OWL *Asio flammeus* 35cm FIELD NOTES: Active at dusk and dawn. Hunts low over vegetation, often hovers before pouncing onto prey. In flight, primaries look dark tipped. VOICE: A short *hoo-hoo* or *bow-wow*; also an emphatic *kee-ow*. HABITAT: Open country. Breeds from April to June. DISTRIBUTION: Cuba, Hispaniola, Puerto Rico and the Cayman Islands, where rare. Also a vagrant recorded from the Bahamas, the Virgin Islands and St Bartholomew.

9 LONG-EARED OWL *Asio otus* 35–37cm FIELD NOTES: Mainly nocturnal. Primary tips show 4 or 5 bars. VOICE: A soft hoot; when alarmed, a barking *bwah bwah bwah*. HABITAT: Woodland. DISTRIBUTION: A vagrant, recorded from Cuba.

10 JAMAICAN OWL *Pseudoscops grammicus* 27–34cm FIELD NOTES: Nocturnal. Arboreal, often has a regular roosting tree. VOICE: A high, quivering hoot and a throaty growl. HABITAT: Open woodland and forest edge. Breeds from December to June. DISTRIBUTION: Endemic to Jamaica.

40 POTOO, NIGHTHAWKS AND NIGHTJARS

1 NORTHERN POTOO *Nyctibius jamaicensis* 43–46cm FIELD NOTES: Nocturnal. Some more reddish brown than shown. VOICE: A harsh, throaty *kwah waugh waugh waugh...* and a hoarse *waark-cucu*. HABITAT: Forests, palm groves and scrubland near open areas. DISTRIBUTION: Jamaica and Hispaniola (race *N. j. abbotti*, fig 1b). Vagrant on islands off Puerto Rico.

2 COMMON NIGHTHAWK *Chordeiles minor* 23–25cm FIELD NOTES: In flight, male shows a prominent white patch at base of primaries and a white subterminal band on all outer tail feathers. Females lack white in tail. VOICE: A nasal, repeated *peent*. HABITAT: Open areas. DISTRIBUTION: A widespread migrant during September, October, April and May.

3 ANTILLEAN NIGHTHAWK *Chordeiles gundlachii* 20–21cm FIELD NOTES: Often forages at dusk and dawn. At rest, wing-tips do not protrude beyond tail. VOICE: A descending *que-re-be-bé*. HABITAT: Open areas. DISTRIBUTION: Breeding resident, from March to October, in the Bahamas, the Greater Antilles and the Virgin Islands, a rare migrant in the rest of the Lesser Antilles.

4 JAMAICAN POORWILL *Siphonorhis americanus* 23–25cm FIELD NOTES: Critically endangered. Nocturnal. Male has outer tail feathers tipped white, female's tipped buff. VOICE: Unrecorded. HABITAT: Possibly dry limestone forest, semiarid woodland and open country. DISTRIBUTION: Endemic to Jamaica.

5 LEAST POORWILL *Siphonorhis brewsteri* 17–20cm FIELD NOTES: Nocturnal. In flight, male shows narrow white tip to outer tail feathers, replaced with buff on female. VOICE: A whistled, rising *toorrrri*, a warbled *tworri* and a throaty *torico torico*. HABITAT: Coniferous forest, arid or semiarid lowlands with cactus and thorn scrub. DISTRIBUTION: Endemic to Hispaniola.

6 CHUCK-WILL'S WIDOW *Caprimulgus carolinensis* 27–34cm FIELD NOTES: Nocturnal. In flight, male shows white inner webs on 3 outer tail feathers, female has buffy tips to outer tail feathers. Rufous phase similar to Rufous Nightjar. VOICE: A whistled *chip wido wido* or *chuck-wills-wid-ow*. HABITAT: Woodlands. DISTRIBUTION: Occurs from September to May on Hispaniola, the Bahamas, Cuba, Jamaica, Saba, Puerto Rico, the Cayman and Virgin Islands. Vagrant on St Martin, St Bartholomew and Barbuda.

7 RUFOUS NIGHTJAR *Caprimulgus rufus* 28cm FIELD NOTES: Nocturnal. Flight pattern similar to Chuck-will's Widow. VOICE: A loud *chuck wee wee weeeo*. HABITAT: Dry scrub forests. DISTRIBUTION: North-east St Lucia.

8 CUBAN NIGHTJAR *Caprimugus cubanensis* 25–29cm FIELD NOTES: Nocturnal. In flight, male shows broad white tips to outer tail feathers, these are lacking in female. VOICE: A short trilled whistle and a plaintive *gua bai ah ro*. HABITAT: Dense forest (Isle of Pines), open woodland and edges of swamps. Breeds from March to July. DISTRIBUTION: Endemic to Cuba.

9 HISPANIOLAN NIGHTJAR *Caprimulgus ekmani* 26–30cm FIELD NOTES: Nocturnal. Flight pattern similar to Cuban Nightjar, tail tips narrower. VOICE: A *tuc* followed by a trilled, rising whistle. HABITAT: Pine forests. Breeds from April to July. DISTRIBUTION: Endemic to Hispaniola.

10 WHIP-POOR-WILL *Caprimulgus vociferus* 23–26cm FIELD NOTES: Nocturnal. In flight, males show broad white tips to outer tail feathers, buff in female. VOICE: *whip-poor-will*. HABITAT: Dry, open woodlands. DISTRIBUTION: Vagrant on Cuba and Jamaica.

11 PUERTO RICAN NIGHTJAR *Caprimulgus noctitherus* 22cm FIELD NOTES: Critically endangered. Nocturnal. In flight, males show broad white tips to outer tail feathers, buff in female. VOICE: A liquid *whilp whilp whilp*. HABITAT: Dry, semi-deciduous forests. DISTRIBUTION: Endemic to south-western Puerto Rico.

12 WHITE-TAILED NIGHTJAR *Caprimulgus cayennensis* 20–23cm FIELD NOTES: Nocturnal. In flight, male shows white bar on primaries and much white on outer tail feathers. VOICE: A high-pitched whistle. HABITAT: Grassy areas. Breeds from January to July. DISTRIBUTION: Martinique. Vagrant on Puerto Rico and Barbados.

41 SWIFTS

1 BLACK SWIFT *Cypseloides niger* 15–18cm FIELD NOTES: Gregarious, often occurs in large flocks feeding high in the air. Flight less erratic than the smaller swifts, wing-beats shallow. VOICE: A soft *chip-chip*. HABITAT: Mountain areas, often occurs near waterfalls, less common in lowlands and coastal areas. Breeds from March to September. DISTRIBUTION: Greater Antilles (rare on Cuba, vagrant on the Cayman Islands) and Lesser Antilles (breeds on St Lucia, St Vincent, Montserrat, Barbados and Grenada, a migrant elsewhere).

2 WHITE-COLLARED SWIFT (COLLARED SWIFT) *Streptoprocne zonaris* 20–22cm FIELD NOTES: Gregarious, often in large flocks; forages, with rapid and agile flight, above forests. VOICE: A shrill *sreee-screee*; also a rapid *chip-chip-chip*. HABITAT: Montane forest areas; less common, except during bad weather, in lowland areas. Breeds in May and June. DISTRIBUTION: Cuba, Jamaica and Hispaniola. Vagrants recorded from Puerto Rico, Saba, St Christopher, Martinique and Grenada.

3 CHIMNEY SWIFT *Chaetura pelagica* 12–14cm FIELD NOTES: Usually gregarious. Wing-beats rapid and with a bat-like fluttering when feeding low down. VOICE: A chattering *chip chip chip chip....* HABITAT: Forages over woodland, fields, villages and towns. DISTRIBUTION: Uncommon to rare migrant, from August to October and April and May, on the Bahamas, Hispaniola, Jamaica, the Cayman Islands and the Virgin Islands (St Croix).

4 SHORT-TAILED SWIFT *Chaetura brachyura* 10cm FIELD NOTES: Gregarious, usually in small loose flocks. Flight rapid and powerful. VOICE: A musical twittering. HABITAT: Forages over towns, open areas, also lowland and hill forests. Breeds from March to September. DISTRIBUTION: Breeding resident on St Vincent, vagrants recorded from the Virgin Islands (St Croix), Barbados, and possibly Grenada and Puerto Rico.

5 GREY-RUMPED SWIFT *Chaetura cinereiventris* 11cm FIELD NOTES: Gregarious, usually in small flocks of 20 to 30 birds. May hover to take insects from treetops. VOICE: A light twittering. HABITAT: Forages over forests. Breeds from March to May. DISTRIBUTION: Grenada, recorded as a vagrant on Hispaniola.

6 LESSER ANTILLEAN SWIFT *Chaetura martinica* 11cm FIELD NOTES: Gregarious, generally in flocks of 20 to 40, often associated with swallows and martins. VOICE: A soft twittering. HABITAT: Mainly over mountain forests, occasionally above lowland forests and open areas. Breeds during May and June. DISTRIBUTION: Dominica, Martinique, St Lucia, St Vincent and Guadeloupe, also a vagrant on Nevis.

7 ALPINE SWIFT *Apus melba* 20–22cm FIELD NOTES: Flight fast and powerful with long glides on slightly drooping wings, making it look falcon-like. Usually associates with other swifts when foraging for insects. VOICE: A high-pitched twittering *trrr-titititititititititityiti-ti-ti-ti...*, which rises and falls in pitch, accelerates and then normally slows at the end. HABITAT: Typically forages over mountain or hill areas but will use virtually any type of country. DISTRIBUTION: A vagrant recorded from Barbados, St Lucia, Guadeloupe and Desecho Island off Puerto Rico.

8 ANTILLEAN PALM SWIFT *Tachornis phoenicobia* 10–11cm FIELD NOTES: Flight rapid and bat-like interspersed with glides. Usually in small groups, which are occasionally joined by swallows and martins. VOICE: A constant, high-pitched, weak twittering. HABITAT: Open cultivated areas and urban areas, all usually with nearby palms. Breeds during March and April. DISTRIBUTION: Resident on Cuba, Jamaica and Hispaniola, and a vagrant on Puerto Rico.

42 HUMMINGBIRDS

1 WHITE-NECKED JACOBIN *Florisuga mellivora* 11–12cm FIELD NOTES: Favours high perches or foraging above the canopy, usually solitary, although small parties have been recorded high above treetops, calling excitedly while indulging in rapid chases. VOICE: A high-pitched *tit-tit-tit-tit*. HABITAT: Various forests, from sea level up to 900m. DISTRIBUTION: Vagrant recorded from Grenada, the Grenadines and Carriacou.

2 RUFOUS-BREASTED HERMIT (HAIRY HERMIT) *Glaucis hirsuta* 10–12cm FIELD NOTES: Generally solitary, aggressive, often seen chasing other hummingbirds through undergrowth. VOICE: A high-pitched *sweep*, *sweep-sweep* or *sweep swee-swee*. HABITAT: Montane forests, forest edge and plantations. Breeds from December to August. DISTRIBUTION: Grenada.

3 RUFOUS HUMMINGBIRD *Selasphorus rufus* 9cm FIELD NOTES: A few males have a green back. Often aggressive in defending a feeding territory. VOICE: A high-pitched, hard *tchup*; also various chipping and buzzy notes and an excited *zee-chupity-chup*. HABITAT: Mixed forests, scrubland and disturbed areas. DISTRIBUTION: Vagrant, recorded from the Bahamas (Grand Bahama).

4 GREEN-BREASTED MANGO *Anthracothorax prevostii* 11–12cm FIELD NOTES: Feeds mainly at flowering trees, although often fly-catches, sallying from a high perch or by hovering and then darting after insect prey. VOICE: A repeated chipping, a high-pitched shrill note and a series of thin *see* notes, often given in flight. HABITAT: Mainly open coastal areas with scattered bushes and trees. DISTRIBUTION: Resident on San Andrés and Providencia.

5 JAMAICAN MANGO (BLACK MANGO) *Anthracothorax mango* 11–13cm FIELD NOTES: Feeds on nectar from a wide variety of flowers including those of cacti, also takes insects. VOICE: A sharp, raspy *tic tic tic....* HABITAT: Forest edge, plantations and gardens. Breeds at any month. DISTRIBUTION: Endemic to Jamaica.

6 GREEN MANGO (PUERTO RICAN MANGO) *Anthracothorax viridis* 11–14cm FIELD NOTES: Feeds, from understorey to canopy, on nectar, spiders and insects, the latter often taken in flight. VOICE: A hard *tic*, a harsh chatter and a trill-like twitter. HABITAT: Mountain forests and coffee plantations. Breeds from October to May. DISTRIBUTION: Puerto Rico.

7 ANTILLEAN MANGO *Anthracothorax dominicus* 11–12.5cm FIELD NOTES: Feeds on the nectar of flowering trees and plants; also takes spiders and insects, the latter often taken in flight. Juvenile like female but with a black central line on underparts. VOICE: Sharp chipping notes and a thin trill. HABITAT: Scrub and clearings in moist and dry areas, also plantations and gardens. Breeds from March to April. DISTRIBUTION: Hispaniola. Race *A. d. aurulentus* (fig 7b) occurs on Puerto Rico and the Virgin Islands (St Thomas, St John and Anegada).

8 PURPLE-THROATED CARIB *Eulampis jugularis* 11–12cm FIELD NOTES: Feeds on flower nectar, spiders and insects, generally foraging from mid-level to canopy. Juvenile has orange throat and breast speckled with red. VOICE: A sharp *chewp*, repeated rapidly when agitated. HABITAT: Mainly mountain forests and banana plantations. Breeds from January to July. DISTRIBUTION: Lesser Antilles, although only a vagrant on St Croix, St John, Barbuda, Barbados and the Grenadines.

9 GREEN-THROATED CARIB *Eulampis holosericeus* 11–12.5cm FIELD NOTES: Feeding habits as Purple-throated Carib. VOICE: A sharp *chewp*. HABITAT: Rainforests, parks and gardens. Breeds from March to July. DISTRIBUTION: North-eastern Puerto Rico and the Lesser Antilles.

10 ANTILLEAN CRESTED HUMMINGBIRD *Orthorhyncus cristatus* 8–9.5cm FIELD NOTES: Feeds on nectar, spiders and insects. The races shown are the nominate from Barbados, *O. c. exilis* (fig 10b) from Puerto Rico south to St Lucia and *O. c. ornatus* (fig 10c) from St Vincent; there is a race *O. c. emigrans* from the Grenadines and Grenada, which is like nominate but more bluish. VOICE: Various notes, which usually include a sharp *pit-chew*. HABITAT: Open vegetation, parks, plantations and forest edge. Breeds from January to August. DISTRIBUTION: Puerto Rico and the Lesser Antilles.

43 HUMMINGBIRDS

1 RUBY TOPAZ HUMMINGBIRD *Chrysolampis mosquitus* 8–9cm FIELD NOTES: Feeds on nectar, spiders and insects. VOICE: A high-pitched *tsip*. HABITAT: Savannah vegetation, from sea level to hills. DISTRIBUTION: Vagrant on Grenada.

2 CUBAN EMERALD *Chlorostilbon ricordii* Male 10.5–11.5cm Female 9.5–10.5cm FIELD NOTES: Feeds on the nectar of flowering trees and shrubs; also insects and spiders. VOICE: A squeaking twitter. HABITAT: Woodland, swamp edge, coastal scrub forest, plantations, parks and gardens. Breeds at any month. DISTRIBUTION: Cuba and the Bahamas (Grand Bahama, Abaco and Andros).

3 HISPANIOLAN EMERALD *Chlorostilbon swainsonii* Male 9.5–10.5cm Female 8.5–9.5cm FIELD NOTES: Feeds on nectar from flowering trees and shrubs; also hawks for insects. VOICE: A metallic *tic tic tic*. HABITAT: Mountain forest and forest edge. DISTRIBUTION: Hispaniola.

4 PUERTO RICAN EMERALD *Chlorostilbon maugaeus* Male 8.5–9.5cm Female 7.5–8.5cm FIELD NOTES: Feeds on the nectar of flowers; also spiders and insects. VOICE: A thin, rapid trill that ends with a high-pitched buzz; also a *tic tic tic* given at varying speeds. HABITAT: Mainly mountain forests, forest edge, lowland woods, coffee plantations and mangroves. Breeds primarily from February to May. DISTRIBUTION: Puerto Rico.

5 BLUE-HEADED HUMMINGBIRD *Cyanophaia bicolor* 9–11cm FIELD NOTES: Feeds on the nectar of flowers; also takes spiders and regularly hawks for insects over streams. VOICE: A metallic *click-click-click*; also shrill notes that rapidly descend in pitch. HABITAT: Moist open areas in mountain forests, along mountain streams and wooded field edges. Breeds from February to May. DISTRIBUTION: Dominica and Martinique.

6 BLACK-BILLED STREAMERTAIL (EASTERN STREAMERTAIL) *Trochilus scitulus* Male 22–24cm Female 10.5cm FIELD NOTES: Feeds on nectar from various flowers, and insects. Juvenile lacks tail streamers, otherwise much like adult male. VOICE: A metallic *ting* or *teet*; also a descending *twink-twink-twink-twink....* In flight, tail streamers create a vibrating hum. HABITAT: Humid forests, banana plantations, parks and gardens. DISTRIBUTION: Eastern Jamaica.

7 RED-BILLED STREAMERTAIL (WESTERN STREAMERTAIL) *Trochilus polytmus* Male 22–25cm Female 10.5cm FIELD NOTES: Feeding habits similar to Black-billed Streamertail. Juvenile like adult male but lacks streamers. VOICE: Similar to Black-billed Streamertail. HABITAT: Forests, forest edge, plantations, parks and gardens, from sea level to mountains. DISTRIBUTION: Jamaica, except the extreme east.

8 RUBY-THROATED HUMMINGBIRD *Archilochus colubris* 8–9.5cm FIELD NOTES: Feeds mainly on nectar from flowering plants, also fly-catches for insects. VOICE: A squeaking *cric-cric*. HABITAT: Woodland edge, copse and gardens. DISTRIBUTION: Rare migrant, during March, April and November to February, in the northern Bahamas and Cuba. A vagrant recorded from Jamaica, Hispaniola, Puerto Rico and the Cayman Islands.

9 BAHAMA WOODSTAR *Calliphlox evelynae* 8–9.5cm FIELD NOTES: Feeds on the nectar of flowering plants and by hawking insects. Inagua race, *C. e. lyrura*, (fig 9b) has purple forehead. VOICE: A dry *prititidee prititidee prititidee*; also a sharp *tit titit tit tit titit*, which often speeds into a rattle. HABITAT: Mixed pine forests, forest edge, clearings, scrub and large gardens. DISTRIBUTION: Resident in the Bahamas.

10 VERVAIN HUMMINGBIRD *Mellisuga minima* 6–7cm FIELD NOTES: Feeds on the nectar from a variety of flowers. VOICE: A throaty buzz and high-pitched squeaks. HABITAT: Open areas that contain small flowers. Breeds primarily from December to May. DISTRIBUTION: A resident on Jamaica and Hispaniola.

11 BEE HUMMINGBIRD *Mellisuga helenae* 5–6cm FIELD NOTES: The world's smallest bird. Feeds on nectar and small insects. Often uses a favourite perch for years. VOICE: A long, high-pitched twitter and a low warbling. HABITAT: Forest, woodland, swampland and gardens. DISTRIBUTION: Resident on Cuba. Vagrant in the Bahamas (Providenciales).

44 TROGONS, TODIES AND KINGFISHERS

1 CUBAN TROGON *Priotelus temnurus* 25–28cm FIELD NOTES: Hovers, flycatcher-like, while feeding on flowers, buds or fruits. Usually in pairs. VOICE: A pleasant *toco-toco-tocoro-tocoro...* and a short mournful note. HABITAT: Shady areas in wet or dry forests. Breeds from May to August. DISTRIBUTION: Endemic to Cuba.

2 HISPANIOLAN TROGON *Priotelus roseigaster* 27–30cm FIELD NOTES: Usually in pairs. Feeds mainly on insects but also takes fruit and small lizards. VOICE: A repeated *toca-loro, coc ca-rao* or *cock-caraow*; also a puppy-like whimpering and cooing. HABITAT: Mature pine and deciduous broadleaf montane forests and occasionally coastal mangroves. Breeds from March to July. DISTRIBUTION: Endemic to Hispaniola.

3 CUBAN TODY *Todus multicolor* 10–11cm FIELD NOTES: Feeds mainly by fly-catching, sallying out from exposed perch to pick insects off leaves or in mid-air; also feeds on caterpillars, spiders and small fruits. VOICE: A soft *pprreeee-pprreeee* and a short *tot-tot-tot-tot*. During courtship flights, wings make a rattling or cracking sound. HABITAT: Forests, woodlands, thickets, gullies and stream sides. Breeds from March to June. DISTRIBUTION: Endemic to Cuba.

4 BROAD-BILLED TODY *Todus subulatus* 11–12cm FIELD NOTES: Feeding actions similar to Cuban Tody, although tends to feed higher up and on larger prey. VOICE: A monotonous, plaintive *terp terp terp*. Wings produce a cracking or rattling sound during courtship flights. HABITAT: Mainly arid and semiarid lowland scrub forest, second-growth forest, coffee plantations and mangroves. Breeds from April to June. DISTRIBUTION: Endemic to Hispaniola.

5 NARROW-BILLED TODY *Todus angustirostris* 11cm FIELD NOTES: Feeding techniques similar to Cuban Tody, although feeding flights can be more of a hop due to it inhabiting dense, tangled vegetation. VOICE: A chattering *chippy-chippy-chippy-chip* and a frequently repeated *chip-chee*. Produces wing noises similar to Cuban Tody. HABITAT: Primarily ravines in dense wet forests, also in coffee plantations. Breeds from April to June. DISTRIBUTION: Endemic to Hispaniola.

6 JAMAICAN TODY *Todus todus* 9–11cm FIELD NOTES: Feeding actions similar to Cuban Tody. Usually feeds in the understorey. VOICE: A rapid, throaty rattle, uttered during display; also a loud *beep* or *cherek*. Produces wing noises similar to Cuban Tody. HABITAT: All types of forest. Breeds from December to July. DISTRIBUTION: Endemic to Jamaica.

7 PUERTO RICAN TODY *Todus mexicanus* 11cm FIELD NOTES: Feeding methods very similar to Cuban Tody. VOICE: A loud, harsh *beep, beep-beep* or *cherek*. Produces wing noises similar to Cuban Tody. HABITAT: From sea-level to mountains in rainforest, arid scrub, dense thickets and shade coffee plantations. Breeds from March to July. DISTRIBUTION: Endemic to Puerto Rico.

8 RINGED KINGFISHER *Megaceryle torquata* 38–41cm FIELD NOTES: Usually shy and solitary. Feeds by diving for fish, either from a perch or by hovering. VOICE: A loud *kek, klek* or *klek-klek*; when alarmed, a rattling *klek-klek-klek-klek-klek....* HABITAT: Edges of large streams and lakes. Breeds from April to August. DISTRIBUTION: Dominica, Martinique and Guadeloupe, recorded as vagrant on Puerto Rico and Montserrat.

9 BELTED KINGFISHER *Megaceryle alcyon* 28–33cm FIELD NOTES: Often uses prominent perch, from where it dives to catch fish; also regularly hovers before diving to seize fish. VOICE: A harsh, rattling *kekity-kek-kek-kek-tk-ticky-kek*. HABITAT: Coastal areas, rivers, lakes and lagoons. DISTRIBUTION: Widespread non-breeding resident, mainly from September to April.

45 PICULET AND WOODPECKERS

1 ANTILLEAN PICULET *Nesoctites micromegas* 14–16cm FIELD NOTES: Feeds primarily in the understorey, gleaning insects from vines, small branches, leaf clusters and the stalks of herbaceous plants, moving agilely and quickly through vegetation. Flight is fast and direct. Gonâve Island race *N. m. abbotti* is greyer above, often with white spots extending onto mantle, and less heavily streaked below. VOICE: A loud *kuk-ki-ki-ki-ke-ku-kuk*. In territorial encounters utters a series of weak *wiii* notes and a noisy, chattering *yeh-yeh-yeh-yeh*. HABITAT: Dry and humid forests, mixed pine and broadleaved forests, thorn forests and mangroves. Breeds from March to July. DISTRIBUTION: Endemic to Hispaniola.

2 GUADELOUPE WOODPECKER *Melanerpes herminieri* 24–29cm FIELD NOTES: Can often be shy and retiring. Forages mainly in the canopy, on the trunk or on large branches, probing for insect larvae; also feeds on fruits when in season. VOICE: A single *kwa*; when excited, a variable *wa-wa-wa* or *kakakaka*. Drums in short, slow rolls. HABITAT: All forest types from sea-level to tree line. Breeds from February to August. DISTRIBUTION: Endemic to Guadeloupe.

3 PUERTO RICAN WOODPECKER *Melanerpes portoricensis* 23–27cm FIELD NOTES: Males forage in the lower and middle parts of trees, on trunks and branches, pecking and probing; females tend to prefer gleaning in the middle to higher parts. Often occurs in small parties. VOICE: A *wek wek wek-wek-wek-wek*, which increases in volume and speed; also a harsh *gurrr-gurrr*, a chicken-like *kuk* and a *mew*. Drumming is weak and infrequent. HABITAT: Woodland, from sea-level to mountains, including mangroves and coffee plantations. Breeds from January to April. DISTRIBUTION: Endemic to Puerto Rico.

4 HISPANIOLAN WOODPECKER *Melanerpes striatus* 20–25cm FIELD NOTES: Often found breeding in loose colonies. Forages at all levels, pecking, probing and gleaning; feeds mainly on insects and insect larvae; also recorded feeding on scorpions, lizards and fruits; noted taking insects by hawking. Females tend more towards gleaning. VOICE: A long rolling series interspersed with throaty notes. Also various short notes such as *wup*, *ta* and *ta-a*. Drums infrequently. HABITAT: Mountain forests, cultivations with palms and trees, wooded swamps, mangroves and coastal scrub. Breeds mainly from February to July. DISTRIBUTION: Endemic to Hispaniola.

5 WEST INDIAN WOODPECKER *Melanerpes superciliaris* 27–32cm FIELD NOTES: Forages at all levels, including the ground; pecks, probes and gleans, searching for insects, spiders and fruit; also recorded taking frogs and lizards. Apart from the depicted Cayman Island race, *M. s. caymanensis* (fig 5b), other races, that vary mainly in size and depth of colour, are found in the Bahamas and on the Isle of Pines. VOICE: A repeated, high-pitched *krruuu-krruu-kruu...*; also various low-pitched notes and a *ke-ke-ke-ke-ke* series. HABITAT: Dry forests, forest and swamp edge, coastal forests, scrub, palm groves and gardens. Breeds from January to August. DISTRIBUTION: Resident on Cuba, the Cayman Islands and the Bahamas (Abaco and San Salvador).

6 JAMAICAN WOODPECKER *Melanerpes radiolatus* 24–26cm FIELD NOTES: Forages mainly at mid-crown level, feeding mostly on insects and fruit; also recorded pecking sugarcane to extract the juice. VOICE: A loud *kaaa*, *kaaa-kaaa* or *kaaa-kaaa-kaaa*; also a parakeet-like *chee-ee-urp* or *wee-cha weecha*. Drums loudly. HABITAT: Wide ranging from lowland copses, including plantations, to mountain rainforest. Breeds from December to August. DISTRIBUTION: Endemic to Jamaica.

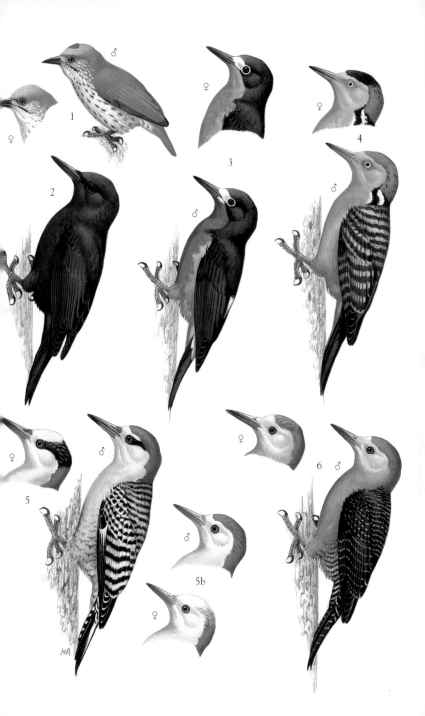

46 SAPSUCKER, WOODPECKERS AND FLICKERS

1 YELLOW-BELLIED SAPSUCKER (COMMON SAPSUCKER) *Sphyrapicus varius* 19–21cm FIELD NOTES: In flight, shows white rump and large white patch on upperwing. Juvenile generally browner with pale throat, crown brown with pale feather tips. Feeds on insects, fruits and buds; also drills a series of holes, horizontally or vertically, to get at the soft under-bark and sap. VOICE: A nasal, squealing *neeah*; also a hoarse *wik-a-wika...*, although usually silent in the West Indies. Drumming consists of about 5 rapid taps then slower, with the odd double tap. HABITAT: Forests, forest edge, woodlands and gardens. DISTRIBUTION: Non-breeding resident, from October to April, in the Bahamas, the Greater Antilles, San Andrés, Puerto Rico and the Virgin Islands; also recorded as a vagrant on St Martin, St Bartholomew and Dominica.

2 CUBAN GREEN WOODPECKER *Xiphidiopicus percussus* 21–25cm FIELD NOTES: Only green-backed woodpecker on Cuba. Forages, usually in pairs, on trunks and branches and among vines or creepers, from low level to canopy, feeding primarily on insects. VOICE: A short, harsh *jorr-jorr-jorr...* and a high-pitched *eh-eh-eh*. HABITAT: Various types of forest, including wet, dry, open and dense, also mangroves. Breeds from February to August. DISTRIBUTION: Endemic to Cuba.

3 HAIRY WOODPECKER *Picoides villosus* 20–23cm FIELD NOTES: The main depiction is the eastern race from North America, which may have occurred in the West Indies, otherwise two endemic races inhabit the region: *P. v. piger* (fig 3b) on Grand Bahama and Abaco; *P. v. maynardi* (fig 3c) on Andros and New Providence. Forages by pecking, hammering, probing and gleaning, feeding mainly on insects, insect larvae, spiders, fruits and seeds. VOICE: A loud *keek* and a rapid whinny. HABITAT: Mainly pine woods. Breeds from March to July. DISTRIBUTION: Resident in the northern Bahamas, also recorded as a vagrant on Puerto Rico.

4 NORTHERN FLICKER *Colaptes auratus* 30–32cm FIELD NOTES: Mainly arboreal, although will descend to forage or dust bathe on the ground; feeds mainly on insects and spiders, with fruit and seeds included in the diet when available. In flight, shows yellow underwing and a white rump. VOICE: A loud, rapid *wik-wik-wik-wik-wik...* and a low-pitched *flick-a-flick-a....* Drum rolls slow and not very loud. HABITAT: Any area with trees. Breeds mainly during April and May. DISTRIBUTION: Resident on Cuba and the Cayman Islands.

5 FERNANDINA'S FLICKER *Colaptes fernandinae* 33–35cm FIELD NOTES: Regularly forages on the ground, feeding on insects, larvae, worms and seeds. In flight, shows yellow underwing. Endangered due to habitat loss. VOICE: A loud *pic-pic-pic-pic-pic-pic*, slightly lower pitched than Northern Flicker; also gives a nasal *ch-ch-ch*. HABITAT: Open woodland, low open country with palms. Breeds from March to June. DISTRIBUTION: Endemic to Cuba.

6 IVORY-BILLED WOODPECKER *Campephilus principalis* 45–50cm FIELD NOTES: Probably extinct, last recorded in 1987. Unmistakable. Favours large dead trees in which to forage for insect larvae. VOICE: A soft, trumpet-like *tut-tut-tut-tut*. HABITAT: Pine woods mixed with deciduous forests; also needs many dead trees. DISTRIBUTION: Cuba.

47 TYRANT FLYCATCHERS

1 WILLOW FLYCATCHER *Empidonax trailli* 15cm FIELD NOTES: Uses a low perch from which it makes sallies to catch insects in the air or from foliage; occasionally takes prey from the ground. VOICE: A buzzy *fi-bo-o*. HABITAT: Woodlands, copse and gardens, often near water. DISTRIBUTION: Rare migrant, during September and October, on Cuba and Jamaica.

2 ACADIAN FLYCATCHER *Empidonax virescens* 12–14cm FIELD NOTES: Slightly more distinct eye ring and longer primary projection than Willow Flycatcher. Feeding actions similar to Willow Flycatcher. VOICE: Generally silent, may utter a soft *weet*. HABITAT: Open woodlands, forest edge, copse and gardens. DISTRIBUTION: An uncommon migrant, mainly in September, October and very rarely April, in the northern Bahamas and Cuba. A vagrant in the Cayman Islands.

3 LEAST FLYCATCHER *Empidonax minimus* 12.5–14cm FIELD NOTES: Distinct pale eye ring and short primary projection. Feeding actions similar to Willow Flycatcher. VOICE: A sharp, dry *pwit* or *pit*. HABITAT: Deciduous and mixed forests edges and clearings. DISTRIBUTION: Vagrant, recorded from the Cayman Islands (Grand Cayman).

4 YELLOW-BELLIED FLYCATCHER *Empidonax flaviventris* 15cm FIELD NOTES: Distinct pale eye ring. Feeding actions similar to Willow Flycatcher. VOICE: Generally silent, may utter an ascending *pee-wee*. HABITAT: Dense vegetation in forests, secondary forest and forest edge, also plantations, copse and gardens. DISTRIBUTION: A rare migrant on Cuba, during September, October and April; also a vagrant recorded from Jamaica.

5 EULER'S FLYCATCHER *Empidonax euleri* 13–14cm FIELD NOTES: The West Indian race *E. e. flaviventris* is probably extinct. Buff wing bars. Feeding actions similar to Willow Flycatcher. VOICE: A murmuring *de-dee-dee-dee-dee*. HABITAT: Moist mountain forests. DISTRIBUTION: Grenada.

6 GREATER ANTILLEAN ELAENIA *Elaenia fallax* 15cm FIELD NOTES: White crown patch usually hidden. Often in pairs or with mixed species flocks. Sallies from perch to take prey from leaves or the air, also feeds on fruit. VOICE: A harsh *pwee-chi-chi-chiup see-ere chewit-chewit*; also a repeated trill, given at dawn. HABITAT: Humid mountain and lowland forest, pine forest, forest edge, thickets and open country with scattered trees. Breeds during May and June. DISTRIBUTION: Resident on Jamaica and Hispaniola.

7 CARIBBEAN ELAENIA *Elaenia martinica* 16–18cm FIELD NOTES: Often sits quietly for long periods. Sallies out to capture prey in the air or from leaves. VOICE: A repetitious *jui-up wit-churr*; also a drawn-out *pee-wee-reecreeree*. HABITAT: Mainly dry lowland forests, woods, scrub and gardens, in southern Lesser Antilles occurs in mountains. Breeds from January to September. DISTRIBUTION: Resident on San Andrés, Providencia, the Cayman Islands, Puerto Rico and the Lesser Antilles.

8 YELLOW-BELLIED ELAENIA *Elaenia flavogaster* 16–17cm FIELD NOTES: Feeds on berries, also takes insects with typical sallying method. Generally noisy. VOICE: A harsh, drawn-out *creup* or *creup-wi-creup*. HABITAT: Lowland forest edge, open woodland, scrub and gardens. Breeds mainly from April to June. DISTRIBUTION: Resident on St Vincent, Grenada and the Grenadines.

9 WESTERN WOOD-PEWEE *Contopus sordidulus* 15–17cm FIELD NOTES: Only reliably distinguished from Eastern Wood-pewee by voice. Makes sallies from perch to catch insects in the air or from foliage, returning to same or nearby perch. VOICE: A nasal, descending *peeyee* or *peeer*. HABITAT: Woodland and river groves. DISTRIBUTION: Rare migrant, during September and October, on Cuba. A vagrant to Jamaica.

10 EASTERN WOOD-PEWEE *Contopus virens* 16cm FIELD NOTES: Feeding actions very similar to Western Wood-pewee. Voice only sure way to differentiate. VOICE: A plaintive *pee-a-wee*, which slurs down and then up; also an up-slurred *pawee* or down-slurred *peeaaa*. HABITAT: Forest edge, mixed woodland, coastal woodland, scrub and gardens. DISTRIBUTION: Rare migrant in September, October, March and April on the Bahamas, Cuba, San Andrés and Providencia. A vagrant on Jamaica, the Virgin Islands (St Croix) and Barbados.

48 TYRANT FLYCATCHERS AND JAMAICAN BECARD

1 JAMAICAN PEWEE *Contopus pallidus* 15cm FIELD NOTES: Generally makes lengthy horizontal sallies, from an exposed perch, to take insects in the air; usually moves to a new perch after capturing prey. VOICE: A plaintive *pee*; also a rising then falling *oéeoh* and, at dawn, 2 alternating phrases *paléet weeléeah*. HABITAT: Mid-elevation to montane forest and forest edge. Breeds from April to June. DISTRIBUTION: Endemic to Jamaica.

2 CRESCENT-EYED PEWEE (CUBAN PEWEE) *Contopus caribaeus* 15–16.5cm FIELD NOTES: Generally uses a low perch from which it makes sallies to capture insects in the air, often returns to the same perch or one nearby. The race found on the Bahamas *C. c. bahamensis* (fig 2b) is generally greyer. VOICE: A prolonged thin whistle; also a feeble *vi-vi* and a repeated *weet* or *dee*. At dawn, gives a squeaky *eeah ooweeah*; the Bahamian race adds a *dee-dee* to the *eeah ooweeah*. HABITAT: Pine and broadleaf forest, forest edge, tree plantations, swamps, bushy scrub and mangroves. Breeds from February to March. DISTRIBUTION: Northern Bahamas and Cuba.

3 HISPANIOLAN PEWEE *Contopus hispaniolensis* 15–16cm FIELD NOTES: Feeding actions similar to Crescent-eyed Pewee. VOICE: A mournful *purr pip-pip-pip-pip*. At dawn gives a rapid *shurr pet-pit pit-pit peet-peet* that rises in pitch. HABITAT: Various wooded areas, including pine and broadleaved forests, forest edge, shade coffee plantations and orchards. Breeds during May and June. DISTRIBUTION: Endemic to Hispaniola. Hurricane-blown vagrant to the Bahamas (Providenciales).

4 ST LUCIA PEWEE *Contopus latirostris* 15cm FIELD NOTES: Makes sallies from a low perch to take insects. VOICE: A rising *pree-e-e* and a high-pitched *peet-peet-peet*. HABITAT: Mainly moist montane forests. Breeds during May and June. DISTRIBUTION: Endemic to St Lucia.

5 PUERTO RICAN PEWEE *Contopus blancoi* 15cm FIELD NOTES: Feeding habits similar to St Lucia Pewee; usually seen in open areas below the forest canopy. VOICE: A high-pitched trill that occasionally rises in pitch; also utters some warbling phrases. At dawn, gives a repetitive trill. HABITAT: Mainly moist forests and woodland at moderate to low elevations. Breeds from March to June. DISTRIBUTION: Endemic to Puerto Rico.

6 LESSER ANTILLEAN PEWEE *Contopus brunneicapillus* 15cm FIELD NOTES: Feeding actions similar St Lucia Pewee. VOICE: A rising *pree-e-e* and a high-pitched, repeated *peet-peet-peet*. HABITAT: Mountain forests and woodland, less often in dry forest, scrub and mangroves. DISTRIBUTION: Guadeloupe, Dominica and Martinique.

7 JAMAICAN ELAENIA *Myiopagis cotta* 12.5cm FIELD NOTES: Forages from the understorey to the canopy, sallying out from a perch to pick insects off foliage while in flight. VOICE: A rapid, high-pitched *ti-si-si-sip*. HABITAT: Middle elevation wet forests, open woods, scrub, shade coffee plantations and dry forest. Breeds from March to June. DISTRIBUTION: Endemic to Jamaica.

8 EASTERN PHOEBE *Sayornis phoebe* 16.5–18cm FIELD NOTES: Makes frequent fly-catching sallies from a prominent perch. Persistently wags and spreads tail. VOICE: A distinctive *fee-be* and a sharp *chip* or *tsyp*. HABITAT: Woodland edge, open and semi-open bushy areas with scattered trees, often near water. DISTRIBUTION: Migrant, from September to February, on Cuba and the Bahamas (Grand Bahama, Bimini, Eleuthera and Great Inagua).

9 JAMAICAN BECARD *Pachyramphus niger* 18cm FIELD NOTES: Forages slowly below the forest canopy, occasionally hovering to pick insects off twigs; also hawks flying insects. VOICE: A hoarse *queeck queeck*, followed by a musical *co-ome and tell me what you hee-ear*, which rises in pitch then lowers pitch on the last 2 syllables. HABITAT: Tall open forests and forest edge in hills and mountains; has been seen in more closed forest, woodland, fields with scattered trees and gardens. Breeds from March to June. DISTRIBUTION: Endemic to Jamaica.

49 TYRANT FLYCATCHERS

1 SAD FLYCATCHER *Myiarchus barbirostris* 16.5cm FIELD NOTES: Makes sallies from a perch, generally 3–9m from the ground, to pick insects from leaves; often returns to the same perch. Only the lower belly is yellow on juveniles. VOICE: A forceful *pip pip-pip* or *pip-pip-pireee* and a single *huit*. HABITAT: Mainly forests and woodland from lowlands to middle elevations. Scarce in semiarid lowland forest and high-elevation forest. Breeds from April to June. DISTRIBUTION: Endemic to Jamaica.

2 GREAT CRESTED FLYCATCHER *Myiarchus crinitus* 18–20.5cm FIELD NOTES: Feeds by sallying from a perch to take insects in the air, from foliage or on the ground; also eats small berries and other fruit. VOICE: A harsh, rising *wheee-eep*, which is often part of a series *whee-up wheee whe-whe-whe-wheee-up*; also a rolling *whir-r-r-r-r-r-up*. At dawn, gives a repeated *wheee-up whir-r-r-r-r-r-up*. HABITAT: Various wooded areas from semiarid to humid. DISTRIBUTION: Migrant or non-breeding resident, from September to April, on Cuba. A migrant to the northern Bahamas and a vagrant on Hispaniola (Dominican Republic) and Puerto Rico.

3 GRENADA FLYCATCHER *Myiarchus nugator* 20cm FIELD NOTES: Catches insects by sallying from a perch; often returns to the same perch, flicking its tail on landing. VOICE: A loud *quip* or harsh *queuk*. HABITAT: Lowland scrub and open areas near settlements, usually near palms, secondary forest and tropical lowland forest. Breeds from March to October. DISTRIBUTION: Resident on St Vincent, Grenada and the Grenadines.

4 RUFOUS-TAILED FLYCATCHER *Myiarchus validus* 24cm FIELD NOTES: Sallies to catch insects from perches situated in dense foliage below forest canopy. Also feeds on fruit. VOICE: A descending, rolling *pree-ee-ee-ee-ee*; also a *chi-chi-chiup* and a *wick-up*. HABITAT: Mainly moist forest, less common in secondary forests and dry scrub. Breeds from April to July. DISTRIBUTION: Endemic to Jamaica.

5 LA SAGRA'S FLYCATCHER *Myiarchus sagrae* 19–22cm FIELD NOTES: Captures caterpillars and insects during hovering flights in the understorey. VOICE: A plaintive *huit*. At dawn, and more often during the breeding season, utters a whistled *tra-hee*. HABITAT: Forests at all elevations, pine woodland, mixed woodland, thickets and mangroves. Breeds from April to July. DISTRIBUTION: Resident in the Bahamas (less common in the southern Bahamas and absent from Turks and Caicos), Cuba and the Cayman Islands (Grand Cayman).

6 STOLID FLYCATCHER *Myiarchus stolidus* 20cm FIELD NOTES: Hovers to snatch insects from a twig or foliage and to pluck small fruits. VOICE: A long, rolling *whee-ee-ee swee-ip bzzrt*. Birds on Hispaniola also give a plaintive *jui*. HABITAT: Lowland forest, forest edge, arid woodlands, scrub and mangrove forest; also in pine forests on Hispaniola. Breeds from April to June. DISTRIBUTION: Resident on Jamaica and Hispaniola, including adjacent islands of Gonâve, Tortue, Beata and Grand Cayemite.

7 PUERTO RICAN FLYCATCHER *Myiarchus antillarum* 18.5–20cm FIELD NOTES: Inconspicuous and inactive. Foraging methods not well documented although known to feed on insects, caterpillars, seeds and berries. VOICE: A plaintive, whistled *whee*. At dawn, utters a *whee-a-wit-whee*; the middle section may be given separately at other times of the day. HABITAT: Tropical deciduous forest, tropical lowland evergreen forest, arid scrub, mangroves, coffee plantations and groves. Breeds from April to July. DISTRIBUTION: Resident on Puerto Rico and the Virgin Islands (St John, St Thomas, Virgin Gorda and Tortola).

8 LESSER ANTILLEAN FLYCATCHER *Myiarchus oberi* 19–22cm FIELD NOTES: Feeds mainly by hovering to glean insects and pick small fruits. Martinique race M. *o. sclateri* lacks rufous in the tail. VOICE: A loud, whistled *peeu-wheeet* and short *oo-ee oo-ee* or *e-oo-ee* whistles. HABITAT: Edges of forests, dense woodlands and tree plantations; also lower altitude scrub or second growth. Breeds from March to July. DISTRIBUTION: Resident on Barbuda, St Christopher, Nevis, Dominica, Martinique, St Lucia and Guadeloupe.

50 TYRANT FLYCATCHERS

1 TROPICAL KINGBIRD *Tyrannus melancholicus* 18–23cm FIELD NOTES: Uses a conspicuous perch from which it launches aerial sallies after insects or to harry other birds; returns to same perch or one nearby. VOICE: A high-pitched trill. At dawn, utters a thin *pit-pit-pit...* interspersed with short trills. HABITAT: Open, semiarid scrubland. DISTRIBUTION: Migrant on Grenada, sometimes breeds. Vagrant on Cuba.

2 WESTERN KINGBIRD *Tyrannus verticalis* 21–24cm FIELD NOTES: Uses a prominent perch to make aerial sallies to capture flying insects; will also glean prey from vegetation or the ground. Also found at fruiting trees. VOICE: A sharp *whit* or *kit*. A rapid, rising *widik-pik-widi-pik-pik-pik* and a lower *kdew-kdew-kdew-kdew*. HABITAT: Open woodland and plantations. DISTRIBUTION: Rare migrant, during October and November, on the northern Bahamas, south to Eleuthera and vagrant on Cuba.

3 EASTERN KINGBIRD *Tyrannus tyrannus* 22–23cm FIELD NOTES: Frequently perches in tall trees. Feeding methods much as Western Kingbird. VOICE: A sharp, buzzy *kzeer*. At dawn, gives a rapid, rattling crescendo ending *kiu kittttttttttttttiu ditide*. HABITAT: Semi-open woodland and urban gardens. DISTRIBUTION: An uncommon or rare migrant, in September, October, April and May, on Cuba, the Cayman Islands and the northern Bahamas, San Andrés and Jamaica. A vagrant in the southern Bahamas, Puerto Rico, St Christopher and Dominica.

4 GREY KINGBIRD *Tyrannus dominicensis* 22–25cm FIELD NOTES: Uses prominent perch, such as bare treetops, telephone posts and wires, to make sallies after flying insects; also feeds by hovering to glean from leaves; sometimes drops to the ground to capture prey. Occasionally forms very large communal roosts. VOICE: A loud *pi-tirr-ri* and a musical *pi-ti-réee pi-ti-rro*. HABITAT: Open areas with scattered trees in lowlands and mountains. Breeds from April to June. DISTRIBUTION: Widespread in the West Indies.

5 LOGGERHEAD KINGBIRD *Tyrannus caudifasciatus* 24–26cm FIELD NOTES: Uses exposed perches from which to make sallies to capture insects, usually from foliage; also eats fruit and small lizards. Most races differ mainly in the amount of yellow-buff wash on the underparts and pattern of tail tip, *see* Bahama race *T. c. bahamensis* (fig 5b). VOICE: A variable, loud chattering such as *jo-bee-beep*. Also a bubbling, repeated *p-p-q*. HABITAT: Forests, mangroves and swamp edges. Breeds from April to June. DISTRIBUTION: Resident on the Greater Antilles and the Bahamas (Grand Bahama, Abaco, Andros and New Providence).

6 GIANT KINGBIRD *Tyrannus cubensis* 23cm FIELD NOTES: Often found in pairs. Uses high exposed perches, feeds on flying insects, fruit and small lizards. VOICE: A loud *tooee-tooee-tooee-tooee-toee*; also a call of 4 distinct syllables. HABITAT: Mixed pine and hardwood forests, semi-open woodland with tall trees, woodlands near rivers and swamps. Breeds from April to June. DISTRIBUTION: Endemic to Cuba.

7 SCISSOR-TAILED FLYCATCHER *Tyrannus forficatus* 31–38cm FIELD NOTES: Feeding techniques similar to others of the genus, although captures prey from the ground more often. Underwing coverts bright pinkish orange. Juvenile paler with shorter tail. VOICE: A low, flat *pik*, *pik-prrr* or *kopik*. At dawn, utters a *pup-pup-pup-pup-pup-perleep*. HABITAT: Open areas with scattered bushes. DISTRIBUTION: Vagrant, recorded from the Bahamas (Grand Bahama, Abaco and San Salvador), western Cuba, Hispaniola and Puerto Rico.

8 FORK-TAILED FLYCATCHER *Tyrannus savana* 33–41cm FIELD NOTES: Uses exposed perch from which to launch sallies in pursuit of flying insects; occasionally takes insects from the ground or water; also feeds on berries and fruits. Female and juvenile duller with shorter tail. VOICE: A very high-pitched *tik-tik-krkrkr....* HABITAT: Open savannah. DISTRIBUTION: Irregular migrant on Grenada in July and August; also a vagrant recorded from the Grenadines (Carriacou), Barbados, St Lucia, St Bartholomew, St Martin, the Cayman Islands, Jamaica and Cuba.

51 SWALLOWS

1 **TREE SWALLOW** *Tachycineta bicolor* 13–15cm FIELD NOTES: Flight light, often straight and direct with sudden dips or turns to catch prey. VOICE: Generally silent in the West Indies but may utter a sharp *cheet* or *chi-veet* and a *duli-duli-duli* contact call. HABITAT: Various wetlands including swamps, marshes and rice fields. DISTRIBUTION: Non-breeding resident on Cuba and the Cayman Islands from September to June; also recorded as a migrant in the Bahamas, Jamaica, Hispaniola, Puerto Rico and the Virgin Islands (St Croix).

2 **BAHAMA SWALLOW** *Tachycineta cyaneoviridis* 15cm FIELD NOTES: Active mainly in the evening or during overcast weather, chasing insects either high up, where gliding seems common, or low over the ground in a rapid darting flight. VOICE: A metallic *chep* or *chi-chep* and a plaintive *seew-seew-seew-seew*. HABITAT: Pine forests, woodland clearings, cliffs, open fields and urban areas. Breeds from April to July. DISTRIBUTION: Endemic to the Bahamas (breeds on Grand Bahama, Abaco and Andros).

3 **GOLDEN SWALLOW** *Tachycineta euchrysea* 12cm FIELD NOTES: Flies low or over pine forests, darting after insects, alone or in small groups. Also noted perched on tall dead pines. Hispaniolan race *T. e. sclateri* (fig 3b) shows less golden wash. VOICE: A soft, repeated *tchee-weet*. HABITAT: On Hispaniola usually in open country, mountain pine forests and rainforests. On Jamaica occurs over open areas such as sugarcane fields. Breeds from April to June. DISTRIBUTION: Jamaica and Hispaniola.

4 **WHITE-WINGED SWALLOW** *Tachycineta albiventer* 14cm FIELD NOTES: Flies low over water or ground, hawking insects. Often perches on branches overhanging water. VOICE: A shrill *wrreeeet* or *chirrup*. HABITAT: Open, wet, lowland areas, primarily mangroves, rivers and lakes. DISTRIBUTION: Vagrant, a 1993 unofficial record from Martinique.

5 **SWALLOW (BARN SWALLOW)** *Hirundo rustica* 15–19cm FIELD NOTES: Often feeds in flocks over open areas; an agile, fast flier that twists and turns to catch flying insects. Juvenile and female generally much paler below, juvenile with much shorter outer tail feathers. VOICE: A thin *vit or vit-vit*; also a sharper *vit-VEET* when alarmed. HABITAT: Open areas, including fields, swamps and coastal areas. DISTRIBUTION: Widespread migrant from September to October and April to May.

6 **CAVE SWALLOW** *Pterochelidon fulva* 12.5–14cm FIELD NOTES: Usually in loose, small or large flocks; flight strong with frequent periods of gliding. Puerto Rican race *P. f. puertoricensis* (fig 6b) tends to be brighter. VOICE: A *weet*, *twit* or *cheweet*; also a chattering or twittering. HABITAT: Over fields, wetlands, around cliffs and urban areas. Breeds colonially from March to July. DISTRIBUTION: Breeds on Jamaica, Hispaniola, Puerto Rico and Cuba; leaves Cuba post breeding from September to February. Migrants recorded from Grand Cayman and the Virgin Islands and vagrants recorded from Martinique, St Lucia, St Vincent and the Grenadines.

7 **CLIFF SWALLOW (AMERICAN CLIFF SWALLOW)** *Petrochelidon pyrrhonota* 13–15cm FIELD NOTES: Usually in flocks, hawking insects both high in the air and near to the ground; frequently soars and glides. VOICE: A soft, husky *verr*, *purr* or *chur*. HABITAT: Mainly along coasts during migration. DISTRIBUTION: A migrant from August to December and from March to May on the Cayman Islands, Barbados, San Andrés, the Bahamas, Cuba, the Virgin Islands, Guadeloupe, Dominica and St Lucia.

52 MARTINS AND NORTHERN ROUGH-WINGED SWALLOW

1 SAND MARTIN (BANK SWALLOW) *Riparia riparia* 12cm FIELD NOTES: Gregarious, often associates with other swallow species. Rapid, light flight usually close to the ground. VOICE: A short, harsh, often repeated *tschr*, *chirr* or *shrit*. HABITAT: Open areas and along coasts on migration. DISTRIBUTION: Fairly widespread, but generally rare, migrant in the region, recorded primarily from September to December and from April to May.

2 NORTHERN ROUGH-WINGED SWALLOW *Stelgidopteryx serripennis* 13cm FIELD NOTES: Flight direct with leisurely but purposeful wing-beats; usually forages low over water or land. Juveniles have bright cinnamon wing-bars on upperwing coverts. VOICE: A low, harsh *prrit*; also a rising *frrip-frrip-frrip....* HABITAT: Open areas and wetlands. DISTRIBUTION: A rare migrant and non-breeding resident, from August to April, in the Bahamas, Cuba, Jamaica, Hispaniola, the Cayman Islands and the Virgin Islands (St Croix); also a vagrant on Guadeloupe.

3 PURPLE MARTIN *Progne subis* 19–22cm FIELD NOTES: Forages high in the air, frequently at 50m or more, often alternates flapping-flight with gliding on outstretched wings; less manoeuvrable than smaller swallows. Often mixes with Cuban Martins. VOICE: A rich *cherr*, a melodious whistle; male also utters a gurgling croak, while the female gives various chortles and whistles. HABITAT: Open areas and villages and towns. DISTRIBUTION: A migrant, from August to October and March, on Cuba, the Cayman Islands and the Bahamas; also a vagrant recorded on Jamaica, Hispaniola, Puerto Rico and the Virgin Islands.

4 CUBAN MARTIN *Progne cryptoleuca* 20–22cm FIELD NOTES: Foraging techniques similar to Purple Martin, which mean high-flying birds are virtually impossible to identify. Has variously been thought to be a race of both Purple Martin and Caribbean Martin. VOICE: A melodious warble and a gurgling that includes a high-pitched *twick-twick*, similar, but said to be distinct from those of Purple and Caribbean Martin. HABITAT: Towns and cities, swamp borders, lowland open areas and occasionally in mountain regions. Breeds from March to July. DISTRIBUTION: Breeding resident, from February to October, on Cuba. Vagrant in the Bahamas (Eleuthera).

5 CARIBBEAN MARTIN *Progne dominicensis* 20cm FIELD NOTES: Forages at high and low level; chases insects that are disturbed by cattle; flights consist of gentle flapping interspersed with gliding. VOICE: Very similar to Purple and Cuban Martin. HABITAT: Open and semi-open areas, usually near water, coasts, cliffs and towns. Breeds from February to August. DISTRIBUTION: Breeding resident, from January to September, on Hispaniola, Jamaica, Puerto Rico and most of the Lesser Antilles; also recorded as a vagrant on the Cayman Islands and the southern Bahamas (Great Inagua, Mayaguana and Grand Turk).

53 CROWS

1 CUBAN PALM CROW *Corvus minutus* 38cm FIELD NOTES: Usually occurs in pairs or small groups, foraging primarily in trees but will feed on the ground. Eats mainly fruit, seeds, insects and small lizards. Flies with rapid, flapping wing-beats. This and the Hispaniolan Palm Crow often considered one species under the name Palm Crow. VOICE: A harsh *craaao*. HABITAT: Forest, scrub and palm savannah. Breeds from March to May. DISTRIBUTION: Endemic to Cuba.

2 HISPANIOLAN PALM CROW *Corvus palmarum* 43cm FIELD NOTES: Forages in small- to medium-sized groups in trees and on the ground, feeding mainly on fruit, seeds, insects and small lizards. Flight similar to Cuban Palm Crow. Often considered, with the Cuban Palm Crow, to be a single species called Palm Crow. VOICE: A harsh, nasal *aaar aaar aaar....* HABITAT: Pine forests, swamp and dry plains with wooded ravines. Breeds from March to May. DISTRIBUTION: Endemic to Hispaniola.

3 CUBAN CROW *Corvus nasicus* 40–46cm FIELD NOTES: Usually occurs in small noisy parties; forages in trees and on the ground, feeding on fruit, seeds, lizards and frogs. Flight is unhurried, with deep wing-beats. VOICE: A high, nasal *caah-caaah*; also a bubbling or turkey-like gobbling. HABITAT: Primarily wooded areas, but also in urban areas where trees are plentiful. Breeds mainly during April and May. DISTRIBUTION: Cuba and the Bahamas (North and Middle Caicos, Providenciales and a vagrant on Grand Turk).

4 FISH CROW *Corvus ossifragus* 36–41cm FIELD NOTES: Usually gregarious, forages in trees and on the ground and is often associated with human habitations. Feeds on a variety of prey and carrion including amphibians, crabs, invertebrates and fruit. VOICE: A short, nasal, dry *ark ark ark* or *arruk*. HABITAT: Marshes, riverine plains with scattered trees, and coastal shores. DISTRIBUTION: Vagrant, recorded from the Bahamas (Grand Bahama).

5 WHITE-NECKED CROW *Corvus leucognaphalus* 48–51cm FIELD NOTES: White bases of body feathers only show during display. Occurs in pairs or small flocks, used to gather in very large flocks; leaves mountain forest roosts to forage in lowland forest on fruit, berries, nestlings and small toads. Flight is graceful and often soars high up. VOICE: Variable, including babbling and squawking, which makes it sound much like a parrot. HABITAT: Mountain and lowland forests and woodlands; also open areas with scattered trees. Breeds from February to June. DISTRIBUTION: Endemic to Hispaniola.

6 JAMAICAN CROW *Corvus jamaicensis* 38cm FIELD NOTES: Mainly arboreal; usually occurs in pairs or small groups that forage in the canopy in search of fruit and invertebrates, the latter found by probing bark and bromeliads. Flight slow and heavy with deliberate wing-beats. VOICE: A loud *craa-craa* and various bubbling, chuckling and gobbling noises strung together in garbled outbursts. HABITAT: Hill and mountain forests, descending to lower levels during dry season. Breeds from April to June. DISTRIBUTION: Endemic to Jamaica.

7 HOUSE CROW (INDIAN HOUSE CROW) *Corvus splendens* 40cm FIELD NOTES: Bold scavenger, usually very sociable and generally associated with human habitations. VOICE: A flat, dry *kaaaa-kaaa*. HABITAT: Villages, towns and cities, often in and around ports. DISTRIBUTION: Vagrant, recorded from Barbados.

54 NUTHATCH, WRENS, RUBY-CROWNED KINGLET, GNATCATCHERS, WHEATEAR AND BLUEBIRD

1 BROWN-HEADED NUTHATCH *Sitta pusilla* 9.5–11cm FIELD NOTES: Climbs up or head down on tree trunks, and often upside down as it forages along branches. VOICE: A weak, high-pitched chattering. HABITAT: Pine barrens. DISTRIBUTION: Endemic race on the Bahamas (Grand Bahama).

2 ZAPATA WREN *Ferminia cerverai* 16cm FIELD NOTES: Very secretive, best located by song. Feeds low down in vegetation and on the ground. Tail is regularly cocked but is held down while singing. VOICE: Utters a clear series of gurgling whistles interspersed with harsh churring notes, which can continue for over a minute; also gives a low, harsh *chut-chut, churr-churr* or similar. HABITAT: Sawgrass marshes. Breeds from January to July. DISTRIBUTION: Endemic to Cuba.

3 MARSH WREN (LONG-BILLED MARSH WREN) *Cistothorus palustris* 11.5–12.5cm FIELD NOTES: Secretive; forages low in marsh vegetation. VOICE: A dry *tek*; when agitated, gives a harsh *shrrr* and a rolling *chrddd*. HABITAT: Marshes with tall reeds or cattails. DISTRIBUTION: Vagrant, recorded from Cuba.

4 SOUTHERN HOUSE WREN (HOUSE WREN) *Troglodytes musculus* 11.5–12.5cm FIELD NOTES: Forages in low vegetation; holds tail down while singing; rarely cocks tail over back. Races depicted are from St Lucia *T. m. mesoleucos* (fig 4a) and from Dominica *T. m. rufescens* (fig 4b). VOICE: A bubbling warble; also a sharp chatter. HABITAT: Moist uplands, arid lowland coastal regions and around human habitations. Breeds from May to August. DISTRIBUTION: Resident on Dominica, Grenada, St Vincent and St Lucia, probably now extinct on Guadeloupe and Martinique. Vagrant on western Cuba. Rare migrant on northern Bahamas.

5 RUBY-CROWNED KINGLET *Regulus calendula* 10cm FIELD NOTES: Restless, acrobatic feeder. Females lack the red crest. VOICE: A series of high notes followed by descending notes, ending in a warble; also utters a thin *ze-zeet*. HABITAT: Woodlands, thickets and scrub. DISTRIBUTION: Rare non-breeding resident, from October to March, in the northern Bahamas; also a vagrant recorded from Cuba, Jamaica and Hispaniola (Dominican Republic).

6 BLUE-GREY GNATCATCHER *Polioptila caerulea* 11cm FIELD NOTES: Active, forages in trees and tall bushes, often fly-catches by making short flits from branches. VOICE: A thin *zpee-zpee, pwee* or *zeef-zeef*; also gives a series of soft warbles. HABITAT: Woodlands, scrub, mangroves and gardens. Breeds from March to June. DISTRIBUTION: Breeding resident on the Bahamas; non-breeding resident, from September to April, on Cuba and the Cayman Islands.

7 CUBAN GNATCATCHER *Polioptila lembeyei* 10.5cm FIELD NOTES: A tame, very active forager in scrub; often occurs in family groups. VOICE: A loud, 4-note whistle followed by a trill and variable whisper, *pss-psss-psss-psss-ttiizzzt-zzzz-ttizzz-tzi-tzi-tzi*; also utters a *speee* and a *pit*. HABITAT: Mainly dense, coastal thorn scrub, occasionally inland in thick scrub. Breeds from March to June. DISTRIBUTION: Endemic to Cuba.

8 WHEATEAR (NORTHERN WHEATEAR) *Oenanthe oenanthe* 14.5–15.5cm FIELD NOTES: In flight, shows white rump and white bases to outer tail feathers. Always seems alert, feeds in stop-start fashion, little runs interspersed with stops to pick up prey or to look around. VOICE: A hard *chak* and *wheet*, often combined as *wheet-chak-chak*. HABITAT: On migration, occurs in open places, especially areas of managed grassland such as pastures, parks and golf courses. DISTRIBUTION: Vagrant, recorded from Cuba, Puerto Rico, Barbados and the Bahamas (Andros and Eleuthera).

9 EASTERN BLUEBIRD *Sialia sialis* 15–16.5cm FIELD NOTES: Usually sits on an exposed perch waiting to pounce upon insects on the ground; occasionally makes short fly-catching sallies. VOICE: A musical *chur-lee, tu-a-wee* or *jeew wiwi*. HABITAT: Open country with hedgerows. DISTRIBUTION: Vagrant, recorded from western Cuba, the Virgin Islands (St John) and the Bahamas (Eleuthera).

55 SOLITAIRES AND THRUSHES

1 CUBAN SOLITAIRE *Myadestes elisabeth* 19cm FIELD NOTES: Perches high in trees, from where it makes sallies to catch flying insects or to pick prey from vegetation; also hovers to pluck fruits. VOICE: Short whistles and a loud, flute-like, far-carrying song, said to sound like a wet finger rubbed on the rim of a fine porcelain cup. HABITAT: Dense, humid mountain and hill forests. Breeds from February to April. DISTRIBUTION: Endemic to Cuba.

2 ST VINCENT SOLITAIRE *Myadestes sibilans* 19cm FIELD NOTES: Arboreal, frequently makes aerial sallies to catch insects, glean prey from vegetation and to pluck fruit; also uses a perch and pounce technique to catch insects on the ground. Considered by many authors to be a race of Rufous-throated Solitaire. VOICE: Similar to Rufous-throated Solitaire? HABITAT: Dense, moist mountain forest. Breeds from April to August. DISTRIBUTION: Endemic to St Vincent.

3 RUFOUS-THROATED SOLITAIRE *Myadestes genibarbis* 19–20.5cm FIELD NOTES: Often sits motionless and silent in dense vegetation. Feeding methods similar to St Vincent Solitaire. Nominate and the Dominican race M. g. *dominicanus* (fig 3b) are depicted. VOICE: A drawn-out *teut* or *toot*; also a series of semi-discordant whistles and trills, highly ventriloquial. HABITAT: Moist, montane forests. Breeds from March to August. DISTRIBUTION: Resident on Hispaniola, Jamaica, Dominica, Martinique and St Lucia.

4 VEERY *Catharus fuscescens* 17–19cm FIELD NOTES: Shy and secretive, forages primarily on the ground. VOICE: A fluted *phew whee-uu*; also a slow, slurred *weee-oo* and sharp *wuck* given when agitated. HABITAT: Open woodland with thick undergrowth, scrub and gardens. DISTRIBUTION: Rare migrant, during September, October, April and May, on the Bahamas, Cuba, Jamaica, Hispaniola and the Cayman Islands; also recorded as a vagrant on St Christopher, Providencia, San Andrés and the Virgin Islands (St John).

5 BICKNELL'S THRUSH *Catharus bicknelli* 16–17cm FIELD NOTES: Wary, forages on or near the ground, occasionally making short sallies to catch flying insects. VOICE: A *wee-ooo*, *pee-oo* or *psee-uuu*; also a sharp *shrip* or *chirp*. HABITAT: High-elevation broadleaved forests, woods and gardens with large trees. DISTRIBUTION: Non-breeding resident, from September to May, on Hispaniola. A rare migrant in the Bahamas, eastern Cuba and Jamaica; also a vagrant with records from Puerto Rico and the Virgin Islands.

6 GREY-CHEEKED THRUSH *Catharus minimus* 16–20cm FIELD NOTES: Actions and habits similar to Bicknell's Thrush. VOICE: A downward slurred *wee-ah* or similar; also a short *what* or *chuck* and a light *pheeu*. HABITAT: Forests and woodlands. DISTRIBUTION: A rare migrant to Cuba and Martinique. Many records from the region are under review due to the splitting of Grey-cheeked and Bicknell's Thrush.

7 SWAINSON'S THRUSH *Catharus ustulatus* 16–20cm FIELD NOTES: Shy and retiring, more arboreal than others of the genus, attracted to fruiting trees and palms; also forages on the ground in thick cover. VOICE: A liquid *whit* or a soft *whup*. HABITAT: Open woods, copse and gardens. DISTRIBUTION: A rare migrant on Cuba, Jamaica, the Cayman Islands and the northern Bahamas.

8 HERMIT THRUSH *Catharus guttatus* 19cm FIELD NOTES: Shy and retiring, forages on the ground. Nervous, constantly flicks wings and tail. VOICE: A low *chuck*, a ringing *cheeeee* or *seeee*, and a harsh *pay*. HABITAT: Forest thickets. DISTRIBUTION: A rare non-breeding resident in the northern Bahamas, from October to April. A vagrant on Cuba.

9 WOOD THRUSH *Catharus (Hylocichla) mustelina* 20cm FIELD NOTES: Generally a shy and retiring ground feeder; frequently flicks wings. VOICE: Utters a liquid *pip-pip-pip* or *kuk-kuk-kuk* and a sharp *pit-pit-pit*. HABITAT: Tree plantations and gardens. DISTRIBUTION: Rare migrant to Cuba and the northern Bahamas, from September to November and March to April. A vagrant on the southern Bahamas, Jamaica, Hispaniola, Puerto Rico and the Cayman Islands.

56 THRUSHES

1 COCOA THRUSH (LESSER ANTILLEAN THRUSH) *Turdus fumigatus* 23cm
FIELD NOTES: Feeds primarily on the ground, although often attracted to fruiting trees. VOICE: A variable series of musical notes, consisting mostly of rapid, repeated phrases; also utters descending *weeo weeo weeo* or *wee-a-wee-a-wee-a*. HABITAT: Forest, cacao plantations and farmland with scattered trees. Breeds from November to June. DISTRIBUTION: Resident on St Vincent and Grenada.

2 BARE-EYED THRUSH (BARE-EYED ROBIN, SPECTACLED or YELLOW-EYED THRUSH) *Turdus nudigenis* 23–25cm FIELD NOTES: Forages in trees and on the ground, feeding mainly on berries and fruit. Often aggressive to other thrushes. VOICE: A loud, liquid *cheerily cheer-up cheerio* or similar; also utters a high *miter-ee*. HABITAT: Open lowland woods, forest edge, secondary growth and plantations. Breeds from April to August. DISTRIBUTION: Resident in the Lesser Antilles (Martinique, St Lucia, St Vincent, Grenada and the Grenadines).

3 WHITE-EYED THRUSH *Turdus jamaicensis* 23cm FIELD NOTES: Usually forages in dense vegetation from ground to treetops; shy and secretive. VOICE: A shrill *dzee* or *dzaw*; song varied and musical with repeated phrases such as a bell-like *hee-haw* and trilling whistles and chimes. HABITAT: Wet mountain forests and shade coffee plantations. Breeds from April to June. DISTRIBUTION: Endemic to Jamaica.

4 AMERICAN ROBIN *Turdus migratorius* 23–28cm FIELD NOTES: Feeds mainly on the ground but also in trees and bushes where attracted to berries and fruit. VOICE: A *tut-tut-tut* and an excited *kli-kli-kli…*. HABITAT: Open woodlands, open scrub, parks and gardens. DISTRIBUTION: Non-breeding resident, from October to April, on Cuba and the northern Bahamas; also a vagrant recorded from Jamaica, Hispaniola and Puerto Rico.

5 LA SELLE THRUSH *Turdus swalesi* 26cm FIELD NOTES: Forages mainly on the ground. Race *T. s. dodae*, from central Dominican Republic, has mantle dark olive-brown. VOICE: A deliberate *tu-re-oo* or *cho-ho-cho*; also a strident *poo-ip poo-ip* or *whewry-whewry'wheury*; also some low chuckling or gurgling notes. HABITAT: Dense understorey of wet forests, including mountain pine forests. Breeds from May to July. DISTRIBUTION: Endemic to Hispaniola.

6 WHITE-CHINNED THRUSH *Turdus aurantius* 24cm FIELD NOTES: Active, especially after rain; forages mainly on the ground. VOICE: Song slow and lilting that includes shrill whistles, which are often give on their own; also utters a clucking *kek*. HABITAT: Mountain and hill woodlands, plantations, road sides and gardens. Breeds from May to July. DISTRIBUTION: Endemic to Jamaica.

7 RED-LEGGED THRUSH *Turdus plumbeus* 26–27cm FIELD NOTES: Forages mainly on the ground; generally shy but becomes more conspicuous during breeding season. Races shown are nominate, from the Bahamas, *T. p. rubripes* (fig 7b), from west and central Cuba, *T. p. ardosiaceus* (fig 7c), from Hispaniola and Puerto Rico and *T. p. albiventris* (fig 7d) from Dominica. VOICE: A high-pitched *weecha weecha weecha*, *cha-cha-cha* or *chu-week chu-week chu-week*; song is a melodious, monotonous series of 1- to 3-syllable phrases. HABITAT: Woodlands, thick undergrowth, scrub, shade coffee plantations and gardens. Breeds from January to September. DISTRIBUTION: Resident in the northern Bahamas (Grand Bahama, Abaco, Andros, New Providence and Cat Island), Cuba, Hispaniola, Puerto Rico, the Cayman Islands and Dominica.

8 FOREST THRUSH *Cichlherminia lherminieri* 24–27cm FIELD NOTES: Shy, often runs into cover when disturbed; forages from ground to tree canopy. Race on Montserrat *C. l. lawrencii* intermediate in colour from the depicted forms, which are nominate, from Guadeloupe and *C. l. dominicensis* (fig 8b), from Dominica. VOICE: A loud *chuck-chuck*, which is often extended into a harsh chatter; song is a fluty, whistled cadence, which may include some harsh notes. HABITAT: Moist mountain forests. DISTRIBUTION: Resident on Montserrat, Guadeloupe, Dominica and St Lucia.

57 CATBIRD, MOCKINGBIRDS AND THRASHERS

1 GREY CATBIRD *Dumetella carolinensis* 23cm FIELD NOTES: Skulks in thick cover, near or on the ground. More often heard than seen. VOICE: An explosive *kak-kak-kak* and a soft cat-like *mew*; song contains sweet, varied phrases interspersed with harsher notes and mewing. HABITAT: Dense undergrowth and thickets. DISTRIBUTION: Non-breeding resident and migrant, from October to April, on the Bahamas, the Cayman Islands, Providencia, Cuba, Jamaica, San Andrés and Hispaniola; also a vagrant on Puerto Rico and Anguilla.

2 NORTHERN MOCKINGBIRD *Mimus polyglottos* 24–28cm FIELD NOTES: Forages mainly on the ground, occasionally uses a perch to pounce on prey or make fly-catching sallies. VOICE: A series of melodious phrases, each repeated several times; often mimics the calls of other birds. When agitated, utters a harsh *tchack*. HABITAT: Open country with scattered trees or bushes, mangroves, parks and gardens. Breeds from January to July. DISTRIBUTION: Resident in the Bahamas, Greater Antilles and the Virgin Islands.

3 TROPICAL MOCKINGBIRD *Mimus gilvus* 23–24cm FIELD NOTES: Forages mostly on the ground or low in vegetation, also hawks for insects. Fig 3b is the race *M. g. magnirostris* from San Andrés. VOICE: Repeated musical whistles and phrases, similar to Northern Mockingbird but slightly more harsh with less mimicry. When agitated, gives a harsh *chuck*. HABITAT: Open areas near habitations, lowland scrub and cultivations. Breeds from February to July and again from September to November. DISTRIBUTION: Lesser Antilles, from Antigua south to Grenada and on San Andrés.

4 BAHAMA MOCKINGBIRD *Mimus gundlachii* 28cm FIELD NOTES: Forages mostly on the ground or in tall dense vegetation. Juvenile more uniform above, flank streaks less prominent. VOICE: A series of repeated phrases, less variable than Northern Mockingbird and lacks mimicry. HABITAT: Woodlands, semiarid scrub and urban areas. Breeds from February to June. DISTRIBUTION: Resident on the Bahamas, the cays of northern Cuba and southern Jamaica.

5 WHITE-BREASTED THRASHER *Ramphocinclus brachyurus* 20–23cm FIELD NOTES: Forages mainly on the ground, usually among leaf litter; also feeds in bushes and trees, especially when they are in fruit. VOICE: Repeated short, mellow phrases of several syllables; also utters a *chek-chek-chek* on Martinique and a *tschhhhhh* on St Lucia. HABITAT: Dry woodland, coastal thickets, wooded stream valleys and scrub forest. Breeds from April to August. DISTRIBUTION: Endangered resident on Martinique and St Lucia.

6 BROWN THRASHER *Toxostoma rufum* 28cm FIELD NOTES: Rather shy, forages in leaf litter under bushes and trees, occasionally feeds in low vegetation. VOICE: A loud *tschek* or *chip*. HABITAT: Dense undergrowth. DISTRIBUTION: Vagrant, recorded from Cuba and the Bahamas (Harbour Island and Grand Bahama).

7 SCALY-BREASTED THRASHER *Margarops fuscus* 23cm FIELD NOTES: Retiring. Mainly arboreal, feeds on fruits. VOICE: Repeated phrases much like those of the Tropical Mockingbird, but less vigorous. HABITAT: Moist and semiarid forests and woodlands. Breeds during May and June. DISTRIBUTION: Lesser Antilles, from St Martin southwards, but probably extinct on St Eustatius, Barbuda and Barbados.

8 PEARLY-EYED THRASHER *Margarops fuscatus* 28–30cm FIELD NOTES: Arboreal, often forages in small groups from the middle level to the canopy. Takes a large variety of food, including fruits, berries, frogs, lizards, land crabs, eggs, nestlings and occasionally adult birds. VOICE: A slow series of 1- to 3-syllable phrases with lengthy pauses between segments; also gives a *craw-craw* or *chook-chook*. Often sings late in the day and occasionally at night. HABITAT: Forests, woodlands, thickets, mangroves, coastal palm groves and urban areas. Breeds from December to September. DISTRIBUTION: Southern and central Bahamas (spreading north?), Puerto Rico and the Lesser Antilles south to St Lucia. A vagrant on Jamaica and Barbados.

58 TREMBLERS, PIPITS, SHRIKE, WAXWING, PALMCHAT, STARLING AND MYNA

1 BROWN TREMBLER *Cinclocerthia ruficauda* 23–26cm FIELD NOTES: Arboreal, searches for food among epiphytic vegetation and tree hollows. Frequently cocks tail over back. Southern Lesser Antilles race (fig 1b) *C. r. tenebrosa* has longer bill and is more suffused with grey on breast. VOICE: A rasping *yeeak* and a series of melodic and harsh phrases. HABITAT: Wet forests, secondary forests and drier woodlands; on St Lucia found only in dry forest or scrub. Breeds during March and April. DISTRIBUTION: Lesser Antilles from the Virgin Islands southwards, although only a vagrant on the Virgin Islands (St Thomas), St Eustatius and Antigua.

2 GREY TREMBLER *Cinclocerthia gutturalis* 23–26cm FIELD NOTES: Actions and foraging methods similar to Brown Trembler. VOICE: Repeated wavering, whistled notes and phrases; also harsh scolding notes. HABITAT: Mainly high-level mature, moist forests. Less common in open woodlands, second growth and dry scrub. Breeds during March and April. DISTRIBUTION: Resident on Martinique and St Lucia.

3 SPRAGUE'S PIPIT *Anthus spragueii* 17cm FIELD NOTES: Solitary and secretive, usually keeps well hidden in grass or other short vegetation. Does not bob tail. In flight, shows white outer tail feathers. VOICE: In flight, gives a sharp, high-pitched *squeet* or *squeet squeet*, occasionally repeated several times in quick succession. HABITAT: Open grassy areas and weedy fields. DISTRIBUTION: Vagrant, recorded on the Bahamas (Grand Bahama, Eleuthera and Exuma).

4 BUFF-BELLIED PIPIT (AMERICAN PIPIT) *Anthus rubescens* 16cm FIELD NOTES: Walks with a light, dainty gait and bobbing tail. Often occurs in flocks. In flight, shows white outer tail feathers. VOICE: In flight, gives a squeaky *sip, sipit* or *tsweep*; when flushed, gives a *si-si-si-si-s-si*. HABITAT: Open fields and sandy areas. DISTRIBUTION: Non-breeding resident, from October to March, in the northern Bahamas. Vagrant on Jamaica, Providencia and San Andrés.

5 LOGGERHEAD SHRIKE *Lanius ludovicianus* 23cm FIELD NOTES: Uses exposed perches from which to drop on to quarry; occasionally hovers to search for prey. In flight, shows white patch at base of primaries. VOICE: A harsh *shack-shack*. HABITAT: Open areas with scattered bushes or trees. DISTRIBUTION: Vagrant, recorded from the Bahamas (Grand Bahama, Great Exuma and Andros).

6 CEDAR WAXWING *Bombycilla cedrorum* 18cm FIELD NOTES: Gregarious. Juvenile duller and streaked below. VOICE: A high-pitched whistled *sreee*. HABITAT: Fruit-bearing trees and bushes in forests, cultivations and gardens. DISTRIBUTION: Non-breeding visitor, in variable numbers, on Cuba, Jamaica, the Bahamas and the Cayman Islands, from October to April. A vagrant on Hispaniola, Puerto Rico, the Virgin Islands, Guadeloupe and Dominica.

7 PALMCHAT *Dulus dominicus* 20cm FIELD NOTES: Gregarious, active forager in the upper levels of trees; occasionally hawks after flying insects. VOICE: A variety of short, harsh notes; also a musical whistle that drops in pitch, given when alarmed. HABITAT: Royal palm savannahs and open areas with scattered trees. Breeds from March to June. DISTRIBUTION: Endemic to Hispaniola.

8 HILL MYNA *Gracula religiosa* 30cm FIELD NOTES: Unmistakable; in flight, shows large white patch on base of primaries. VOICE: Various whistles, squawks and chirps; can also mimic virtually any sound. HABITAT: Open woodlands. Breeds from February to June. DISTRIBUTION: Puerto Rico (introduced).

9 STARLING (EUROPEAN STARLING) *Sturnus vulgaris* 22cm FIELD NOTES: Highly gregarious, generally feeds on the ground. Juvenile grey-brown above, slightly paler below, especially on the throat. VOICE: A medley of clicks, chirrups, warbles etc., interspersed with drawn-out whistles and mimicry; also various harsh or grating notes. HABITAT: Varied, including woodland edge, parks and gardens. Breeds from April to June. DISTRIBUTION: Resident (introduced) on Jamaica and the Bahamas (Grand Bahama and Bimini); also recorded from the Cayman Islands, Puerto Rico and the Virgin Islands (St Croix).

59 VIREOS

1 WHITE-EYED VIREO *Vireo griseus* 12.5cm FIELD NOTES: Sluggish and rather secretive when moving about in dense vegetation. VOICE: The song is a repeated *chip-a-tee-weeo-chip* or similar; calls include a *rik* or *rikrikrikrik-rik-rik-rik-rik*. HABITAT: Bushy woodlands, undergrowth, scrub and coastal thickets. DISTRIBUTION: Uncommon or rare non-breeding resident, from October to March, on the Bahamas, the Greater Antilles and the Virgin Islands (St John).

2 THICK-BILLED VIREO *Vireo crassirostris* 13cm FIELD NOTES: Slow and secretive, more often heard than seen. Underpart colour varies, being yellow on southern Bahamas, greyish on the northern Bahamas and Cayman Islands (fig 2b) and buff on Île Tortue (fig 2c). VOICE: Song and calls are very similar to that of the White-eyed Vireo, but generally slower; the calls are usually longer. HABITAT: Woodland edge, bushes and undergrowth. Breeds from April to July. DISTRIBUTION: Resident on the Bahamas, Hispaniola (Île Tortue), the Cayman Islands and Providencia; also a migrant in north central Cuba during October.

3 MANGROVE VIREO *Vireo pallens* 12cm FIELD NOTES: Occurs singly or in pairs, associates with mixed species flocks. VOICE: Song variable; includes a series of rapid, nasal twanging notes. Call also varied, includes a buzzy, scolding *chi-chi-chi-chi...*, a forceful *tckrrr* and a drawn-out *tchrrrirrr*. HABITAT: Mangroves. DISTRIBUTION: Providencia.

4 ST ANDREW VIREO *Vireo caribaeus* 12cm FIELD NOTES: Active forager in bushes and trees, from ground level up to 10m. VOICE: Three different songs, a chatter made up by repeating a single syllable note from 2 to 20 or more times, a 2-syllable phrase *se-wi se-wi se-wi...* repeated up to 15 times and a variable 3-syllable call. HABITAT: Mangroves, bushes and scrubby pasture. Breeds from May to July. DISTRIBUTION: Endemic to San Andrés.

5 JAMAICAN VIREO *Vireo modestus* 13cm FIELD NOTES: Active but secretive, keeps to dense vegetation. VOICE: Various repeated phrases such as *sewi-sewi*, *twee-weet-weet-wuu* or *pee-eu*; also gives a rapid, scolding *chi-chi-chi-chi-chi*. HABITAT: Forests, forest edge and thickets, primarily in the arid lowlands. Breeds from April to June. DISTRIBUTION: Endemic to Jamaica.

6 CUBAN VIREO *Vireo gundlachii* 13cm FIELD NOTES: Sluggish, usually encountered in pairs or among mixed species feeding flocks, often alongside Yellow-headed or Oriente Warblers. VOICE: A high-pitched, repeated *wi-chiví wi-chiví wi-chiví*, and a guttural *shruo* given when agitated. HABITAT: Brushland, forest edge, thickets and dense scrub, mainly in the lowlands but also found in hills and mountains. Breeds from April to June. DISTRIBUTION: Endemic to Cuba.

7 YELLOW-THROATED VIREO *Vireo flavifrons* 13cm FIELD NOTES: Usually forages alone in the canopy of trees. VOICE: Song is a slow, slurred *rrreeyoo rreeooee three-eight* or *de-ar-ie come-here three-eight*, on average repeated every 3 seconds. Call is a harsh, descending *chi-chi-chur-chur-chur-chur-chur* or *ship-shep-shep-shep-shep-shep-shep*. HABITAT: Various types of forests, woodlands, coastal scrub and second growth. DISTRIBUTION: Uncommon, or rare non-breeding resident on Cuba, the Bahamas, the Cayman Islands, Puerto Rico, Barbados and the Virgin Islands (St John and St Thomas), from September to April. Vagrant on Jamaica, Hispaniola, Antigua, Dominica, St Lucia, St Vincent and Grenada.

8 FLAT-BILLED VIREO *Vireo nanus* 12–13cm FIELD NOTES: Forages slowly through bushes, occasionally feeds on the ground or pursues insects in flight. VOICE: A high-pitched, chattering *weet-weet-weet-weet-weet-weet-weet*. Also a slower, repeated version. HABITAT: Mainly semiarid scrub and undergrowth. Breeds from February to June. DISTRIBUTION: Endemic to Hispaniola.

60 VIREOS

1 BLUE-MOUNTAIN VIREO *Vireo osburni* 13cm FIELD NOTES: Secretive, heard more often than seen due to its habit of foraging in dense vegetation. VOICE: A slightly descending, trilling whistle. When agitated gives a harsh, descending *burr*. HABITAT: Primarily moist and humid mountain forest; also upland woods and shade coffee plantations. Breeds from March to July. DISTRIBUTION: Endemic to Jamaica.

2 PUERTO RICAN VIREO *Vireo latimeri* 13cm FIELD NOTES: Inactive, best located by frequent calls. VOICE: A melodious 3- or 4-syllable whistle; also a rattling *chur-chur-churr-rrr*. Other calls include a *tup tup* and a grating, cat-like *mew*. HABITAT: All types of forest including mangroves, shade coffee plantations and coastal scrub. Breeds from March to June. DISTRIBUTION: Endemic to western Puerto Rico.

3 BLUE-HEADED VIREO *Vireo solitarius* 13–15cm FIELD NOTES: Forages slowly and deliberately in shrubs and trees. VOICE: Sweet, slurred phrases such as *see you cheerio be-seein-u so-long seeya...*, repeated every few seconds. HABITAT: Trees, shrubs and dense bushes. DISTRIBUTION: Rare non-breeding resident, from September to April, in the northern Bahamas and Cuba. A vagrant on Jamaica.

4 WARBLING VIREO *Vireo gilvus* 13–15cm FIELD NOTES: Forages as others of the genus, often occurs in mixed species flocks. VOICE: A flowing, warbled phrase *brig-adier brig-adier brigate*. Calls include a harsh *quee*, a slightly 2-syllabled *meeerish* and a short *git or gwit*. HABITAT: Woodland, scrub and plantations. DISTRIBUTION: Vagrant, during September and October, in western Cuba and Jamaica.

5 PHILADELPHIA VIREO *Vireo philadelphicus* 13cm FIELD NOTES: Feeds in low to middle level of trees; recorded hovering, or fluttering to pick insects from vegetation. VOICE: Song very similar to Red-eyed Vireo but higher-pitched and weaker. Call is a descending *weeej weeezh weeezh weeezh*. HABITAT: Forests, woods and gardens. DISTRIBUTION: Rare migrant in the Bahamas, Cuba and Jamaica, mainly during October. Vagrant in the Cayman Islands and Antigua.

6 YELLOW-GREEN VIREO *Vireo flavoviridis* 14–15cm FIELD NOTES: Sluggish forager in the mid to upper levels of trees. VOICE: Song like Red-eyed Vireo but shorter and more rapid. Calls include a dry chatter and a rough mewing. HABITAT: Woodland, scrubby forest edge and plantations. DISTRIBUTION: Vagrant recorded on Providencia.

7 RED-EYED VIREO *Vireo olivaceus* 14–15cm FIELD NOTES: Active but with heavy movements; forages mainly in tree canopy. VOICE: Rambling, warbled phrases that often end abruptly *teeduee-tueedee-teeudeeu...* or *here-I-am in-the-tree look-up at-the-top...*, each phrase given every 2 seconds. Calls include a soft mewing *meerf* and a nasal *tshay*. HABITAT: Wet and dry forests, open woodlands, scrub and gardens. DISTRIBUTION: Uncommon migrant, from September to November and also in April, in the Bahamas, Cuba, Jamaica, the Cayman Islands (Grand Cayman) and Hispaniola. A vagrant recorded from Puerto Rico, the Virgin Islands, Guadeloupe, Martinique, St Lucia and Barbados.

8 BLACK-WHISKERED VIREO *Vireo altiloquus* 15–16cm FIELD NOTES: Often sits motionless, best located by song. VOICE: A monotonous *chip-john-phillip chiip-phillip...chillip phillip*. Calls include a nasal mew, a thin *tsit* and a nasal chatter. HABITAT: All types of forest. Breeds in May and June. DISTRIBUTION: Widespread throughout the region, absent from Grand Cayman and San Salvador. Birds from the Bahamas, Cuba, Jamaica, Puerto Rico and the Cayman Islands migrate to South America post-breeding, September to January.

9 YUCATAN VIREO *Vireo magister* 15cm FIELD NOTES: More often heard than seen due to its slow movements in thick vegetation. VOICE: A 2-note whistle and a 3-syllabled *sweet brid-get*. HABITAT: Low-elevation woodlands and mangroves. Breeds from April to August. DISTRIBUTION: Cayman Islands (Grand Cayman).

61 AMERICAN WARBLERS

1 NORTHERN PARULA *Parula americana* 11cm FIELD NOTES: Very agile, often hangs upside down whilst foraging in the tree canopy. VOICE: Song is an ascending buzzing trill, ending with an abrupt *tship*. Calls include a sharp *chip* and a weak *tsif* given in flight. HABITAT: Mainly lowland dry forests and scrub, but also damp mountain forests. DISTRIBUTION: Non-breeding resident, from August to May, throughout the region.

2 BLUE-WINGED WARBLER *Vermivora pinus* 12cm FIELD NOTES: Agile acrobatic forager, usually in middle level of trees. VOICE: A buzzy *bzeeee bzzzz*; also a sharp musical *tchip* and a high-pitched *zzee* uttered in flight. HABITAT: Rainforest edge, second growth with a rich understorey, and bushes and hedgerows. DISTRIBUTION: Rare non-breeding resident, from October to March, in the Bahamas, Cuba, Jamaica, Hispaniola, the Cayman Islands and the larger Virgin Islands. Vagrant on St Bartholomew and Guadeloupe.

3 GOLDEN-WINGED WARBLER *Vermivora chrysoptera* 12cm FIELD NOTES: Very agile, often feeding tit-like in bushes and trees. Probes dead leaf clumps for insects. VOICE: A soft, buzzy *zee-bee-bee-bee*, which is occasionally more trilling; also a short *tchip*. HABITAT: High forests, woodlands and gardens. DISTRIBUTION: Mainly a migrant, during September, October and April, on Puerto Rico, Cuba, the Virgin and Cayman Islands, Cuba, Jamaica and Hispaniola.

4 TENNESSEE WARBLER *Vermivora peregrina* 12cm FIELD NOTES: Usually forages high in the tree canopy, although will descend to feed in bushes; agile and active. VOICE: A loud, staccato series of double and single notes ending in a trill. Calls include a sharp *tsip* and a thin *see*. HABITAT: Woodlands, scrub and gardens. DISTRIBUTION: Uncommon or rare non-breeding resident, from September to May, in the Bahamas, Cuba, the Cayman Islands, San Andrés, Jamaica, Hispaniola and Providencia. A vagrant on the Virgins Islands (St John) and Barbados.

5 ORANGE-CROWNED WARBLER *Vermivora celata* 13cm FIELD NOTES: Feeds from low to high levels on insects and small berries. Western race *V. c. lutescens* (fig 5b) may occur. VOICE: A high-pitched trill followed by a lower, slower trill. Calls include a sharp *chet* and a clear *see* uttered in flight. HABITAT: Woodlands with scrubby undergrowth. DISTRIBUTION: A rare winter resident on the northern Bahamas, mainly from October to January. A vagrant on Cuba, Jamaica and the Cayman Islands.

6 NASHVILLE WARBLER *Vermivora ruficapilla* 12cm FIELD NOTES: Found mainly at low levels feeding on insects, nectar and berries. VOICE: Song consists of a series of high-pitched *tsee* notes followed by a low trill. Call is a metallic *tink* or *spink*; in flight, gives a high, clear *see* or *swit*. HABITAT: Pine woodland and scrub woodland in highlands; also in wooded areas in coastal lowlands. DISTRIBUTION: A rare non-breeding resident, from September to April in the northern Bahamas and the Cayman Islands. A vagrant in the southern Bahamas, Cuba, Jamaica, Hispaniola and Puerto Rico.

7 VIRGINIA'S WARBLER *Vermivora virginiae* 12cm FIELD NOTES: Actions and habits similar to Nashville Warbler. VOICE: Song starts with a series of rapid, accelerating, thin notes and ends with several lower notes. Calls similar, although a little rougher, to those of Nashville Warbler. HABITAT: Dense semiarid scrub. DISTRIBUTION: Vagrant, recorded from Cuba and the Bahamas (Grand Bahama).

8 BACHMAN'S WARBLER *Vermivora bachmanii* 12cm FIELD NOTES: Probably extinct. Often feeds high in treetops, gleaning insects from clumps of leaves or twigs. VOICE: Song is a buzzy, pulsating trill; only call recorded is a low, hissing *zee-e-eep*. HABITAT: Undergrowth in moist woods, forest edge near swamps and canebrakes. DISTRIBUTION: Rare non-breeding resident on Cuba, from September to April. Vagrant on the Bahamas (Cay Sal).

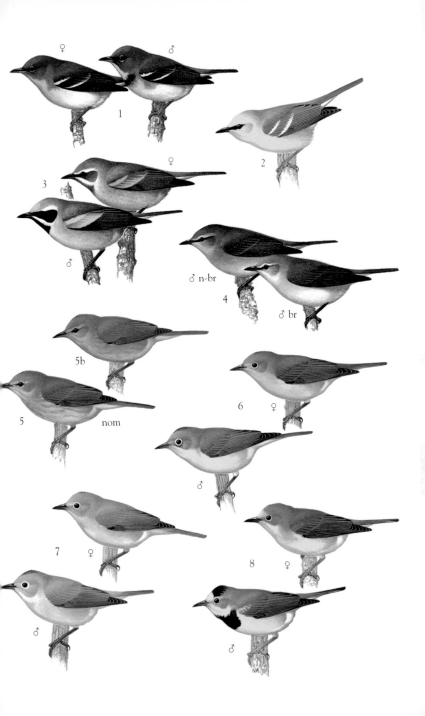

62 AMERICAN WARBLERS

1 YELLOW WARBLER *Dendroica petechia* 13cm FIELD NOTES: Agile, active feeder in trees, bushes and on the ground. Races depicted are the nominate from Barbados, *D. p. aestiva* (fig 1b) migrant from North America and *D. p. ruficapilla* (fig 1c) from Martinique. Other races occur with the rufous on the crown varying in intensity. VOICE: Song is a loud, clear and rapid *sweet-sweet-sweet-ti-ti-ti-weet*. Calls include a loud *tship* and a high *zzee*, usually given in flight. HABITAT: Mangroves, coastal scrub and also in mountain forest on Martinique. Breeds from March to July. DISTRIBUTION: Widespread throughout the region.

2 CHESTNUT-SIDED WARBLER *Dendroica pensylvanica* 13cm FIELD NOTES: Agile forager at low to medium levels in shrubs and lower branches of trees. VOICE: Song transcribed as *pleased-pleased-pleased-to-meecha*. Calls with a low, flat *tchip* and in flight, utters a rough *zeet*. HABITAT: Open woodlands and gardens with trees. DISTRIBUTION: Uncommon or rare non-breeding resident, from September to May, on Cuba, the Bahamas, Jamaica, Hispaniola, Puerto Rico, the Cayman Islands, the Virgin Islands and San Andrés. A vagrant on Antigua, Dominica, Barbados and St Vincent.

3 MAGNOLIA WARBLER *Dendroica magnolia* 13cm FIELD NOTES: Agile forager in tree foliage at low to mid levels. VOICE: Song is a short musical *weety-weety-wee* or *weet-weety-weety-wee*; the last note is occasionally higher-pitched. Calls include a full *tship*, a harsh *tshekk* and a buzzy *zee* given in flight. HABITAT: Open woodlands, swamp edges, bushes and gardens. DISTRIBUTION: A common to rare migrant throughout the region, occasionally remaining during the non-breeding season, September to May.

4 CAPE MAY WARBLER *Dendroica tigrina* 13cm FIELD NOTES: Active forager around flowering plants and in treetops. VOICE: Song is a high-pitched *seet-seet-seet*. Calls include a high *tsip* and a descending *tsee-tsee* that is often given in flight. HABITAT: Mountain forests, shade coffee plantations, coastal thickets, mangroves and gardens. DISTRIBUTION: A non-breeding resident throughout the region from October to April.

5 YELLOW-RUMPED WARBLER (MYRTLE WARBLER) *Dendroica coronata* 14cm FIELD NOTES: Often encountered in small parties feeding in low vegetation, bushes and treetops. VOICE: Song is a slow trill. Call note is a sharp *chek*; in flight, utters a thin *tsee*. HABITAT: Woodlands, thickets, mangroves, swamp edges, gardens and areas with scattered vegetation. DISTRIBUTION: Non-breeding resident, from October to April, throughout the region.

6 GOLDEN-CHEEKED WARBLER *Dendroica chrysoparia* 14cm FIELD NOTES: Forages primarily at medium to high levels, gleaning or fly-catching for insects. VOICE: Call is a high *tchip*; the song is a buzzy *bzzzz layzee dazzee*. HABITAT: High-level coniferous or mixed forest. DISTRIBUTION: A vagrant recorded from the Virgin Islands (St Croix).

7 TOWNSEND'S WARBLER *Dendroica townsendi* 13cm FIELD NOTES: Gleans and fly-catches insects from low level to the canopy. Often part of mixed species flocks. VOICE: Calls include a metallic *tick* or *tip*. Song consists of a series of high *zee* notes followed by 2 or 3 high-pitched buzzy notes. HABITAT: Mountain coniferous or mixed forest. DISTRIBUTION: Vagrant, recorded from the Bahamas (Grand Bahama and Grand Turk).

8 BLACK-THROATED GREEN WARBLER *Dendroica virens* 13cm FIELD NOTES: Forages primarily from mid to high levels, feeding on insects and caterpillars by gleaning, hovering to pick from vegetation or by fly-catching. VOICE: Call very similar Townsend's Warbler. Song is a lisping *zee zee zee zo zee*. HABITAT: Low- to middle-elevation forests, shade coffee plantations, woodlands and gardens. DISTRIBUTION: A widespread migrant, during September, October, April and May, throughout most of the region; rare in the Lesser Antilles where only recorded from the Virgin Islands, St Martin, St Bartholomew, Antigua, Guadeloupe, Dominica and Barbados.

1

1b

nom

♂

♀

1c

n-br

2

♂ br

3

♂ n-br

♂ br

♂ n-br

4

♂ br

♂ n-br

5

♂ br

6

♀

♂

♀

7

♀

8

♂

♂

63 AMERICAN WARBLERS

1 BLACK-THROATED BLUE WARBLER *Dendroica caerulescens* 13cm FIELD NOTES: Forages from low level to the canopy; males prefer tall mature trees and females shrubby second growth. VOICE: A dull *stip* or *chup* and a metallic *twik* given in flight. Song is a wheezy *zweea-zweea-zweea-zwee*. HABITAT: Mountain forests, woodlands, forest edge, moist lowland forest and occasionally dry forests. DISTRIBUTION: Non-breeding resident, from September to May, throughout the region, although rare in the Lesser Antilles.

2 BLACKBURNIAN WARBLER *Dendroica fusca* 13cm FIELD NOTES: Tends to forage high in the canopy. VOICE: A high, sharp *tsip* and a thin *seet* given in flight. The variable song consists of a series of *swee* notes followed by a high-pitched trill. HABITAT: Conifers, high trees, woodlands and tall bushes. DISTRIBUTION: Migrant, during September, October, April and May, to the Bahamas, Greater Antilles and the Virgin Islands (St John); also a vagrant, recorded from Dominica, Barbados and Grenada.

3 YELLOW-THROATED WARBLER *Dendroica dominica* 13cm FIELD NOTES: Generally feeds high in trees, although does forage in bushes. *D. d. flavescens* (fig 3b) is resident on Grand Bahama and Abaco. VOICE: A sharp *chip* and a high *see* given in flight. Song consists of a descending series of whistles, ending in a flourish. HABITAT: Pine forests (resident race), lowland forests, palms and gardens. DISTRIBUTION: The resident race occurs on the northern Bahamas. These birds are joined, from August to March, by migrants of the North American race that frequent the Bahamas and the Greater Antilles. Vagrants recorded from the Virgin Islands, Montserrat, Barbados and Guadeloupe.

4 ADELAIDE'S WARBLER *Dendroica adelaidae* 12.5cm FIELD NOTES: Forages mainly at high levels. Often forms part of mixed species flocks. The 3 races that occur in the West Indies are the nominate on Puerto Rico, *D. a. delicata* (fig 4b) on St Lucia and *D. a. subita* on Barbuda, which is browner grey above and lacks the black lateral crown-stripe, and are thought by some authorities to be separate species. VOICE: A *chick*. Song is a variable trill, said to be more melodious in the Lesser Antillean races. HABITAT: Puerto Rican Birds occur mainly in dry coastal scrub and thickets, St Lucia birds in forests, Barbuda birds in thickets near water. Breeds from March to June. DISTRIBUTION: Resident on western Puerto Rico, Barbuda and St Lucia. Vagrant on Martinique.

5 OLIVE-CAPPED WARBLER *Dendroica pityophila* 13cm FIELD NOTES: Feeds from ground level to the treetops. VOICE: A *tsip*. Song is a series of shrill, whistled notes. HABITAT: Primarily pine forests. Breeds from March to August. DISTRIBUTION: Cuba and the Bahamas (Grand Bahama and Abaco).

6 PINE WARBLER *Dendroica pinus* 14cm FIELD NOTES: Often occurs in small parties, foraging from ground level to treetops. VOICE: A sharp *chip* and a *zeet* given in flight. Song is a simple, 1-pitched trill. HABITAT: Mature pine forests. Breeds from March to June. DISTRIBUTION: Resident on the northern Bahamas and Hispaniola, wanders to Cuba and the Cayman Islands, during October and November. Vagrants recorded from Jamaica, Puerto Rico (Mona Island) and Martinique.

7 KIRTLAND'S WARBLER *Dendroica kirtlandii* 15cm FIELD NOTES: Solitary, generally forages low down in dense scrub. VOICE: A loud *tchip*. Song is an emphatic *flip lip lip-lip-tip-tip-CHIDIP*. HABITAT: Mainly understorey, broadleaved scrub and thickets. DISTRIBUTION: The Bahamas, from October to April. The main wintering area for this very rare warbler.

8 PRAIRIE WARBLER *Dendroica discolor* 12cm FIELD NOTES: Forages from the ground to middle levels; often joins mixed species feeding flocks. VOICE: A low, sharp *tchip* or *tsup*. Song is a series of rising buzzy notes. HABITAT: Dry coastal forest, thickets, agricultural areas with scattered trees, mangroves and gardens. DISTRIBUTION: Non-breeding resident, from August to April, in the Bahamas and the Greater and Lesser Antilles.

134

64 AMERICAN WARBLERS

1 VITELLINE WARBLER *Dendroica vitellina* 13cm FIELD NOTES: Forages from the ground to the canopy. Quite tame on Little Cayman. VOICE: Song is a wheezy *szwee-szwee-szwee-zee*. HABITAT: Dry woodland, scrub and urban areas. Breeds from April to August. DISTRIBUTION: Endemic to the Cayman Islands and Swan Island.

2 PALM WARBLER *Dendroica palmarum* 14cm FIELD NOTES: Forages low in vegetation or on the ground; hops, does not run or walk. VOICE: A sharp *chek*, *tick* or *sup*, and a high *seep* given in flight; the song consists of a series of buzzy *tsee* notes. HABITAT: Coastal brush and bushes, mangroves, open areas with scattered bushes and gardens. DISTRIBUTION: Non-breeding resident, from October to April, on the Bahamas, Greater Antilles, San Andrés and the Virgin Islands. Vagrant on Saba, Dominica, St Lucia and Barbados.

3 BAY-BREASTED WARBLER *Dendroica castanea* 14cm FIELD NOTES: A deliberate forager from middle to high levels. VOICE: Calls include a high-pitched *sip* or *see*, and occasionally a loud *chip*. Song is a series of high *see* notes, all on one pitch. HABITAT: Forest edge, woodlands, open areas with scattered trees and gardens. DISTRIBUTION: A rare migrant, during October, November, April and May, in the Bahamas, Cuba, Jamaica and San Andrés. Vagrants recorded from Hispaniola, Puerto Rico, the Virgin Islands (St Croix), Antigua, Dominica, Barbados and St Vincent.

4 CERULEAN WARBLER *Dendroica cerulea* 12cm FIELD NOTES: Active and agile; feeds mainly in the canopy. VOICE: A sharp *chip* and a loud *zzee* flight note. Song consists of a short series of buzzy notes ending in a high buzzing trill. HABITAT: Forests, also low bushes and small trees. DISTRIBUTION: A rare migrant in the Bahamas, western Cuba, Jamaica and the Cayman Islands (Grand Cayman), during September, October and April. Vagrants recorded from Puerto Rico (Mona Island) and Barbados.

5 PLUMBEOUS WARBLER *Dendroica plumbea* 13cm FIELD NOTES: Generally tame; constantly flicks tail as it forages, mainly in the understorey. VOICE: Calls include a rattle and a short *chek*. Song is a simple, melodic *pa-pi-a* or *de-de-diu*. HABITAT: Moist mountain forests and occasionally scrub forests and mangroves. Breeds from March to July. DISTRIBUTION: Resident on Guadeloupe and Dominica.

6 BLACKPOLL WARBLER *Dendroica striata* 14cm FIELD NOTES: Constantly on the move, often part of mixed species feeding flocks. VOICE: Calls include a thin *ssts*, a high-pitched *sip* and occasionally a *chip*. Song consists of a series of 1-pitched, high *si* notes. HABITAT: Wide range of woodland, thickets and scrubby areas. DISTRIBUTION: A migrant throughout the region during October, November and May.

7 ARROW-HEADED WARBLER *Dendroica pharetra* 13cm FIELD NOTES: Forages at high levels; constantly flicks tail downwards. VOICE: A metallic *tic*; song is a high-pitched *sww-sw-swee sww-sw-swee sww-sw-swee-swee-swee*, generally given at dawn. HABITAT: Moist humid forests. Breeds in May and June. DISTRIBUTION: Endemic to Jamaica.

8 ELFIN WOODS WARBLER *Dendroica angelae* 11–13.5cm FIELD NOTES: Very active, constantly flicks its tail as it forages high in the canopy, often with other species, in a search for insects. VOICE: A metallic *chip*. The song is made up of a number of rapid, unmusical notes, on 1 pitch, that increases in volume and ends with a short series of double notes. HABITAT: Humid montane and lower montane elfin forests. Breeds from March to June. DISTRIBUTION: Endemic to Puerto Rico.

9 BLACK-AND-WHITE WARBLER *Mniotilta varia* 13cm FIELD NOTES: Climbs up and down trunks and large branches, nuthatch-like, probing bark for food. VOICE: A sharp *tick* and a thin *tsip* or *tzeet*. Song transcribed as *see wee-see wee-see wee-see wee-see wee-see wee-see*. HABITAT: Forests and woodlands. DISTRIBUTION: Non-breeding resident, from August to April, throughout the region.

♀

1

♂ n-br

♂ br

2

3

♀ br

♂ n-br

♂ br

♀

4

♂

5

♂ n-br

6

♂ br

7

♂ br

8

♀ br

9

♂ br

65 AMERICAN WARBLERS

1 WHISTLING WARBLER *Catharopeza bishopi* 14.5cm FIELD NOTES: Generally shy and secretive. Forages purposely and fairly actively from low levels to tree canopy. VOICE: A soft *tuk* or *tchurk*. Song starts with a series of rich, rising notes, ending with 2 or 3 emphatic notes. HABITAT: Rainforest, palm brakes, humid secondary forest, elfin forest and forest edges. Breeds from April to July. DISTRIBUTION: Endemic to St Vincent.

2 AMERICAN REDSTART *Setophaga ruticilla* 13cm FIELD NOTES: Very active, frequently makes fly-catching sallies to capture insects. Regularly fans wings and tail. VOICE: A sweet *chip* and a high-pitched, rising *sweet* flight note. Song very variable, usually a high-pitched series ending with an emphatic low note. HABITAT: Forests, woodlands, shrubby areas and gardens. DISTRIBUTION: Non-breeding resident, from August to May, throughout the region. Recorded breeding in Cuba.

3 PROTHONOTARY WARBLER *Protonotaria citrea* 14cm FIELD NOTES: Forages on trunks and branches much like a Black-and-White Warbler. VOICE: Song consists of a series of ringing *zweet* notes. Calls include a loud, ringing *tsip*, a softer *psit* and, in flight, a long, thin *seet*. HABITAT: Mangrove swamps, tree clumps and gardens. DISTRIBUTION: Uncommon or rare migrant, from August to October and March to April, throughout the region.

4 WORM-EATING WARBLER *Helmitheros vermivorus* 14cm FIELD NOTES: Forages in undergrowth and among dead leaf clumps in trees. VOICE: Song is a monotonous, 1-pitched trill. Calls include a sharp *tchip* and a buzzy *zeet-zeet*. HABITAT: Dense forests. DISTRIBUTION: A non-breeding resident, from September to April, on the Bahamas, Greater Antilles, Providencia and the Virgin Islands. Vagrant on St Martin, St Bartholomew, Antigua and Guadeloupe.

5 SWAINSON'S WARBLER *Limnothlypis swainsonii* 14cm FIELD NOTES: Forages on the ground and in low bushes and on logs. VOICE: Song transcribed as *wee wee wee wee-tu-weeu*. Call is a strong, long *sship*. HABITAT: Leaf litter in forests, woodland, thickets etc. DISTRIBUTION: Uncommon or rare non-breeding resident on Cuba, Jamaica, the Bahamas and Puerto Rico, from September to April. A rare migrant in the Cayman Islands and a vagrant on Hispaniola and the Virgin Islands (St John).

6 OVENBIRD *Seiurus aurocapillus* 15cm FIELD NOTES: Walks on the forest floor, foraging among leaf litter. VOICE: Song is an emphatic *teecher- teecher- teecher- teecher*, rising in pitch and volume. Call is a *chuk* or *tsuk*, often repeated. HABITAT: Closed canopy woodland with dense undergrowth, often near water. DISTRIBUTION: Non-breeding resident, from August to May, in the Bahamas, Greater Antilles, San Andrés and Providencia; uncommon or rare in the Lesser Antilles south to St Vincent.

7 NORTHERN WATERTHRUSH *Seiurus noveboracensis* 12.5–15cm FIELD NOTES: Constantly bobs rear end as it walks on the ground searching for prey among leaves and on logs. Long-distance migrant, greyer race *S. n. notablis* (fig 7b) may start its journey in Alaska. VOICE: Song transcribed as *swee-swee-chit-weedleo*, the last note down-slurred. Call is a loud, metallic *chink*. HABITAT: Watery borders of mangroves and coastal scrub. DISTRIBUTION: Widespread, mainly from September to April.

8 LOUISIANA WATERTHRUSH *Seiurus motacilla* 14.5–16cm FIELD NOTES: Actions and habits similar to Northern Waterthrush. VOICE: A high-pitched *chink*. The song is loud and consists of a short series of descending notes followed by a warbling twitter. HABITAT: Primarily occurs at the edges of flowing water, mainly at higher elevations. DISTRIBUTION: Widespread, from August to March, less common in the Lesser Antilles, south to St Vincent.

66 AMERICAN WARBLERS

1 KENTUCKY WARBLER *Oporornis formosus* 13cm FIELD NOTES: Shy and skulking, forages on the ground and in low bushes. VOICE: A low, sharp *tship* or *chip*, and a buzzy *zeep*. The song consists of a series of loud, whistled *churree* notes. HABITAT: Woodland with dense undergrowth. DISTRIBUTION: Rare migrant or very rare non-breeding resident on the Bahamas, the Greater Antilles, the Virgin Islands and Providencia. Vagrants recorded from Antigua and Guadeloupe.

2 MOURNING WARBLER *Oporornis philadelphia* 13cm FIELD NOTES: Skulking, forages mainly on the ground or in low, dense undergrowth. VOICE: A flat *jik* or *chip*, and a buzzy *zee* flight call. The song is a rich, churring *churree churree churree turi turi*. HABITAT: Second-growth, wet thickets and swamp edges. DISTRIBUTION: Vagrant, recorded on the Bahamas, Cuba, Jamaica, Hispaniola (Dominican Republic), Puerto Rico and the Virgin Islands.

3 CONNECTICUT WARBLER *Oporornis agilis* 13–15cm FIELD NOTES: Shy and skulking, forages on the ground or in low bushes. Walks, much in the manner of an Ovenbird. VOICE: A metallic *plink* and a high-pitched buzzy *zee* flight note. The song is a loud *wee-cher-cher wee-cher-cher wee-cher-cher wee*. HABITAT: Moist woodland understorey, usually near water. DISTRIBUTION: Rare migrant in the Bahamas, Cuba, Hispaniola, Puerto Rico, the Virgin Islands (St Croix), St Bartholomew and St Martin, mainly during September and October.

4 COMMON YELLOWTHROAT *Geothlypis trichas* 13cm FIELD NOTES: Skulking forager in thick vegetation, usually in damp areas. Often cocks tail. VOICE: A dry *chep* or *tchuk*. Song variable, usually transcribed as *wichity-wichity-wichity-wich*. HABITAT: Bushes and thick vegetation at the edge of various water bodies. DISTRIBUTION: Non-breeding resident, from October to May, on the Bahamas, the Greater Antilles, the Virgin Islands, San Andrés and Providencia. Vagrants recorded from St Martin, Antigua, Dominica and Guadeloupe.

5 BAHAMA YELLOWTHROAT *Geothlypis rostrata* 15cm FIELD NOTES: Actions and habits similar to Common Yellowthroat, although a little less sprightly. Shown are the nominate race, from Andros and New Providence and *G. r. coryi* (fig 5b) from Eleuthera and Cat Island. The race on Grand Bahama and the Great Abaco islands, *G. r. tanneri*, has the pale band behind the black mask tinged yellow. VOICE: A sharp *tchit*. The song is a loud *wichity-wichity-wichit*, similar to the song of the Common Yellowthroat. HABITAT: Dense low scrub and shrubs, also pine woods with thatch palm understorey. Breeds from May to July. DISTRIBUTION: Endemic to the northern Bahamas.

6 ORIENTE WARBLER *Teretistris fornsi* 13cm FIELD NOTES: Regularly forages in noisy flocks, probing bark crevices and gleaning vegetation for insects; often joins mixed species flocks. VOICE: A sharp *tchip* and a shrill *tsi-tsi-tsi....* All calls are similar to those of Yellow-headed Warbler. HABITAT: Forest scrub and swamp borders. Breeds in April and May. DISTRIBUTION: Endemic to eastern Cuba.

7 YELLOW-HEADED WARBLER *Teretistris fernandinae* 13cm FIELD NOTES: Usually forages in small noisy flocks, probing and gleaning in search of various prey items, such as insects, spiders, caterpillars and small fruits. Regularly forms part of mixed species feeding flocks, often with migrant warblers, Cuban Vireos and Crescent-eyed Peewees. VOICE: A shrill, chattering *tsi-tsi-tsi....* All calls are similar to those of the Oriente Warbler. HABITAT: All forests with good understorey, scrubby thickets and occasionally open forests. Breeds from April to June. DISTRIBUTION: Endemic to west and central Cuba.

67 AMERICAN WARBLERS

1 HOODED WARBLER *Wilsonia citrina* 13cm FIELD NOTES: Active forager, often makes fly-catching sallies; constantly flicks wings and spreads tail to reveal white in the outer feathers. VOICE: A sharp *tchip* or *tchink* and buzzy *zrr*. Song is a loud *too-ee too-ee too-ee tee-ch*. HABITAT: Moist forest undergrowth and mangrove swamps. DISTRIBUTION: Uncommon or rare non-breeding resident in the Bahamas, Cuba, Hispaniola, Puerto Rico, the Cayman Islands and the Virgin Islands. A migrant on Jamaica and San Andrés and a vagrant elsewhere.

2 WILSON'S WARBLER *Wilsonia pusilla* 12cm FIELD NOTES: Active, constantly flicks wings and tail as it forages in thick undergrowth; feeds on insects by gleaning from vegetation or by making fly-catching sallies. VOICE: A loud, low *chet*, a hard *tik* and a down-slurred *tsip* flight call. Song is a staccato *chi-chi-chi-chi-chi-chet-chet*. HABITAT: Dense vegetation at all elevations, although mainly occurs in the lowlands. DISTRIBUTION: A rare migrant and very rarely a non-breeding resident to the Bahamas, Cuba and Jamaica, from September to April. Vagrants recorded from Hispaniola and Puerto Rico (Mona Island).

3 CANADA WARBLER *Wilsonia canadensis* 13cm FIELD NOTES: Feeds on insects by fly-catching or gleaning from vegetation in the understorey; active, often cocks tail. VOICE: A sharp *chick* or *tyup*; flight call recorded both as a low *plik* or a high *zzee*. Song is a variable warble. HABITAT: Open vegetation among scattered trees, often near water or swamps. DISTRIBUTION: Rare migrant and very rare non-breeding resident on the Bahamas and Cuba, from September to April, but primarily during September and October. Vagrants recorded from Jamaica, Hispaniola, Puerto Rico, the Cayman Islands, the Virgin Islands, St Lucia and Guadeloupe.

4 YELLOW-BREASTED CHAT *Icteria virens* 19cm FIELD NOTES: Shy and retiring, forages in low dense cover searching for various invertebrates, berries and fruit. VOICE: A harsh grating *chack*, a nasal *cheewb* and a soft *tuk*. Song consists of a loud jumble of rattles, cackles, squeals and whistles. HABITAT: Woodland edges, thickets and scrub. DISTRIBUTION: Rare migrant and very rare non-breeding resident to the northern Bahamas, Cuba and the Cayman Islands (Grand Cayman), from August to May.

5 WHITE-WINGED WARBLER (HISPANIOLAN HIGHLAND TANAGER) *Xenoligea montana* 13.5–14.5cm FIELD NOTES: Actively forages for seeds and insects, from undergrowth to understorey. After breeding season becomes a regular member of mixed species feeding flocks. VOICE: A thin *tseep* and a low chattering *suit suit suit chir suit suit suit chir chi....* Song made up of a short series of squeaky notes, delivered slowly and sometimes accelerating at the end. HABITAT: Humid broadleaf forest with dense understorey, scrub, thickets and wet shrubs in mountain areas. Probably breeds from April to June. DISTRIBUTION: Endemic to Hispaniola. Endangered.

6 GREEN-TAILED WARBLER (GREEN-TAILED GROUND WARBLER or TANAGER) *Microligea palustris* 12–14.5cm FIELD NOTES: Forages, often in small groups, in dense undergrowth and thickets. VOICE: A regularly repeated short rasping note. Song transcribed as *sip-sip-sip*. HABITAT: Thickets and dense undergrowth in montane forest; in the Dominican Republic also found in semiarid areas. Breeds in May and June. DISTRIBUTION: Endemic to Hispaniola.

7 SEMPER'S WARBLER *Leucopeza semperi* 14.5cm FIELD NOTES: Forages on or close to the ground. VOICE: The only call recorded is a chattering *tuck-tick-tick-tuck*, given when alarmed. HABITAT: Thick undergrowth in moist, mid-elevation forests, mountain thickets and dwarf forests. DISTRIBUTION: Endemic to St Lucia. Critically endangered, possibly extinct.

68 BANANAQUIT, HONEYCREEPER, EUPHONIAS, TANAGERS AND SPINDALIS

1 BANANAQUIT *Coereba flaveola* 10–12.5cm FIELD NOTES: Pairs or small groups feed on nectar from flowering trees and plants. Races shown are the nominate from Jamaica, *C. f. bahamensis* (fig 1b) from the Bahamas, *C. f. portoricensis* (fig 1c) from Puerto Rico, *C. f. barbadensis* (fig 1d) from Barbados, *C. f. martinicana* (fig 1e) from Martinique and St Lucia and *C. f. atrata* (fig 1f) from St Vincent. VOICE: A metallic *tsip*. Song variable, Bahamian birds give a series of ticks followed by a rapid clicking, Jamaican birds utter a series of single-pitched thin notes, Puerto Rican and Virgin Island birds give an insect-like buzz that ends in a tumbling trill. HABITAT: Almost anywhere there are flowering plants. Breeds mainly from March to June. DISTRIBUTION: Throughout the region, although only a vagrant to Cuba.

2 RED-LEGGED HONEYCREEPER *Cyanerpes cyaneus* 13cm FIELD NOTES: Pairs or small groups forage in trees or shrubs. VOICE: A thin *tsip* and a harsh *chrik-chrik*. HABITAT: Forests and forest edge. Breeds in May and June. DISTRIBUTION: Resident, although rare and local, on Cuba.

3 ANTILLEAN EUPHONIA *Euphonia musica* 12cm FIELD NOTES: Feeds in the canopy, primarily on mistletoe berries; best located by calls. Depicted are the nominate race from Hispaniola, *E. m. sclateri* (fig 3b) from Puerto Rico and *E. m. flavifrons* (fig 3c) from the Lesser Antilles. VOICE: A rapid, tinkling *ti-tit*, a hard *chi-chink* and a plaintive *whee*. Song is a jumbled tinkling, interspersed with explosive notes. HABITAT: Dense forests. Breeds from January to July. DISTRIBUTION: Resident on Hispaniola, Puerto Rico; uncommon or a vagrant in the Lesser Antilles; does not occur on the Virgin Islands.

4 JAMAICAN EUPHONIA *Euphonia jamaica* 11.5cm FIELD NOTES: Arboreal, feeds on mistletoe berries, small fruits, buds and flowers; often seen in small parties. VOICE: A staccato *chur-chur-chur...*; occasionally ends with a rising *chip*. Song is a pleasant, squeaky whistle. HABITAT: Woodlands, forest edge, shrubbery and gardens. Breeds from March to May. DISTRIBUTION: Endemic to Jamaica.

5 LESSER ANTILLEAN TANAGER (HOODED TANAGER) *Tangara cucullata* 15cm FIELD NOTES: Attracted to fruiting trees, usually in pairs or small flocks. Fig 5b is the St Vincent race *T. c. versicolor*. VOICE: A weak *weet-weet-weet-witwitwitwit*. HABITAT: Moist and dry forests, second growth and gardens. Breeds from April to July. DISTRIBUTION: Resident on Grenada and St Vincent.

6 WESTERN SPINDALIS *Spindalis zena* 15cm FIELD NOTES: This and the following 3 species used to be combined as Stripe-headed Tanager. Feeds on plants and fruit. Fig 6b is the green-backed race *S. z. pretrei* from Cuba. VOICE: A descending, high-pitched *see see see see...*, a strong *seee* and a sharp *tit*. Song consists of a series of thin, high notes leading to buzzier phrases. HABITAT: Wooded areas from the coast to mountains. Breeds from April to August. DISTRIBUTION: Resident on the Bahamas, Cuba and Grand Cayman.

7 JAMAICAN SPINDALIS *Spindalis nigricephalus* 18cm FIELD NOTES: Feeds on fruit and plant parts. VOICE: A soft *seep* and a rapid *chi-chi-chi....* HABITAT: Forests, woods and bushy areas. Breeds from April to July. DISTRIBUTION: Endemic to Jamaica.

8 HISPANIOLAN SPINDALIS *Spindalis dominicensis* 17cm FIELD NOTES: Feeds on various fruits and plant parts. VOICE: A high-pitched *thseep*. The song is a thin, high-pitched whistle. HABITAT: Pine, hardwood, mixed and mangrove forests. Breeds from April to June. DISTRIBUTION: Endemic to Hispaniola.

9 PUERTO RICAN SPINDALIS *Spindalis portoricensis* 17cm FIELD NOTES: Feeds on fruit and buds. VOICE: A soft *teweep*, a thin trill and a short twitter. Song is a thin, high-pitched whistle *zée-tit-zée-tittit-zée*. HABITAT: Forests and woodlands. Breeds mainly from March to June. DISTRIBUTION: Endemic to Puerto Rico.

1b

1c

1f

♂ n-br

1

nom

1e

1d

2

♀

♂ br

3

3b

4

♀

♀

♂

♂ nom

5

♀

6b

♀

5b

6

♂ nom

♂ nom

7

♀

8

♀

9

♀

♂

♂

♂

NA

69 TANAGERS, PALM-TANAGERS AND CHAT-TANAGERS

1 SWALLOW TANAGER *Tersina viridis* 15cm FIELD NOTES: Arboreal, often perches on open branches within the canopy; regularly makes fly-catching sallies. Flight swallow-like. VOICE: A high thin *tsee*. The song is a squeaky twitter. HABITAT: Moist forest, light woodland, forest and woodland edge. DISTRIBUTION: Vagrant recorded on the Cayman Islands (Grand Cayman).

2 SCARLET TANAGER *Piranga olivacea* 18cm FIELD NOTES: Forages primarily in the tops of trees, but will descend to feed on the ground. VOICE: A hoarse *chip-burr*; in flight, utters a clear *puwi*. Song is a raspy *querit-queer-query-querit-queer*. HABITAT: Open woods, forest edges and gardens. DISTRIBUTION: A rare migrant, during September, October and March to May, in the Bahamas, Cuba, Jamaica, the Cayman islands, Puerto Rico, the Lesser Antilles south to Antigua; generally a vagrant to the rest of the Lesser Antilles.

3 SUMMER TANAGER *Piranga rubra* 19cm FIELD NOTES: Mainly arboreal, usually singly or in pairs, regularly encountered in the company of migrating vireos, warblers and thrushes. VOICE: Song is a thrush-like series of sweet, clear notes. Calls include a *chick* and a chattering *pit-a-chuck piki-i-tuck* or *piki-i-tuck-i-tuck*. HABITAT: Woodlands, forest edge and gardens. DISTRIBUTION: Uncommon migrant and rare non-breeding resident in the Bahamas, Cuba, Jamaica and the Cayman Islands, from September to May. A vagrant on Hispaniola, Saba, Guadeloupe, Barbados, the Grenadines (Mustique) and Grenada.

4 WESTERN TANAGER *Piranga ludoviciana* 18cm FIELD NOTES: Arboreal, often in mixed feeding flocks. Non-breeding male has orange confined to face. VOICE: A soft, rising rattle and soft, whistled *howee* or *weet* given in flight. Song similar to Scarlet Tanager. HABITAT: Forest and forest edge. DISTRIBUTION: Vagrant, recorded on Cuba and the Bahamas (New Providence).

5 BLACK-CROWNED PALM-TANAGER *Phaenicophilus palmarum* 18cm FIELD NOTES: Slow, deliberate forager in thick cover, often part of mixed species feeding flocks. Feeds on insects, seeds and fruit. VOICE: A low *chep* and a nasal *pe-u*. HABITAT: Anywhere there are trees, forests, woodlands and thickets, and urban areas. Breeds from April to June. DISTRIBUTION: Endemic to Hispaniola.

6 GREY-CROWNED PALM-TANAGER *Phaenicophilus poliocephalus* 18cm FIELD NOTES: Habits similar to the Black-crowned Palm-tanager. VOICE: A short *peu*. A canary-like whisper song is given during the breeding season. HABITAT: Forest and woodland, from sea level to mountains. Breeds during May and June. DISTRIBUTION: Endemic to Hispaniola's southern peninsular.

7 EASTERN CHAT-TANAGER *Calyptophilus frugivorus* 17cm FIELD NOTES: Mainly terrestrial and generally very secretive; forages among leaf litter in dense undergrowth. Until recently, combined with Western Chat-tanager and called Chat Tanager; there still seem to be mixed opinions concerning this split and the allocation of subspecies. VOICE: A sharp *chick*. Song is a loud and clear whistling. HABITAT: Thick undergrowth along streams in moist mountain broadleaf forest. Breeds from May to July. DISTRIBUTION: Endemic to Hispaniola.

8 WESTERN CHAT-TANAGER *Calyptophilus tertius* 20cm FIELD NOTES: Habits similar to Eastern Chat-tanager. VOICE: Similar to Eastern Chat-tanager? HABITAT: Dense undergrowth along watercourses in moist mountain broadleaf forests; the race on Gonâve Island occurs in semiarid scrub. DISTRIBUTION: Endemic to Hispaniola.

9 PUERTO RICAN TANAGER *Nesospingus speculiferus* 18–20cm FIELD NOTES: Regularly occurs in noisy flocks, often with other species, foraging in forest canopy. VOICE: A harsh, loud *chewp, chuck* or *chi-chi-chit*. During the breeding season, utters a soft warble. HABITAT: Mountain forests. Breeds from January to August. DISTRIBUTION: Endemic to Puerto Rico.

70 CARDINAL, SALTATOR, GROSBEAKS, BUNTINGS AND HOUSE SPARROW

1 NORTHERN CARDINAL *Cardinalis cardinalis* 22cm FIELD NOTES: Forages in trees, shrubs and on the ground, sometimes in small groups. VOICE: A high-pitched, hard *tik* and a softer, rising *twik*. Song variable, consisting of a series of high, clear and slurred whistles, transcribed as *pichew pichew tiw tiw tiw tiw tiw tiw* or *woit woit woit chew chew chew chew chew*. HABITAT: Woodland edges, thickets, swamps and gardens. DISTRIBUTION: Vagrant, recorded from the Cayman Islands (Grand Cayman and Cayman Brac).

2 LESSER ANTILLEAN SALTATOR *Saltator albicollis* 22cm FIELD NOTES: Arboreal, feeds primarily on fruit and seeds. Used to be lumped with the Streaked Saltator. VOICE: A series of rising and falling harsh, loud notes. HABITAT: Forest-edge undergrowth, second growth, thickets and dry scrub. Breeds from April to July. DISTRIBUTION: Resident on Guadeloupe, Dominica, Martinique and St Lucia. A vagrant on Nevis.

3 ROSE-BREASTED GROSBEAK *Pheucticus ludovicianus* 19cm FIELD NOTES: Forages in trees and bushes, often in small parties mixed with other species. In flight, male shows rosy underwing coverts and the female buffy-yellow underwing coverts. VOICE: A squeaky *iik* or *eek*; also a soft, wheezy *wheek* flight call. The song is a thrush-like slow, whistled warble. HABITAT: Forest edge, woodlands, shade coffee plantations, scrub and gardens. DISTRIBUTION: Uncommon or rare non-breeding resident, from October to April, in the Bahamas, the Greater Antilles and the Virgin Islands; a vagrant on the rest of the larger Lesser Antillean islands. A migrant on San Andrés and Providencia.

4 BLUE GROSBEAK *Passerina caerulea* 17cm FIELD NOTES: Forages in trees, shrubs and on the ground. Regularly twitches and flares tail. VOICE: A metallic *chink* and a harsh buzzing flight call. Song is made up of a rapid warble with short rising and falling phrases. HABITAT: Forest edge, Casuarina groves, rice fields, seeding grass areas near thickets and woods, and gardens. DISTRIBUTION: Uncommon or rare non-breeding resident, from September to April, on the Bahamas, the Greater Antilles and the Virgin Islands.

5 INDIGO BUNTING *Passerina cyanea* 14cm FIELD NOTES: Feeds in trees, bushes and on the ground, often in flocks. VOICE: A sharp *tsick*. The song is a high-pitched *sweet-sweet where-where here-here see-it-see-it*. HABITAT: Rich fields, pasture borders, grassy areas near thickets, woods and dry scrub. DISTRIBUTION: Non-breeding resident, from October to May, on the Bahamas, the Greater Antilles, the Virgin Islands, San Andrés and Providencia. Vagrants recorded on Saba and Antigua.

6 LAZULI BUNTING *Passerina amoena* 14cm FIELD NOTES: Feeds on or near the ground, often in loose flocks. VOICE: A sharp *tzip* or *pit* and a dry *buzz* uttered in flight. The song is a rapid *see-see-sweert-sweert-sweert-zee-sweet-zeer-see-see*. HABITAT: Thickets and overgrown fields. DISTRIBUTION: Vagrant, recorded from Cuba.

7 PAINTED BUNTING *Passerina ciris* 13cm FIELD NOTES: Forages primarily on or near the ground in thick vegetation, often in small flocks of both same or mixed species. VOICE: A loud *chip* or *pwich*. The song is a sweet, continuous warble. HABITAT: Thickets, brush and grassy places in semiarid areas, usually with water nearby. DISTRIBUTION: Non-breeding resident on Cuba and the Bahamas, from October to April. Vagrants recorded on Jamaica and the Cayman Islands.

8 HOUSE SPARROW *Passer domesticus* 15cm FIELD NOTES: Usually tame, forages on the ground, feeding on seeds or virtually any edible scraps left by man. VOICE: Calls variable, e.g. *chirrup, chirp, chissick*, a soft *swee-swee* and a rolling *chur-r-r- it-It* given when alarmed. The song, consisting mainly of call notes, is an excited *chirrup-chirrup-cheep-chirp-chirrup...* etc. HABITAT: Urban areas, often feeds in grassy areas away from buildings. Breeds mainly from March to September. DISTRIBUTION: The Bahamas, the Greater Antilles and the Virgin Islands.

1 ♀

♂

2

3 ♀

♂

4 ♂ br

♀

5 ♂ n-br

♂ br

6 ♂

♀

7 ♂ n-br

8 ♂ n-br

♀

♀ br

7 ♀

♂

NA

71 ORANGEQUIT, SEEDEATER, GRASSQUITS AND DICKCISSEL

1 ORANGEQUIT *Euneornis campestris* 14cm FIELD NOTES: Forages at low to medium levels, searching for nectar, fruits and sap oozing from holes made by Yellow-bellied Sapsucker. VOICE: A thin, high-pitched *tseet*, *swee* or *fi-swee*. HABITAT: Humid forests and woodlands, mainly at mid elevations. Breeds from April to June. DISTRIBUTION: Endemic to Jamaica.

2 BLUE-BLACK GRASSQUIT *Volatinia jacarina* 11cm FIELD NOTES: Forages in low vegetation in search of seeds and insects. In display, male perches on an exposed branch and jumps up and down with tail spread and wings open showing white axillaries. VOICE: A loud *eee-slick*; during display jump utters a wheezing *jweee*. HABITAT: Shrubby fields, farmland, scrubby second growth and roadsides. Breeds in July and August. DISTRIBUTION: Breeding resident on Grenada, from June to September.

3 YELLOW-BELLIED SEEDEATER *Sporophila nigricollis* 10.5cm FIELD NOTES: Forages for seeds and insects in low vegetation. VOICE: A short *cheep* and a chittering when excited. The song is a short warble followed by buzzy notes. HABITAT: Forest edge, thickets, roadsides, shrubby fields and field edges. Breeds from March to August. DISTRIBUTION: Breeding resident on Grenada and the Grenadines (Carriacou), from March to November. Vagrant on St Vincent.

4 CUBAN GRASSQUIT *Tiaris canora* 11.5cm FIELD NOTES: Forages on the ground, searching out small seeds, generally in flocks. VOICE: A simple *chip* and a shrill, rasping *chiri-wichi-wichi chibiri-wichi-wichi*. HABITAT: Semiarid country near the coast, pine undergrowth, woodland edge, plantations and farmland. Breeds from March to October. DISTRIBUTION: Endemic to Cuba. Introduced on the Bahamas (New Providence).

5 YELLOW-FACED GRASSQUIT *Tiaris olivacea* 11.5cm FIELD NOTES: Singles or small parties forage on grass seed-heads or on the ground. Conspicuous when singing from a cane or tall grass spike. VOICE: A soft *tek*. The song is a weak, rapid trill. HABITAT: Open grassy areas. Breeds in any month. DISTRIBUTION: Resident on the Greater Antilles.

6 BLACK-FACED GRASSQUIT *Tiaris bicolor* 11.5cm FIELD NOTES: Forages in pairs or small flocks, searching for small seeds and occasionally insects. In display, male flies a short distance with rapidly beating wings, giving a buzzing call. VOICE: A soft, musical *tsip*. The song is a loud, buzzing *dik-zeezeezee*. HABITAT: Almost any open area with grasses and shrubs. Breeds at any time of the year. DISTRIBUTION: Resident throughout the region, but rare and local on Cuba and absent from the Cayman Islands.

7 YELLOW-SHOULDERED GRASSQUIT *Loxipasser anoxanthus* 10cm FIELD NOTES: Forages in small parties in shrubs and trees, searching for fruits and seeds. VOICE: A descending, insect-like *zwee-ze-ze-ze-ze*. HABITAT: Forest-edge shrubs, woodlands and gardens near wooded areas. Breeds from March to July. DISTRIBUTION: Endemic to Jamaica.

8 DICKCISSEL *Spiza americana* 15–18cm FIELD NOTES: Gregarious, often mixes with other species, foraging mostly on the ground. Non-breeding male's bib greyish. VOICE: A dry *chek* or *pwik*, and a buzzing *dzzrrrt* given in flight. The song is a staccato, insect-like *dik-dik-serr-si-si* or *dick- dick-ciss-ciss-ciss*. HABITAT: Open grassland and weedy areas with scattered trees. DISTRIBUTION: A rare migrant, from September to November and during March and April, on the Bahamas, Cuba, Jamaica, San Andrés and Providencia. Vagrants recorded on Puerto Rico, the Cayman Islands and Barbados.

72 BULLFINCHES, FINCHES, ZAPATA SPARROW AND TOWEE

1 PUERTO RICAN BULLFINCH *Loxigilla portoricensis* 16.5cm FIELD NOTES: Juvenile dark brownish olive with dull red under-tail coverts. Secretive, more often heard than seen. VOICE: A soft *tseet* or *check*. Song is a rising whistle of 2 to 10 notes. HABITAT: Dense mountain forest, coffee plantations, coastal thickets and mangroves. Breeds from February to June. DISTRIBUTION: Endemic to Puerto Rico.

2 GREATER ANTILLEAN BULLFINCH *Loxigilla violacea* 15–18cm FIELD NOTES: Keeps to dense cover, where it feeds on fruit, seeds and plant parts. VOICE: An insect-like *zeet* and a thin *split* given in alarm. The song is a repetition of the call note. HABITAT: Dense thickets and undergrowth, from coastal scrub to wet mountain forests. Breeds from March to June. DISTRIBUTION: Resident on the larger Bahamian islands, Hispaniola and Jamaica.

3 BARBADOS BULLFINCH *Loxigilla barbadensis* 15cm FIELD NOTES: Very tame; actions and habits as Lesser Antillean Bullfinch, from which it has recently been split. VOICE: A simple twittering and a sharp trill. HABITAT: Undergrowth, shrubbery and gardens. Breeds from February to August? DISTRIBUTION: Endemic to Barbados.

4 LESSER ANTILLEAN BULLFINCH *Loxigilla noctis* 14–15.5cm FIELD NOTES: Conspicuous and fairly tame; feeds on fruit and seeds. *L. n. sclateri* (fig 4b) is from St Lucia. VOICE: A harsh *chuck*, a thin *tseep tseep*, a crisp trill and a lengthy twitter. HABITAT: Shrubbery, thickets, forest understorey and gardens. Breeds from February to August. DISTRIBUTION: Throughout most of the Lesser Antilles, absent from Barbados and the Grenadines. Vagrant on Cuba.

5 CUBAN BULLFINCH *Melopyrrha nigra* 14–15cm FIELD NOTES: Forages from near the ground to the canopy, usually in small flocks; often mixes with other species. VOICE: A buzzing *chip*. The song is a long, descending then ascending trill. HABITAT: Forests, woods, bushes, undergrowth in pine woods and mangroves. Breeds from March to July. DISTRIBUTION: Resident on Cuba and the Cayman Islands (Grand Cayman).

6 ST LUCIA BLACK FINCH *Melanospiza richardsoni* 13–14cm FIELD NOTES: Forages on or near the ground, primarily among leaf litter. VOICE: A burry *tick-zwee-swisiwis-you*, with the accents on the second and last note. HABITAT: Moist and semiarid forests. Breeds from November to June. DISTRIBUTION: Endemic to St Lucia.

7 SAFFRON FINCH *Sicalis flaveola* 14cm FIELD NOTES: Feeds on the ground. Female has crown more yellowish. VOICE: A soft or loud *pink* and a whistled *wheat*. The song is a melodious, slightly harsh *chit chit chit chit-chit*, varying in length. HABITAT: Open country and gardens, where grasses are seeding. Breeds from August to October on Puerto Rico and from March to July on Jamaica. DISTRIBUTION: Introduced to Jamaica and Puerto Rico, also a record from Cuba.

8 GRASSLAND YELLOW-FINCH *Sicalis luteola* 12cm FIELD NOTES: Feeds in grass or on the ground. Female duller. VOICE: A buzzy trill. HABITAT: Open grassy areas. Breeds from February to June. DISTRIBUTION: Resident on Antigua, Guadeloupe, Martinique, St Lucia, Barbados, St Vincent and Grenada. A vagrant in the Grenadines (Mustique).

9 ZAPATA SPARROW *Torreornis inexpectata* 16.5cm FIELD NOTES: Forages on or near the ground. Race *T. i. sigmani* has plain grey mantle and duller, greyer crown. VOICE: A buzzing *zeee* and a thin *tsip* or *tsip-tsip*. The song is a buzzing trill, interspersed with chattering notes. HABITAT: Sawgrass with scattered bushes in the Zapata Swamp (*T. i. inexpectata*), dry vegetation in arid areas east of Guantanamo Bay (*T. i. sigmani*), woods and swampy areas on Cayo Coco (*T. i. varonai*). Breeds from March to June. DISTRIBUTION: Endemic to Cuba.

10 GREEN-TAILED TOWEE *Pipilo chlorurus* 18cm FIELD NOTES: Forages on or near to the ground. VOICE: A cat-like *mew*. HABITAT: Scrubby semiarid areas. DISTRIBUTION: Vagrant on Cuba.

73 DARK-EYED JUNCO AND AMERICAN SPARROWS

1 DARK-EYED JUNCO (SLATE-COLOURED JUNCO) *Junco hyemalis* 16cm FIELD NOTES: Forages on the ground, often in flocks. In flight, shows white outer tail feathers. VOICE: A liquid *chek*, a sharp *dit* and a dry, twittering flight call. The song is a rapid, loose trill. HABITAT: Farmland, scrub, parks and gardens. DISTRIBUTION: Vagrant to the northern Bahamas, Jamaica, Puerto Rico and the Virgin Islands.

2 CHIPPING SPARROW *Spizella passerina* 13cm FIELD NOTES: Forages on the ground or in bushes; often associated with other seed-eating species. VOICE: A short *chip* or *tsip*, and a rising *tsiis* given in flight. The song is a monotonous, dry trill. HABITAT: Open grassy areas, thickets and the bushy parts of parks and gardens. DISTRIBUTION: Rare non-breeding resident, from October to April, on the northern Bahamas and Cuba. Vagrant to the southern Bahamas.

3 CLAY-COLOURED SPARROW *Spizella pallida* 14cm FIELD NOTES: Forages on the ground or in bushes; regularly mixes with other seed-eating species, especially Chipping Sparrows. VOICE: A weak *chip* and a rising *swit* flight call. The song is a short series of insect-like buzzes. HABITAT: Semiarid open areas with scattered bushes, coastal thickets and the borders of salt ponds. DISTRIBUTION: Vagrant, recorded from the northern Bahamas and Cuba.

4 VESPER SPARROW *Pooectes gramineus* 16cm FIELD NOTES: Forages on the ground, retreats into trees or bushes when disturbed. In flight, shows white outer tail feathers. VOICE: A loud *hsip* and a buzzy *ssit* or *seet* flight call. The song is rich and melodious, consisting of 2 long slurred notes followed by 2 higher notes and then ending with a short series of descending trills. HABITAT: Semiarid scrub, weedy fields and open grasslands. DISTRIBUTION: Vagrant, recorded from the Bahamas (Grand Bahama).

5 BLACK-THROATED SPARROW *Amphispiza bilineata* 14cm FIELD NOTES: Forages on the ground and in bushes, calling constantly and regularly flicking tail. In flight, shows white outer tail feathers. Juvenile lacks black bib, breast has indistinct streaks. VOICE: A high-pitched, tinkling *tip*. The song is rapid, starting with 2 bell-like notes followed by a trill. HABITAT: Arid areas with scattered scrub. DISTRIBUTION: Vagrant, recorded from the Bahamas (Andros).

6 LARK SPARROW *Chondestes grammacus* 15cm FIELD NOTES: Forages on the ground. In flight, shows a large amount of white on outer tail feathers and tips of inner tail feathers. Juvenile much duller, with streaked flanks. VOICE: A metallic *tink* and a high *tsewp*, often repeated when alarmed. The song starts with 2 loud, clear notes followed by a series of melodious notes, trills and unmusical buzzes. HABITAT: Semiarid, open areas with scattered bushes. DISTRIBUTION: Vagrant, recorded from the northern Bahamas, Cuba and Jamaica.

7 GRASSHOPPER SPARROW *Ammodramus savannarum* 13cm FIELD NOTES: Secretive, forages on the ground, more conspicuous when singing from grass stem or low perch. Juvenile has fine streaks on breast and flanks. VOICE: A high, thin *tip* and a *titip*, and a rising *tswees* flight call. The song is a thin, insect-like buzz that starts with 2 sharp *tik* notes; also utters a high-pitched tinkling. HABITAT: Weedy fields with tall grass. Breeds mainly from August to May. DISTRIBUTION: Resident on Jamaica, Hispaniola and Puerto Rico. A non-breeding resident, from October to April, on Cuba, the Bahamas and the Cayman Islands.

8 SAVANNAH SPARROW *Passerculus sandwichensis* 14–16cm FIELD NOTES: Forages on the ground in bushes or low in trees. VOICE: A sharp *chack*. The song is a buzzy *ti ti ti tseeeeeee tisoooo* or similar. HABITAT: Open grassy areas, bushy savannahs and coastal thickets. DISTRIBUTION: Non-breeding resident, from October to April, on the northern Bahamas, Cuba and the Cayman Islands (Grand Cayman).

74 AMERICAN SPARROWS, SNOW BUNTING AND BOBOLINK

1 SONG SPARROW *Melospiza melodia* 16cm FIELD NOTES: Skulking, forages on the ground, usually under cover. Hops with tail slightly raised. Pumps tail in flight. VOICE: A nasal *tchep* or *jimp*, and a thin *seet* flight call. The song is a series of clear notes followed by a buzzing rattle and trill. HABITAT: Thickets, waterside undergrowth, hedgerows and forest edge. DISTRIBUTION: Vagrant, recorded from the Bahamas (Grand Bahama, Great Abaco and New Providence) and Hispaniola (Dominican Republic).

2 LINCOLN'S SPARROW *Melospiza lincolnii* 15cm FIELD NOTES: Secretive, forages on the ground usually near cover. Pumps tail in flight. VOICE: A nasal *tschup*, repeated when agitated; in flight, utters a buzzy *zeeet*. The song is a continuous jumble of husky, chirping trills with many pitch changes. HABITAT: Clearings in moist highland thickets, forest borders and coastal thickets. DISTRIBUTION: Rare migrant or non-breeding resident on the Bahamas, Cuba and Jamaica, from October to April. Vagrant on Hispaniola and Puerto Rico.

3 SWAMP SPARROW *Melospiza georgiana* 15cm FIELD NOTES: Shy and nervous; forages on the ground or in low vegetation and also in shallow water. Pumps tail in flight. VOICE: A hard *chip*; in flight, gives a buzzy *zeeet*. The song is a slow, musical, 1-pitched trill. HABITAT: Marshy and bushy areas. DISTRIBUTION: Vagrant on the Bahamas (New Providence, Exuma and Mayaguana).

4 WHITE-CROWNED SPARROW *Zonotrichia lecophrys* 16cm FIELD NOTES: Forages on the ground, both in the open and in undergrowth; readily perches in trees and bushes. Often raises crown feathers when agitated. VOICE: A metallic *pink* and a high *seeep* flight call. The song is a sad *more-wet-wetter-chee-zee*. HABITAT: Open woodlands, forest edge, bushy fields and treed gardens. DISTRIBUTION: Rare migrant or non-breeding resident on the Bahamas and Cuba, from October to April. Vagrant on Jamaica.

5 WHITE-THROATED SPARROW *Zonotrichia albicollis* 16cm FIELD NOTES: Ground forager, but never far from cover; readily perches on bushes. VOICE: A sharp *chink* and a long *seeeet* flight call. The song is a series of clear whistles, often transcribed as *Old-Sam-Peabody-Peabody-Peabody*. HABITAT: Woodland, woodland edge, clearings, parks and gardens. DISTRIBUTION: Vagrant, recorded from Puerto Rico.

6 RUFOUS-COLLARED SPARROW *Zonotrichia capensis* 15–16.5cm FIELD NOTES: Shy, forages on the ground, usually in pairs. Juvenile has indistinct head pattern and is spotted below. VOICE: A sharp *chip*. The song is an accelerating trill, transcribed as *whis-whis-whis-whis-whiswhisu-whiswhis*. HABITAT: Mountain forest edges, stream-side thickets and the undergrowth of pine forests. Breeds during May and June. DISTRIBUTION: Resident on Hispaniola.

7 SNOW BUNTING *Plectrophenax nivalis* 17cm FIELD NOTES: Forages on the ground, usually in small flocks, often with other species. VOICE: A harsh *djee*; in flight, utters a rippling *tiririririt* often followed by a ringing *pyu*. HABITAT: Open country, coastal marshes and beaches. DISTRIBUTION: Vagrant, recorded from the Bahamas (Cat Island).

8 BOBOLINK *Dolichonyx oryzivorus* 18cm FIELD NOTES: Forages on or near the ground, among grasses and weeds, generally in flocks. Non-breeding males similar to breeding female although generally more yellowish buff. VOICE: A soft, low *chuk*; in flight, utters a musical *pink*, *bink* or *bwink*. The song is a bubbling, jangling warble. HABITAT: Arable fields, open grassland, weedy areas and rich fields. DISTRIBUTION: Migrant, from August to December and from February to May, throughout the region, although uncommon or rare on Hispaniola, Puerto Rico and the Lesser Antilles.

75 MEADOWLARK AND AMERICAN BLACKBIRDS

1 EASTERN MEADOWLARK *Sturnella magna* 23cm FIELD NOTES: Forages on the ground; typically rests and sings from posts and overhead wires. In flight, shows much white in outer tail feathers. Non-breeding birds have breast band less distinct. VOICE: A loud, harsh *dziit*. The song consists of simple slurred whistles *seeeeoooaaa seeeeadoo* or similar. HABITAT: Open grasslands, savannahs, marshes and pastures with scattered bushes or trees. Breeds from January to July. DISTRIBUTION: Resident on Cuba.

2 YELLOW-HEADED BLACKBIRD *Xanthocephalus xanthocephalus* 24cm FIELD NOTES: In flight, the male shows distinct white patches on primary coverts of upperwing, females only show a pale crescent. Forages mainly on the ground. VOICE: A croaking *kruck, kack* or *ktuk*. The song consists of low, hoarse rasping notes, ending with a buzz. HABITAT: Marshes and reed-beds, farmland and pasture. DISTRIBUTION: Vagrant, recorded from the Bahamas (Grand Bahama and San Salvador), Cuba and the Cayman Islands.

3 YELLOW-HOODED BLACKBIRD *Agelaius icterocephalus* 19cm FIELD NOTES: Usually in small flocks, often associated with cowbirds and grackles. VOICE: A dry *chek* and a descending whistled *tieeewww*. The song is a wheezy, drawn-out *took-TOOAEEEEE tik* or similar. HABITAT: Marshes, rich fields, pastures and agricultural areas. DISTRIBUTION: Vagrant, recorded from Barbados.

4 RED-SHOULDERED BLACKBIRD *Agelaius assimilis* 19–23cm FIELD NOTES: Occasionally occurs in large flocks, especially in the non-breeding season; forages in marshes and agricultural fields and pastures. VOICE: A short *cheep, chek* or *chek-chek-chek*. The song is a shrill, non-melodious *o-wi-hiii*. HABITAT: Swamps and marshes. Breeds from April to June. DISTRIBUTION: Endemic resident to western Cuba.

5 RED-WINGED BLACKBIRD *Agelaius phoeniceus* 19–23cm FIELD NOTES: Often encountered in large flocks foraging in marshes where they feed on seeds, fruit, insects and small vertebrates. Females of the endemic race on the Bahamas have a whiter throat than those from North America. VOICE: A sharp, throaty *check* and a whistled *cheer* or *peet* given in alarm. The song is a repeated, bubbling and shrill *ok-a-lee*. HABITAT: Swamps and marshes. Breeds from April to July. DISTRIBUTION: Resident on the northern Bahamas and a vagrant on the southern Bahamas.

6 TAWNY-SHOULDERED BLACKBIRD *Agelaius humeralis* 19–22cm FIELD NOTES: Usually occurs in flocks, especially in the non-breeding season. Forages on the ground and in trees, feeding on seeds, rice and nectar. In parts of Cuba very tame, scavenging on scraps in and around restaurants. VOICE: A loud, short *chic-chic* or *chup-chup*, a nasal *whaap* or *nhyaap* and a high *pleeet* or *tweeep*. The song is a buzzy, drawn-out note, sometimes preceded by a higher pitched buzz, transcribed as *preeee-whaaaaaaa*. HABITAT: Woodlands, farmland with scattered trees, mangroves and rich fields. Breeds during April and May. DISTRIBUTION: Resident on Cuba and Hispaniola (Haiti).

7 YELLOW-SHOULDERED BLACKBIRD *Agelaius xanthomus* 19–22cm FIELD NOTES: Usually forages in the upper or mid-levels of mangrove or other woodland, probing into epiphytes, bark crevices or holes etc. Feeds mostly on arthropods and fruit when available, will descend to feed on the ground where it feeds on grain or seeds. VOICE: A *check* and nasal *chwip*; when alarmed, gives a *cut-zee*. The song is a nasal rasp, transcribed as *nhyaaaaaaaaa* or *ttnyyaaa*. HABITAT: Mainly mangroves and arid scrublands. Breeds from March to September. DISTRIBUTION: Endemic to Puerto Rico, most regular on Mona Island. Critically endangered.

76 AMERICAN BLACKBIRDS, COWBIRDS AND GRACKLES

1 RUSTY BLACKBIRD *Euphagus carolinus* 23cm FIELD NOTES: Forages on the ground, often with flocks of grackles or other blackbirds; when disturbed, refuge is taken in a nearby tree or bush. VOICE: A loud *chack*. The song is a creaky *kush-a-lee*. HABITAT: Wooded swamps, lake shores and open fields. DISTRIBUTION: Vagrant, recorded from the Bahamas (Grand Bahama).

2 BREWER'S BLACKBIRD *Euphagus cyanocephalus* 23cm FIELD NOTES: Forages on the ground; often seen in flocks with other blackbirds. VOICE: A short *ket*, *chak* or *chuk*. The song is a short, high, crackling *t-kzzz* or *t-zherr*. HABITAT: Open grasslands, marshes, beaches and urban areas. DISTRIBUTION: Vagrant, recorded from the Bahamas (Grand Bahama).

3 JAMAICAN BLACKBIRD *Nesopsar nigerrimus* 18cm FIELD NOTES: Arboreal, seeks food among epiphytes and tree ferns. VOICE: A *check* or *dzik*; when alarmed, gives a thin, high *seee seee* or *chet-chet-chet....* The song is a buzzy *zwheezoo-whezoo whee* or similar. HABITAT: Wet mountain forests, occasionally in humid woodlands at lower elevations. DISTRIBUTION: Endemic to Jamaica.

4 CUBAN BLACKBIRD *Dives atroviolacea* 25–28cm FIELD NOTES: Regularly forages on the ground, on buildings and even on cattle. Gathers into flocks, sometimes in the company of Greater Antillean Grackles and Tawny-shouldered Blackbirds. VOICE: A loud, repeated *to-teee* or *tí-o*; also various whistles and mews. The song is variable, consisting of a repeated single sharp note or mellow phrases and a nasal call similar to that of a braying sheep. HABITAT: Woodlands, agricultural and open areas, parks and gardens. Breeds from April to June. DISTRIBUTION: Endemic to Cuba.

5 BROWN-HEADED COWBIRD *Molothrus ater* 19cm FIELD NOTES: Forages on the ground. Juveniles like pale female with streaked underparts. VOICE: A harsh *chuk* and a squeaky *weee-titi* often given in flight. The song is a bubbly *glug-glug-gleeee*, followed by thin, slurred whistles. HABITAT: Farmland, open woodland, parks and gardens. DISTRIBUTION: Non-breeding resident to the Bahamas, from October to February. Vagrant on Cuba.

6 SHINY COWBIRD *Molothrus bonariensis* 18–20cm FIELD NOTES: Forages on the ground, often seen around livestock. Roost communally, especially in the non-breeding season, often in marshland. VOICE: A rolling rattle. The song consists of several liquid purrs, followed by a high whistle. HABITAT: Woodland edge, open country and agricultural areas. Breeds from March to July. DISTRIBUTION: Resident almost throughout the region, missing from a few islands in the Lesser Antilles and on San Andrés and Providencia.

7 COMMON GRACKLE *Quiscalus quiscula* 32cm FIELD NOTES: Usually in flocks, forages primarily on the ground. Feeds on virtually anything, from grain to young birds and crayfish. Juvenile brown. VOICE: A loud *chuck*. The song is a short, creaky *koguba-leek*. HABITAT: Almost any type, including woods, bogs, fields and gardens. DISTRIBUTION: Vagrant on the Bahamas (Andros).

8 GREATER ANTILLEAN GRACKLE *Quiscalus niger* 25–30cm FIELD NOTES: Typically encountered in flocks; forages on the ground, often around livestock; also scavenges scraps in urban areas. VOICE: A loud *chak-chak* and *chin-chin-chi-lin*. The song is a variable 4-syllabled phrase. HABITAT: Any type of open situation, including farmland, mangrove edge and urban areas. Breeds from April to August. DISTRIBUTION: The Greater Antilles.

9 CARIB GRACKLE *Quiscalus lugubris* 24–28cm FIELD NOTES: Typically occurs in noisy flocks; can become very bold and tame in urban areas. VOICE: A *chuck* and various whistles. The song is a series of 3- to 7-syllable squeaky notes, ending with a ringing bell-like note; varies on each island. HABITAT: Lowland open situations and residential areas. Breeds from February to July. DISTRIBUTION: Resident on most islands in the Lesser Antilles from Anguilla south to Grenada.

77 AMERICAN ORIOLES

1 GREATER ANTILLEAN ORIOLE (BLACK-COWLED ORIOLE) *Icterus dominicensis* 20–22cm FIELD NOTES: Usually encountered in pairs, foraging, sometimes acrobatically in palms and tees in search of insects, fruit and nectar. The 4 races shown are the nominate *I. d. dominicensis* from Hispaniola, *I. d. northropi* (fig 1b) from the Bahamas, *I. d. melanopsis* (fig 1c) from Cuba and *I. d. portoricensis* (fig 1d) from Puerto Rico. Although recently split from the Black-cowled Oriole it may well be that all should be split again to form 4 full species. VOICE: Variable, each island form has a different song; Hispaniola birds are said to give a clear and pleasant whistle, although some authors do not agree and think the song is weak; Bahamian birds give 8 or 9 sweet whistles; Puerto Rican birds give high long whistles; Cuban birds give clear whistles that last for 2 to 3 seconds. Calls are also variable, a *chur-r-churr-r* on Hispaniola, a plaintive double note on the Bahamas, a sharp *chip* and nasal *wheenk* on Cuba and a musical *chup* on Puerto Rico. HABITAT: Forests, forest edge, woodlands and gardens, usually near palms. Breeds from March to June. DISTRIBUTION: Resident on Hispaniola, Cuba, Puerto Rico and the Bahamas (Andros and Abaco).

2 JAMAICAN ORIOLE *Icterus leucopteryx* 21cm FIELD NOTES: Arboreal, gleans, probes bromeliads and peels bark in a search for insects; also feeds on fruit and nectar. Juvenile has the white wing-patch split by a black bar. The brighter yellow race *I. l. bairdi* from Grand Cayman is almost certainly extinct. VOICE: Calls variously transcribed as *you cheat you cheat*, *cheat-you*, and *Auntie Katie*. The song is a series of rapid whistles, repeated over and over. HABITAT: Montane subtropical forest, lowland forest, forest edge, wooded cultivated areas and gardens. Breeds from March to August. DISTRIBUTION: Resident on Jamaica and San Andrés.

3 ST LUCIA ORIOLE *Icterus laudabilis* 20–22cm FIELD NOTES: Usually occurs in pairs or small parties; forages in trees looking for insects and fruit. VOICE: A harsh *chwee* and a soft *chup*. The song consists of a short series of sweet, varied whistles that are repeated a number of times. HABITAT: Humid forest, dry coastal scrub forest and adjoining mangroves. Breeds from April to July. DISTRIBUTION: Endemic to St Lucia.

4 MONTSERRAT ORIOLE *Icterus oberi* 20–22cm FIELD NOTES: Generally occurs singly or in pairs; forages in the canopy of moist montane forest searching for insects. VOICE: A sharp *chic* or a sharper *chuck* and a scolding *chuur*. The song, only heard during the breeding season, is a loud series of melodious whistles. HABITAT: Moist montane forest. Breeds from April to July. DISTRIBUTION: Endemic to Montserrat.

5 MARTINIQUE ORIOLE *Icterus bonana* 18–21cm FIELD NOTES: Forages in family groups, pairs or singly, mainly in the forest canopy where insects and fruit are the main food items. VOICE: A harsh *cheeo* or *cheeo-cheeo*. The song is described as a variable soft warbling; a series of clear whistles and shrill like a Carib Grackle. HABITAT: Mangroves, dry forest, humid forest, forest edge, dense scrub, plantations and urban areas. Breeds from February to June. DISTRIBUTION: Endemic to Martinique.

78 AMERICAN ORIOLES

1 ORCHARD ORIOLE *Icterus spurius* 18cm FIELD NOTES: Arboreal, forages in trees and shrubs for insects and small fruits. VOICE: A clear, whistled *tweeo*, a soft *chut*, rasping *jarrsh* and a low, soft *yeeep* given in flight. The song is a lively warbling with a distinctive, ringing *plit titi zheeeer* ending. HABITAT: Woodlands, thickets and gardens. DISTRIBUTION: Rare migrant on Cuba in October, April and May. A vagrant to the Bahamas and Jamaica.

2 HOODED ORIOLE *Icterus cucullatus* 20cm FIELD NOTES: Arboreal with a liking for palms. First-summer birds like female but with a black throat and bib, very similar to first-summer Orchard Oriole. VOICE: A hard *chet*, a descending *chairr*, a rising *wheet* and a sharp *veek* flight call. The song is a rapid series of throaty whistles, trills and rattles. HABITAT: Dry open woodland, parks and gardens. DISTRIBUTION: A vagrant, recorded from Cuba.

3 BALTIMORE ORIOLE (NORTHERN ORIOLE) *Icterus galbula* 18–20cm FIELD NOTES: Forages in trees, seems to be attracted to those with colourful flowers or dense foliage; feeds mainly on insects and insect larvae as well as small fruits and nectar. VOICE: A harsh rattling *cher-r-r-r-r-r*; also a tinny *veeet* given in flight. The song is variable, consisting of clear whistled notes, transcribed as *pidoo tewdl tewdl yewdi tew tidew*; also gives a series of *hew-li* notes. HABITAT: Open woodlands, forest edge, semiarid scrub, swamps and gardens. DISTRIBUTION: Uncommon migrant and rare non-breeding resident on the Bahamas, Greater Antilles and the Virgin Islands. Vagrants recorded on St Bartholomew, St Christopher, St Lucia, Barbados, St Vincent and Grenada.

4 TROUPIAL *Icterus icterus* 25cm FIELD NOTES: Usually seen singly or in pairs foraging in trees or bushes, will pick fallen fruit from the ground; often sings from the top of a bush or cactus. VOICE: Mellow whistles and nasal sounds. The song is a repetitive series of whistles *troup troup troup*, *troup-ial troup-ial troup-ial* or *cheer taw cheer*. HABITAT: Primarily arid scrubland. Breeds from March to June. DISTRIBUTION: Puerto Rico, the Virgin Islands (St Thomas, Water Island and St John), Antigua, Dominica and Grenada.

5 AUDUBON'S ORIOLE (BLACK-HEADED ORIOLE) *Icterus graduacauda* 24cm FIELD NOTES: Shy and retiring, generally seen in pairs foraging in trees, often the shady densely vegetated parts. VOICE: A whistled *tooo* or *oooeh* and a husky, rising *jeeek jeeek*.... The song is a melancholy, slurred *hooooo heeeowee heeew heweee*. HABITAT: Edges of dense forests and riparian thickets. DISTRIBUTION: Vagrant, recorded from Puerto Rico.

6 YELLOW ORIOLE *Icterus nigrogularis* 20–22cm FIELD NOTES: Usually solitary or in family groups; forages primarily in trees searching out invertebrates, fruit and nectar. VOICE: A hesitant chattering *chuck-uch-ch-ch* and a *chet-chet-chet* or *retch-retch-retch* given when alarmed. The song is a flute-like *tjee-tjü tjee-tjü tjee tjee*; also adds some buzzes and *tik* notes. HABITAT: Open woodlands, semi-open savannahs, mangroves, suburban areas and gardens. DISTRIBUTION: Vagrant, recorded from Grenada.

7 YELLOW-TAILED ORIOLE *Icterus mesomelas* 24cm FIELD NOTES: Skulking, forages in dense vegetation. Occurs in pairs or small groups. VOICE: A nasal *chew* or *cheuk* and a hard *chuk* or *chook* that may be repeated. The song consists of beautiful phrases of sweet whistles, each phrase repeated several times; may also include some trills. HABITAT: Humid to semi-humid second growth, forest edge, often near water. DISTRIBUTION: Vagrant, recorded from Cuba.

1st summer

1 ♂ ♀

2 ♀ ♂

3 ♂ ♀

4

5

6

7

NA

79 CROSSBILL, REDPOLL, SISKINS, AMERICAN GOLDFINCH, CANARY, WEAVER AND BISHOPS

1 HISPANIOLAN CROSSBILL *Loxia megaplaga* 15cm FIELD NOTES: Usually secretive, although sometimes in noisy flocks; feeds acrobatically, even upside-down to extract pine seeds. Recently split from Two-barred Crossbill. VOICE: A high-pitched, repeated *chu-chu-chu-chu*, usually given by feeding flocks. HABITAT: Pine forests in high mountains. Breeds from December to April. DISTRIBUTION: Resident on Hispaniola. Vagrant on Jamaica.

2 REDPOLL (COMMON REDPOLL) *Carduelis flammea* 13cm FIELD NOTES: Usually in pairs or small parties. An acrobatic forager that searches trees for seeds; also picks up fallen seeds from the ground. VOICE: A metallic twittering *chuch-uch-uch-uch* and a ringing *tsooeet* or *djueee*. HABITAT: Thickets, seed-bearing trees or shrubs, weedy areas and pine forests. DISTRIBUTION: Vagrant, recorded from Jamaica and the Bahamas (Eleuthera).

3 RED SISKIN *Carduelis cucullata* 10cm FIELD NOTES: Usually encountered in small flocks, feeding on the seeds of trees, shrubs and grasses. VOICE: A high-pitched twitter and a sharp *chi-tit* or *chut-chut*. The song is rambling, complicated semi-musical twitters, trills and chattering. HABITAT: Thick scrub on dry hills. DISTRIBUTION: Resident on Puerto Rico. Introduced.

4 ANTILLEAN SISKIN *Carduelis dominicensis* 11cm FIELD NOTES: Usually found in flocks, actively searching for seeds in trees, shrubs and on the ground. VOICE: In flight, utters a low *chut-chut* or a high-pitched *swee-ee*; also gives a *seee-ip* and a *chit chit chee-ee-o*. The song is a low twittering trill. HABITAT: Mountain forest edge and pine forests close to grassy clearings; also wanders, in the non-breeding season, to agricultural areas with nearby scrub forest. Breeds during May and July. DISTRIBUTION: Endemic to Hispaniola.

5 AMERICAN GOLDFINCH *Carduelis tristis* 11–12cm FIELD NOTES: Usually encountered in flocks, foraging on plants, bushes and trees. VOICE: In flight, gives a soft, descending *ti did i di*, *chi-dup chi-dee-dup* or *per-chik-o-ree*. The song a lively series of twitters, trill and *swee* notes. HABITAT: Weedy areas, thickets and second growth. DISTRIBUTION: Vagrant, recorded on the Bahamas (Grand Bahama, Abaco and Eleuthera) and Cuba.

6 YELLOW-FRONTED CANARY *Serinus mozambicus* 11.5cm FIELD NOTES: Forages in bushes, trees and on the ground, searching for seeds, buds and flowers. VOICE: A *tsssp* or *tsssp tsssp*; also a *tseeuu*, *swee-et* or *zeee-zereee-chereeo*. The song is lively, clear, whistled warble. HABITAT: Coastal sea-grape forests. DISTRIBUTION: Resident on Puerto Rico. Introduced.

7 VILLAGE WEAVER *Ploceus cucullatus* 17cm FIELD NOTES: Gregarious when foraging and breeding, colonies can number up to 100 nests in one tree. VOICE: A high-pitched chatter interspersed with squeaks and churrs. HABITAT: Bushes and scrub near water, rice fields, open woodland and trees around urban areas. Breeds from December to June. DISTRIBUTION: Hispaniola and Martinique. Introduced.

8 YELLOW CROWNED BISHOP *Euplectes afer* 12cm FIELD NOTES: Generally occurs in flocks. Non-breeding males and juveniles look very similar to breeding females. VOICE: An unmusical, monotonous chipping, given perched or during display flight. HABITAT: Reeds and tall grass near fresh water. Probably breeds from June to October. DISTRIBUTION: Puerto Rico and Jamaica. Introduced.

9 NORTHERN RED BISHOP (ORANGE BISHOP) *Euplectes franciscanus* 12.5cm FIELD NOTES: Forages in small to large flocks, searching out seeds on grass stems or the ground; probably also feeds on grain crops and rice. Non-breeding males and juveniles look very similar to breeding females. VOICE: A simple tuneless chipping and trilling, given perched or in display flight. HABITAT: Grassy borders of sugarcane fields. Breeds from March to November. DISTRIBUTION: Resident on Puerto Rico, Martinique and Guadeloupe, also recorded from Jamaica and the Virgin Islands (St Croix). Introduced.

80 WAXBILLS, WHYDAH AND SEEDFINCH

1 ORANGE-CHEEKED WAXBILL *Estrilda melpoda* 10cm FIELD NOTES: Gregarious. Juvenile has pale orange face and a dark bill. VOICE: A high *pee* or *pee pee pee pee...*, an excited *sree-sree-sree-sree* and a shrill *tsit tsit* or *tseet tseet* given in alarm. The song consists of several short notes. HABITAT: Tall grass areas at agricultural stations, sugarcane borders and roadsides. Breeds from June to August. DISTRIBUTION: Resident on Puerto Rico; also recorded from Guadeloupe and Martinique. Introduced.

2 BLACK-RUMPED WAXBILL *Estrilda troglodytes* 10cm FIELD NOTES: Forages in flocks, never far from cover. Juvenile has a dark bill and greyish band through eye. VOICE: A loud, repeated *cheu-cheu*, *chit-chit* or *chihooee*. In flight, gives a *tiup-tiup-tiup*. The song is an explosive *tche-tcheer che-eeer* or similar. HABITAT: Tall grass bordering sugarcane fields. Breeds from September to November. DISTRIBUTION: Puerto Rico, Guadeloupe and Martinique; also recorded on the Virgin Islands (St Thomas).

3 PIN-TAILED WHYDAH *Vidua macroura* Male 31cm Female and Non-breeding male 11.5cm FIELD NOTES: Forms flocks in the non-breeding season. Non-breeding male similar to breeding female, but with stronger face markings and a red bill. VOICE: A loud *sweet*. The song is a jumble of harsh squeaks and chirps that form a rhythmic twittering. HABITAT: Short grass areas, including fields and garden lawns. Breeds from April to November. DISTRIBUTION: Resident on Puerto Rico. Introduced.

4 RED AVADAVAT *Amandava amandava* 10cm FIELD NOTES: Usually occurs in flocks. VOICE: A thin *sweet*, *sweet-sweet*, *teei* or *tsi*. The song is a high warble with soft sweet twittering notes. HABITAT: Grassy borders of swamps, drainage canals and sugarcane fields. DISTRIBUTION: Resident on Puerto Rico, Guadeloupe, Martinique and Hispaniola (Dominican Republic). Introduced.

5 INDIAN SILVERBILL (WARBLING SILVERBILL) *Lonchura malabarica* 11cm FIELD NOTES: Gregarious. VOICE: A sharp *cheep* or *cheep cheep*, a soft *seepsip* and a trilling *zip-zip*. The song is a rambling twittering. HABITAT: Arid scrub, grassy areas. Breeds from June to November. DISTRIBUTION: Resident on Puerto Rico and perhaps the Virgin Islands (St Croix). Introduced.

6 SCALY-BREASTED MUNIA (NUTMEG MANNIKIN) *Lonchura punctulata* 11cm FIELD NOTES: Highly social. VOICE: A repeated *kitty-kitty-kitty* and a soft, fading whistled *peet*. The song is a melody of high flute-like whistles and low slurred notes. HABITAT: Open areas with seeding grass, including borders of sugarcane fields, parks and gardens. Breeds from June to October. DISTRIBUTION: Resident on the Greater Antilles (not the Cayman Islands), the Virgin Islands (St Croix), Martinique and Guadeloupe. Introduced.

7 CHESTNUT MUNIA (CHESTNUT MANNIKIN) *Lonchura malacca* 12cm FIELD NOTES: Gregarious. VOICE: A weak, nasal *peekt*. In flight, utters a triple *chirp* note. HABITAT: Grass borders of sugarcane fields, swamps etc. Breeds from June to September. DISTRIBUTION: Resident on Martinique and the Greater Antilles (not the Cayman Islands). Introduced.

8 BRONZE MANNIKIN *Lonchura cucullata* 10cm FIELD NOTES: Gregarious, forages on the ground and on grass heads. Juveniles are plain brownish, paler on underparts. VOICE: A coarse *crrit*; also rapid delivery short burry chips. HABITAT: Grassy areas. Breeds from March to October. DISTRIBUTION: Resident on Puerto Rico and perhaps the Virgin Islands (St Croix). Introduced.

9 CHESTNUT-BELLIED SEEDFINCH *Oryzoborus angolensis* 12.5cm FIELD NOTES: Retiring, usually seen singly or in pairs. VOICE: A nasal *chihk* or *jiit*. The song is a long rich warble, sometimes interspersed with chattering notes. HABITAT: Forests and forest edge. DISTRIBUTION: Martinique. Introduced.

10 JAVA SPARROW *Padda oryzivora* 17cm FIELD NOTES: Highly sociable. Juvenile generally brownish. VOICE: A *tup*, *t'luk* or *tack*. The song is a series of bell-like notes ending in a long whistle. HABITAT: Urban areas. Breeds from July to February. DISTRIBUTION: Puerto Rico and perhaps Jamaica. Introduced.

chestnut-bellied
form

white-bellied
form

SPECIES DISTRIBUTION MAPS

Key to Maps

	Land	Sea
Breeding season		
Non-breeding season		
Resident season		

Vagrants and most introduced species are not included in the distribution maps section.

Cory's Shearwater, Plate 1.4

Jamaican Petrel, Plate 1.5

Black-capped Petrel, Plate 1.6

Manx Shearwater, Plate 2.1

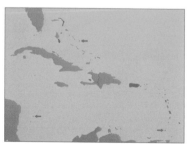

Audubon's Shearwater, Plate 2.2

Great Shearwater, Plate 2.4

170

Sooty Shearwater, Plate 2.5

Wilson's Storm-petrel, Plate 2.6

Leach's Storm-petrel, Plate 2.7

Madeiran Storm-petrel, Plate 2.8

Magnificent Frigatebird, Plate 3.1

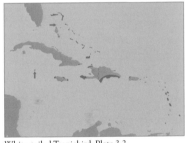

White-tailed Tropicbird, Plate 3.2

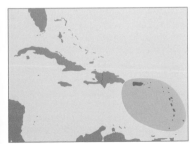

Red-billed Tropicbird, Plate 3.3

Brown Booby, Plate 3.4

171

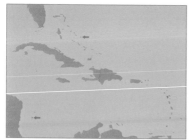

Red-footed Booby, Plate 3.5

Masked Booby, Plate 3.6

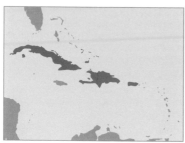

Brown Pelican, Plate 4.2

Double-crested Cormorant, Plate 4.3

Neotropic Cormorant, Plate 4.4

Anhinga, Plate 4.5

American Bittern, Plate 5.1

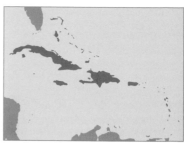

Least Bittern, Plate 5.2

Green Heron, Plate 5.4

Yellow-crowned Night-heron, Plate 5.6

Night Heron, Plate 5.7

Great Blue Heron, Plate 6.1

Little Blue Heron, Plate 6.3

Tricoloured Heron, Plate 6.4

Reddish Egret, Plate 6.5

Great White Egret, Plate 7.1

173

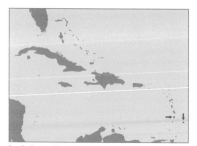

Little Egret, Plate 7.2

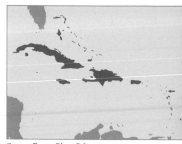

Snowy Egret, Plate 7.3

Western Reef Egret, Plate 7.4

Cattle Egret, Plate 7.5

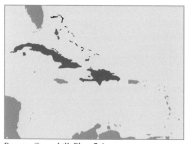

Roseate Spoonbill, Plate 7.6

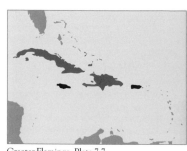

Greater Flamingo, Plate 7.7

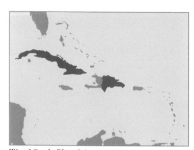

Wood Stork, Plate 8.1

White Ibis, Plate 8.4

174

Glossy Ibis, Plate 8.6

Sandhill Crane, Plate 8.7

Limpkin, Plate 8.8

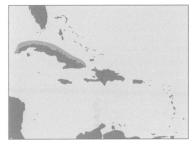

Great Northern Diver, Plate 9.1

Least Grebe, Plate 9.2

Pied-billed Grebe, Plate 9.3

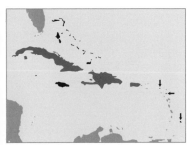

Fulvous Whistling Duck, Plate 9.5

West Indian Whistling Duck, Plate 9.6

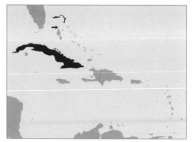

Snow Goose, Plate 10.2

Wood Duck, Plate 11.1

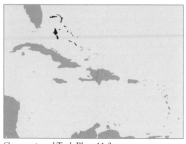

Green-winged Teal, Plate 11.2

Mallard, Plate 11.4

White-cheeked Pintail, Plate 11.5

Pintail, Plate 11.6

Blue-winged Teal, Plate 11.7

Shoveler, Plate 12.2

176

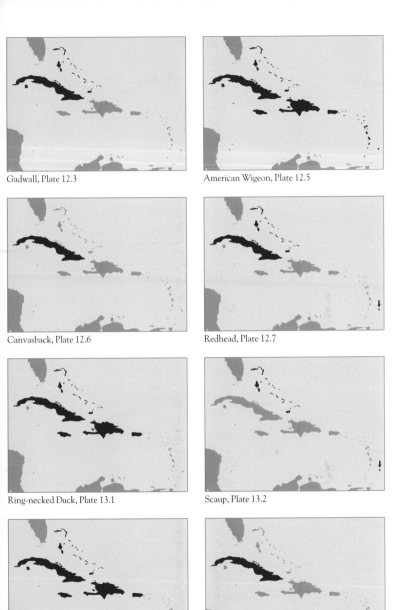

Gadwall, Plate 12.3

American Wigeon, Plate 12.5

Canvasback, Plate 12.6

Redhead, Plate 12.7

Ring-necked Duck, Plate 13.1

Scaup, Plate 13.2

Lesser Scaup, Plate 13.3

Bufflehead, Plate 13.4

Hooded Merganser, Plate 13.6

Red-breasted Merganser, Plate 13.7

Masked Duck, Plate 13.8

Ruddy Duck, Plate 13.9

Turkey Vulture, Plate 14.2

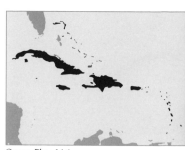
Osprey, Plate 14.4

Crested Caracara, Plate 14.5

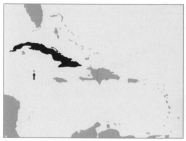
Swallow-tailed Kite, Plate 14.6

Hen Harrier, Plate 14.7

Hook-billed Kite, Plate 15.1

Cuban Kite, Plate 15.2

Snail Kite, Plate 15.3

Common Black Hawk, Plate 15.4

Ridgway's Hawk, Plate 15.5

Broad-winged Hawk, Plate 15.6

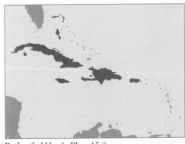

Red-tailed Hawk, Plate 15.8

Sharp-shinned Hawk, Plate 16.1

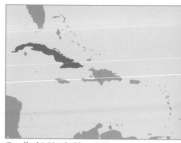

Gundlach's Hawk, Plate 16.2

American Kestrel, Plate 16.3

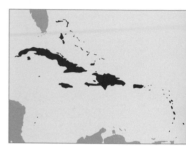

Peregrine Falcon, Plate 16.5

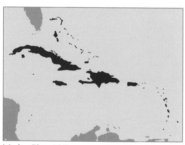

Merlin, Plate 16.6

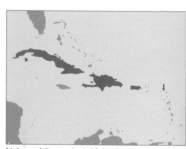

Helmeted Guineafowl, Plate 17.3

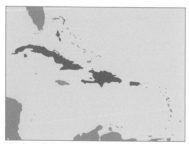

Northern Bobwhite, Plate 17.5

Crested Bobwhite, Plate 17.6

Rufous-vented Chachalaca, Plate 17.7

King Rail, Plate 18.1

Clapper Rail, Plate 18.2

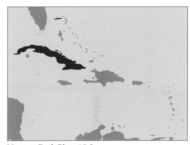

Virginia Rail, Plate 18.3

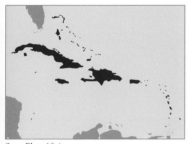

Sora, Plate 18.4

Yellow-breasted Crake, Plate 18.6

Zapata Rail, Plate 18.7

Black Rail, Plate 19.1

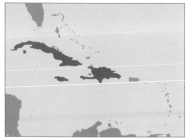

Spotted Rail, Plate 19.3

Purple Gallinule, Plate 19.4

Moorhen, Plate 19.5

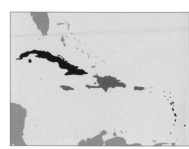

Caribbean Coot, Plate 19.6

American Coot, Plate 19.7

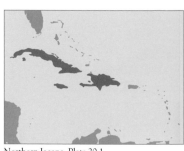

Northern Jacana, Plate 20.1

Double-striped Thick-knee, Plate 20.3

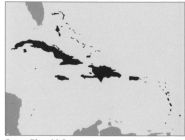

Snipe, Plate 20.5

182

Turnstone, Plate 20.6

Wilson's Phalarope, Plate 20.7

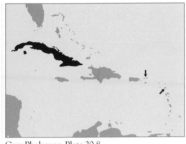

Grey Phalarope, Plate 20.8

Red-necked Phalarope, Plate 20.9

American Oystercatcher, Plate 21.1

Black-necked Stilt, Plate 21.2

American Avocet, Plate 21.3

Grey Plover, Plate 21.5

American Golden Plover, Plate 21.6

Buff-breasted Sandpiper, Plate 21.8

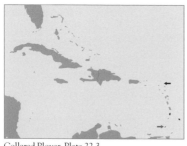

Piping Plover, Plate 22.1

Snowy Plover, Plate 22.2

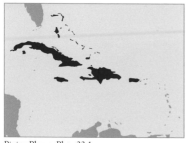

Collared Plover, Plate 22.3

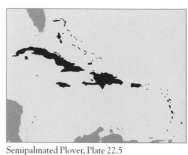

Semipalmated Plover, Plate 22.5

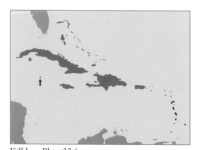

Killdeer, Plate 22.6

Wilson's Plover, Plate 22.7

Willet, Plate 23.2

Greater Yellowlegs, Plate 23.3

Lesser Yellowlegs, Plate 23.4

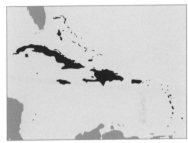

Solitary Sandpiper, Plate 23.7

Spotted Sandpiper, Plate 23.8

Ruff, Plate 24.1

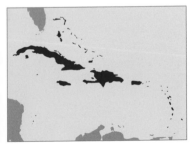

Upland Sandpiper, Plate 24.2

Whimbrel, Plate 24.4

185

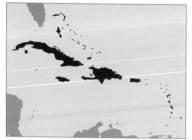

Short-billed Dowitcher, Plate 25.1

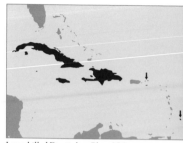

Long-billed Dowitcher, Plate 25.2

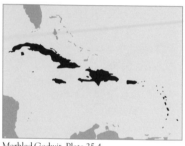

Marbled Godwit, Plate 25.4

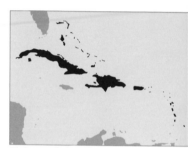

Hudsonian Godwit, Plate 25.5

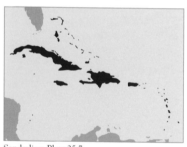

Sanderling, Plate 25.7

Knot, Plate 25.8

Semipalmated Sandpiper, Plate 26.1

Western Sandpiper, Plate 26.2

Least Sandpiper, Plate 26.4

White-rumped Sandpiper, Plate 26.5

Baird's Sandpiper, Plate 26.6

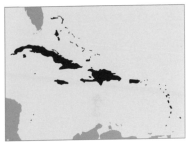

Pectoral Sandpiper, Plate 26.7

Dunlin, Plate 26.8

Stilt Sandpiper, Plate 26.10

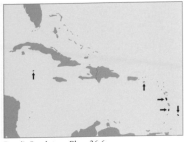

Pomarine Skua, Plate 27.1

Arctic Skua, Plate 27.2

Long-tailed Skua, Plate 27.3

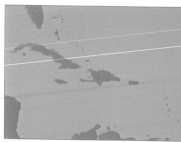

Great Skua, Plate 27.4

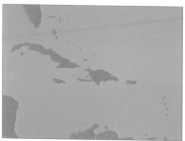

South Polar Skua, Plate 27.5

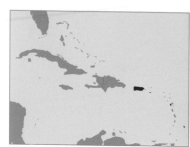

Black-headed Gull, Plate 28.1

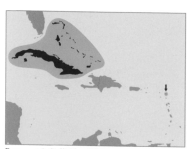

Bonaparte's Gull, Plate 28.3

Kittiwake, Plate 28.6

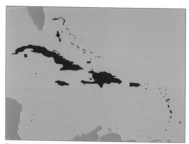

Ring-billed Gull, Plate 29.1

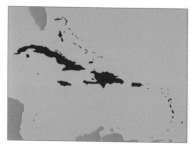

American Herring Gull, Plate 29.2

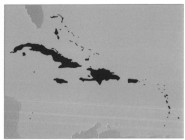

Lesser Black-backed Gull, Plate 29.3

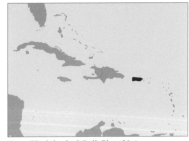

Great Black-backed Gull, Plate 29.4

Laughing Gull, Plate 29.5

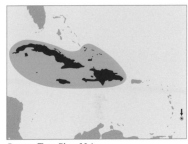

Caspian Tern, Plate 30.1

Royal Tern, Plate 30.2

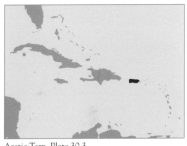

Arctic Tern, Plate 30.3

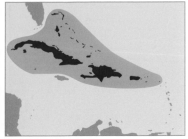

Forster's Tern, Plate 30.4

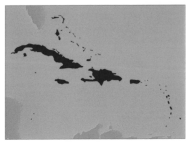

Common Tern, Plate 30.5

189

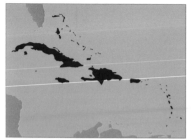

Roseate Tern, Plate 30.6

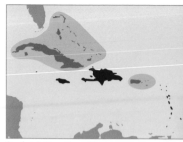

Sandwich Tern, Plate 30.7

Least Tern, Plate 31.1

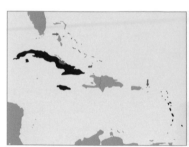

Gull-billed Tern, Plate 31.2

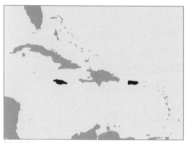

Black Tern, Plate 31.3

Bridled Tern, Plate 31.6

Sooty Tern, Plate 31.7

Brown Noddy, Plate 31.8

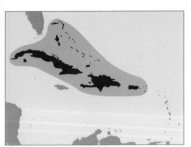

Black Skimmer, Plate 31.10

Rock Dove, Plate 32.1

Scaly-naped Pigeon, Plate 32.2

White-crowned Pigeon, Plate 32.3

Plain Pigeon, Plate 32.4

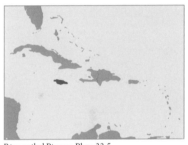

Ring-tailed Pigeon, Plate 32.5

Bridled Quail-dove, Plate 32.6

Key West Quail-dove, Plate 32.7

191

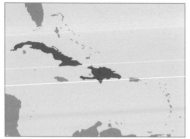

Grey-headed Quail-dove, Plate 32.8

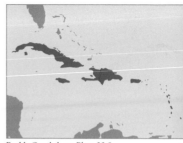

Ruddy Quail-dove, Plate 32.9

Crested Quail-dove, Plate 32.10

Blue-headed Quail-dove, Plate 32.11

Collared Dove, Plate 33.1

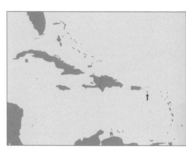

Spotted Dove, Plate 33.2

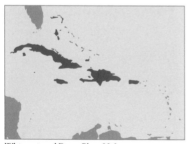

White-winged Dove, Plate 33.3

Zenaida Dove, Plate 33.4

Mourning Dove, Plate 33.5

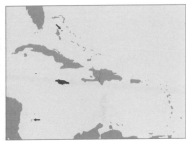

Eared Dove, Plate 33.6

Common Ground-dove, Plate 33.7

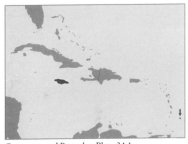

Caribbean Dove, Plate 33.8

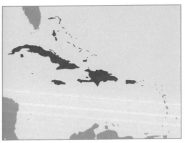

Grenada Dove, Plate 33.9

Green-rumped Parrotlet, Plate 34.1

Olive-throated Parakeet, Plate 34.6

Brown-throated Parakeet, Plate 34.8

Hispaniolan Parakeet, Plate 35.1

Cuban Parakeet, Plate 35.2

Rose-throated Parrot, Plate 35.3

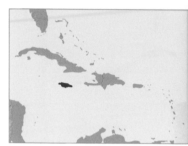

Yellow-billed Parrot, Plate 35.4

Hispaniolan Parrot, Plate 35.5

Puerto Rican Parrot, Plate 35.6

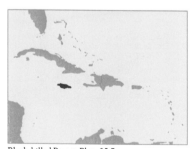

Black-billed Parrot, Plate 35.7

Red-necked Parrot, Plate 36.4

194

St Vincent Parrot, Plate 36.5

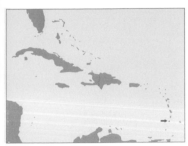

St Lucia Parrot, Plate 36.6

Imperial Parrot, Plate 36.7

Smooth-billed Ani, Plate 37.1

Black-billed Cuckoo, Plate 37.3

Yellow-billed Cuckoo, Plate 37.4

Mangrove Cuckoo, Plate 37.6

Great Lizard-cuckoo, Plate 38.1

195

Puerto Rican Lizard-cuckoo, Plate 38.2

Hispaniolan Lizard-cuckoo, Plate 38.3

Jamaican Lizard-cuckoo, Plate 38.4

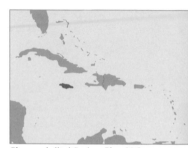

Chestnut-bellied Cuckoo, Plate 38.5

Bay-breasted Cuckoo, Plate 38.6

Barn Owl, Plate 39.1

Ashy-faced Owl, Plate 39.2

Bare-legged Owl, Plate 39.3

Puerto Rican Screech-owl, Plate 39.4

Cuban Pygmy Owl, Plate 39.5

Burrowing Owl, Plate 39.6

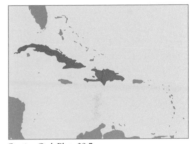

Stygian Owl, Plate 39.7

Short-eared Owl, Plate 39.8

Jamaican Owl, Plate 39.10

Northern Potoo, Plate 40.1

Common Nighthawk, Plate 40.2

197

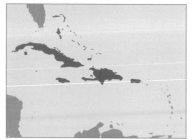

Antillean Nighthawk, Plate 40.3

Jamaican Poorwill, Plate 40.4

Least Poorwill, Plate 40.5

Chuck-will's Widow, Plate 40.6

Rufous Nightjar, Plate 40.7

Cuban Nightjar, Plate 40.8

Hispaniolan Nightjar, Plate 40.9

Puerto Rican Nightjar, Plate 40.11

White-tailed Nightjar, Plate 40.12

Black Swift, Plate 41.1

White-collared Swift, Plate 41.2

Chimney Swift, Plate 41.3

Short-tailed Swift, Plate 41.4

Grey-rumped Swift, Plate 41.5

Lesser Antillean Swift, Plate 41.6

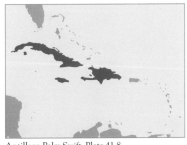

Antillean Palm Swift, Plate 41.8

199

Rufous Breasted Hermit, Plate 42.2

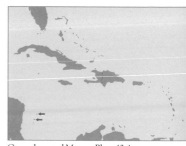

Green-breasted Mango, Plate 42.4

Jamaican Mango, Plate 42.5

Green Mango, Plate 42.6

Antillean Mango, Plate 42.7

Purple-throated Carib, Plate 42.8

Green-throated Carib, Plate 42.9

Antillean Crested Hummingbird, Plate 42.10

Cuban Emerald, Plate 43.2

Hispaniolan Emerald, Plate 43.3

Puerto Rican Emerald, Plate 43.4

Blue-headed Hummingbird, Plate 43.5

Black-billed Streamertail, Plate 43.6

Red-billed Streamertail, Plate 43.7

Ruby-throated Hummingbird, Plate 43.8

Bahama Woodstar, Plate 43.9

201

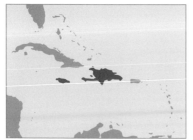

Vervain Hummingbird, Plate 43.10

Bee Hummingbird, Plate 43.11

Cuban Trogon, Plate 44.1

Hispaniolan Trogon, Plate 44.2

Cuban Tody, Plate 44.3

Broad-billed Tody, Plate 44.4

Narrow-billed Tody, Plate 44.5

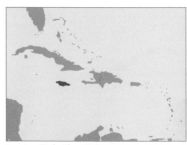

Jamaican Tody, Plate 44.6

Puerto Rican Tody, Plate 44.7

Ringed Kingfisher, Plate 44.8

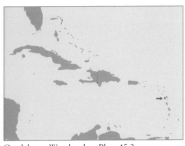

Belted Kingfisher, Plate 44.9

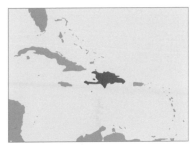

Antillean Piculet, Plate 45.1

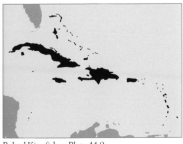

Guadeloupe Woodpecker, Plate 45.2

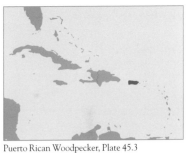

Puerto Rican Woodpecker, Plate 45.3

Hispaniolan Woodpecker, Plate 45.4

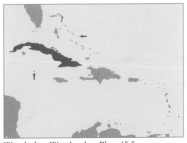

West Indian Woodpecker, Plate 45.5

Jamaican Woodpecker, Plate 45.6

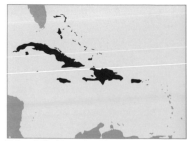

Yellow-bellied Sapsucker, Plate 46.1

Cuban Green Woodpecker, Plate 46.2

Hairy Woodpecker, Plate 46.3

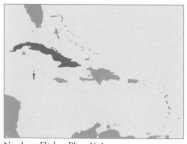

Northern Flicker, Plate 46.4

Fernandina's Flicker, Plate 46.5

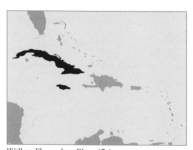

Willow Flycatcher, Plate 47.1

Acadian Flycatcher, Plate 47.2

Yellow-bellied Flycatcher, Plate 47.4

Euler's Flycatcher, Plate 47.5

Greater Antillean Elaenia, Plate 47.6

Caribbean Elaenia, Plate 47.7

Yellow-bellied Elaenia, Plate 47.8

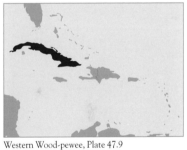

Western Wood-pewee, Plate 47.9

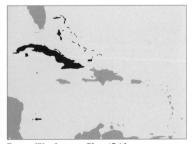

Eastern Wood-pewee, Plate 47.10

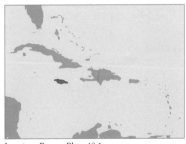

Jamaican Pewee, Plate 48.1

205

Crescent-eyed Pewee, Plate 48.2

Hispaniolan Pewee, Plate 48.3

St Lucia Pewee, Plate 48.4

Puerto Rican Pewee, Plate 48.5

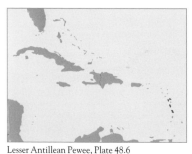

Lesser Antillean Pewee, Plate 48.6

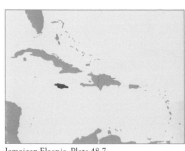

Jamaican Elaenia, Plate 48.7

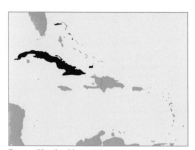

Eastern Phoebe, Plate 48.8

Jamaican Becard, Plate 48.9

Sad Flycatcher, Plate 49.1

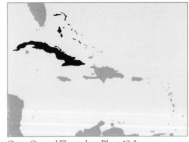
Great Crested Flycatcher, Plate 49.2

Grenada Flycatcher, Plate 49.3

Rufous-tailed Flycatcher, Plate 49.4

La Sagra's Flycatcher, Plate 49.5

Stolid Flycatcher, Plate 49.6

Puerto Rican Flycatcher, Plate 49.7

Lesser Antillean Flycatcher, Plate 49.8

Tropical Kingbird, Plate 50.1

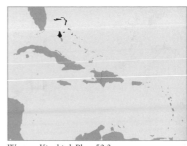

Western Kingbird, Plate 50.2

Eastern Kingbird, Plate 50.3

Grey Kingbird, Plate 50.4

Loggerhead Kingbird, Plate 50.5

Giant Kingbird, Plate 50.6

Fork-tailed Flycatcher, Plate 50.8

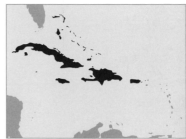

Tree Swallow, Plate 51.1

208

Bahama Swallow, Plate 51.2

Golden Swallow, Plate 51.3

Swallow, Plate 51.5

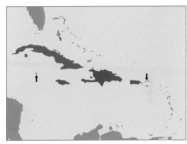

Cave Swallow, Plate 51.6

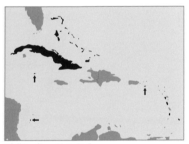

Cliff Swallow, Plate 51.7

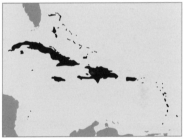

Sand Martin, Plate 52.1

Northern Rough-winged Swallow, Plate 52.2

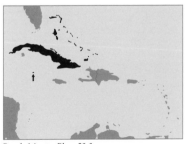

Purple Martin, Plate 52.3

209

Cuban Martin, Plate 52.4

Caribbean Martin, Plate 52.5

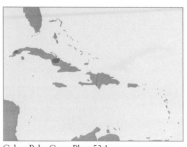

Cuban Palm Crow, Plate 53.1

Hispaniolan Palm Crow, Plate 53.2

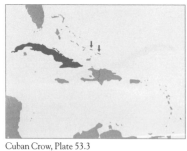

Cuban Crow, Plate 53.3

White-necked Crow, Plate 53.5

Jamaican Crow, Plate 53.6

Zapata Wren, Plate 54.2

Southern House Wren, Plate 54.4

Ruby-crowned Kinglet, Plate 54.5

Blue-grey Gnatcatcher, Plate 54.6

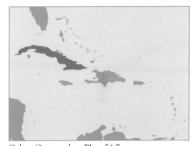
Cuban Gnatcatcher, Plate 54.7

Cuban Solitaire, Plate 55.1

St Vincent Solitaire, Plate 55.2

Rufous-throated Solitaire, Plate 55.3

Veery, Plate 55.4

Bicknell's Thrush, Plate 55.5

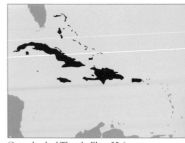

Grey-cheeked Thrush, Plate 55.6

Swainson's Thrush, Plate 55.7

Hermit Thrush, Plate 55.8

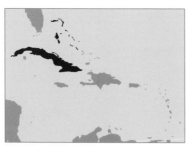

Wood Thrush, Plate 55.9

Cocoa Thrush, Plate 56.1

Bare-eyed Thrush, Plate 56.2

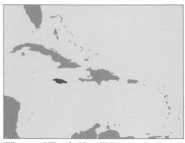

White-eyed Thrush, Plate 56.3

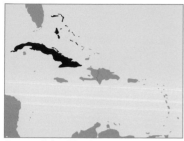

American Robin, Plate 56.4

La Selle Thrush, Plate 56.5

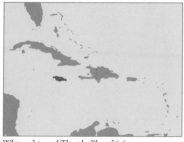

White-chinned Thrush, Plate 56.6

Red-legged Thrush, Plate 56.7

Forest Thrush, Plate 56.8

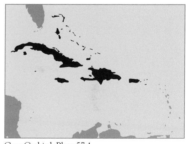

Grey Catbird, Plate 57.1

Northern Mockingbird, Plate 57.2

Tropical Mockingbird, Plate 57.3

Bahama Mockingbird, Plate 57.4

White-breasted Thrasher, Plate 57.5

Scaly-breasted Thrasher, Plate 57.7

Pearly-eyed Thrasher, Plate 57.8

Brown Trembler, Plate 58.1

Grey Trembler, Plate 58.2

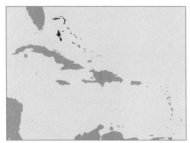

Buff-bellied Pipit, Plate 58.4

Cedar Waxwing, Plate 58.6

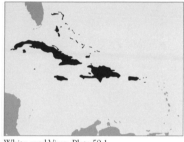

Palmchat, Plate 58.7

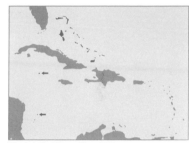

Starling, Plate 58.9

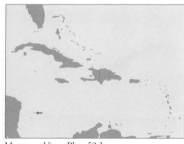

White-eyed Vireo, Plate 59.1

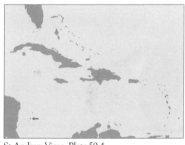

Thick-billed Vireo, Plate 59.2

Mangrove Vireo, Plate 59.3

St Andrew Vireo, Plate 59.4

Jamaican Vireo, Plate 59.5

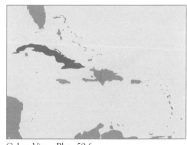

Cuban Vireo, Plate 59.6

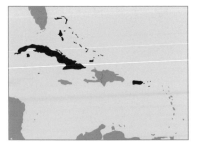

Yellow-throated Vireo, Plate 59.7

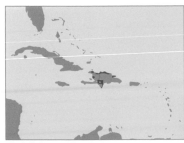

Flat-billed Vireo, Plate 59.8

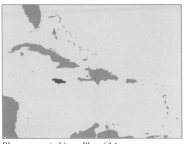

Blue-mountain Vireo, Plate 60.1

Puerto Rican Vireo, Plate 60.2

Blue-headed Vireo, Plate 60.3

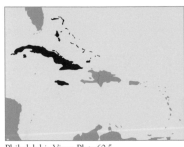

Philadelphia Vireo, Plate 60.5

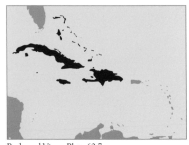

Red-eyed Vireo, Plate 60.7

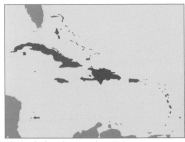

Black-whiskered Vireo, Plate 60.8

216

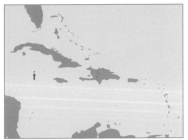
Yucatan Vireo, Plate 60.9

Northern Parula, Plate 61.1

Blue-winged Warbler, Plate 61.2

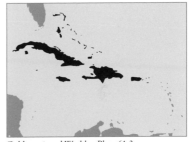
Golden-winged Warbler, Plate 61.3

Tennessee Warbler, Plate 61.4

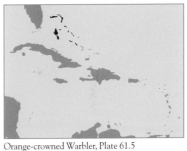
Orange-crowned Warbler, Plate 61.5

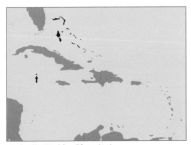
Nashville Warbler, Plate 61.6

Bachman's Warbler, Plate 61.8

Yellow Warbler, Plate 62.1

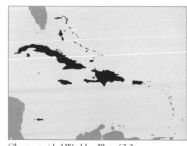

Chestnut-sided Warbler, Plate 62.2

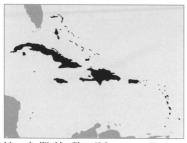

Magnolia Warbler, Plate 62.3

Cape May Warbler, Plate 62.4

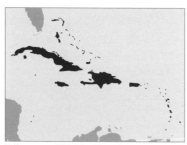

Yellow-rumped Warbler, Plate 62.5

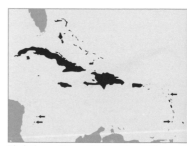

Black-throated Green Warbler, Plate 62.8

Black-throated Blue Warbler, Plate 63.1

Blackburnian Warbler, Plate 63.2

Yellow-throated Warbler, Plate 63.3

Adelaide's Warbler, Plate 63.4

Olive-capped Warbler, Plate 63.5

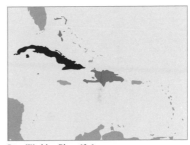

Pine Warbler, Plate 63.6

Kirtland's Warbler, Plate 63.7

Prairie Warbler, Plate 63.8

Vitelline Warbler, Plate 64.1

Palm Warbler, Plate 64.2

219

Bay-breasted Warbler, Plate 64.3

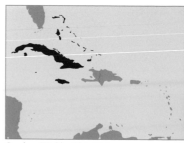

Cerulean Warbler, Plate 64.4

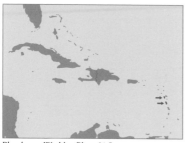

Plumbeous Warbler, Plate 64.5

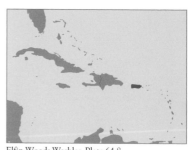

Blackpoll Warbler, Plate 64.6

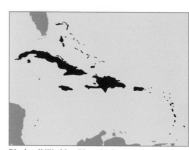

Arrow-headed Warbler, Plate 64.7

Elfin Woods Warbler, Plate 64.8

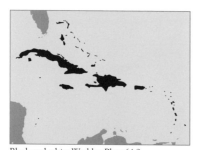

Black-and-white Warbler, Plate 64.9

Whistling Warbler, Plate 65.1

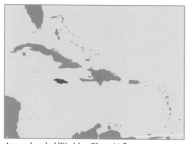

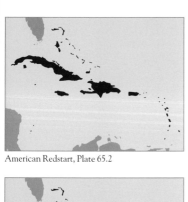

American Redstart, Plate 65.2

Prothonotary Warbler, Plate 65.3

Worm-eating Warbler, Plate 65.4

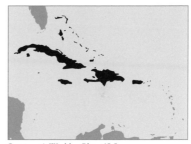

Swainson's Warbler, Plate 65.5

Ovenbird, Plate 65.6

Northern Waterthrush, Plate 65.7

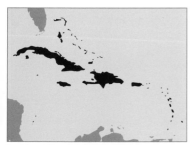

Louisiana Waterthrush, Plate 65.8

Kentucky Warbler, Plate 66.1

221

Connecticut Warbler, Plate 66.3

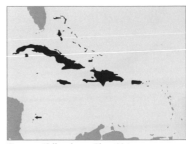

Common Yellowthroat, Plate 66.4

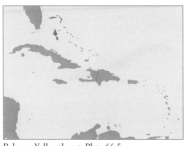

Bahama Yellowthroat, Plate 66.5

Oriente Warbler, Plate 66.6

Yellow-headed Warbler, Plate 66.7

Hooded Warbler, Plate 67.1

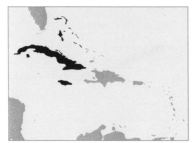

Wilson's Warbler, Plate 67.2

Canada Warbler, Plate 67.3

Yellow-breasted Chat, Plate 67.4

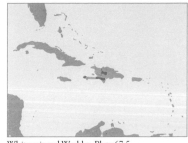

White-winged Warbler, Plate 67.5

Green-tailed Warbler, Plate 67.6

Semper's Warbler, Plate 67.7

Bananaquit, Plate 68.1

Red-legged Honeycreeper, Plate 68.2

Antillean Euphonia, Plate 68.3

Jamaican Euphonia, Plate 68.4

223

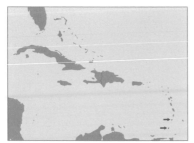

Lesser Antillean Tanager, Plate 68.5

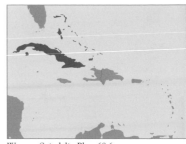

Western Spindalis, Plate 68.6

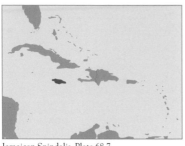

Jamaican Spindalis, Plate 68.7

Hispaniolan Spindalis, Plate 68.8

Puerto Rican Spindalis, Plate 68.9

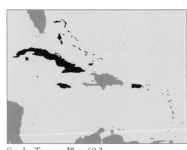

Scarlet Tanager, Plate 69.2

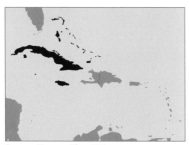

Summer Tanager, Plate 69.3

Black-crowned Palm-tanager, Plate 69.5

Grey-crowned Palm-tanager, Plate 69.6

Eastern Chat-tanager, Plate 69.7

Western Chat-tanager, Plate 69.8

Puerto Rican Tanager, Plate 69.9

Lesser Antillean Saltator, Plate 70.2

Rose-breasted Grosbeak, Plate 70.3

Blue Grosbeak, Plate 70.4

Indigo Bunting, Plate 70.5

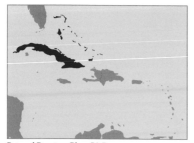

Painted Bunting, Plate 70.7

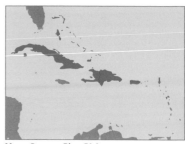

House Sparrow, Plate 70.8

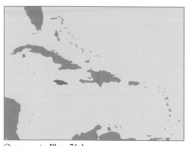

Orangequit, Plate 71.1

Blue-black Grassquit, Plate 71.2

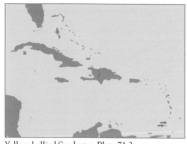

Yellow-bellied Seedeater, Plate 71.3

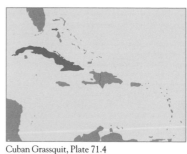

Cuban Grassquit, Plate 71.4

Yellow-faced Grassquit, Plate 71.5

Black-faced Grassquit, Plate 71.6

Yellow-shouldered Grassquit, Plate 71.7

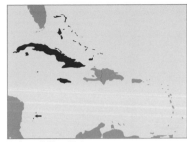

Dickcissel, Plate 71.8

Puerto Rican Bullfinch, Plate 72.1

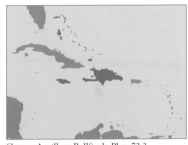

Greater Antillean Bullfinch, Plate 72.2

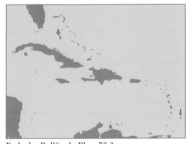

Barbados Bullfinch, Plate 72.3

Lesser Antillean Bullfinch, Plate 72.4

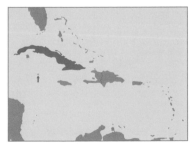

Cuban Bullfinch, Plate 72.5

St Lucia Black Finch, Plate 72.6

Saffron Finch, Plate 72.7

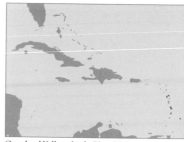
Grassland Yellow-finch, Plate 72.8

Zapata Sparrow, Plate 72.9

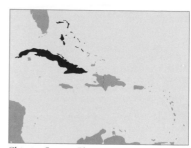
Chipping Sparrow, Plate 73.2

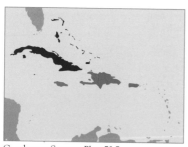
Grasshopper Sparrow, Plate 73.7

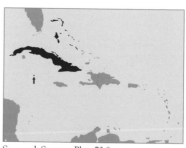
Savannah Sparrow, Plate 73.8

Lincoln's Sparrow, Plate 74.2

White-crowned Sparrow, Plate 74.4

Rufous-collared Sparrow, Plate 74.6

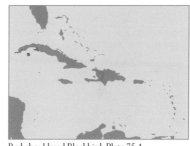

Bobolink, Plate 74.8

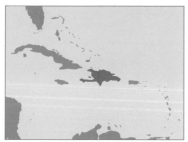

Eastern Meadowlark, Plate 75.1

Red-shouldered Blackbird, Plate 75.4

Red-winged Blackbird, Plate 75.5

Tawny-shouldered Blackbird, Plate 75.6

Yellow-shouldered Blackbird, Plate 75.7

Jamaican Blackbird, Plate 76.3

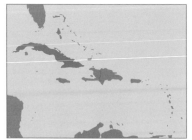

Cuban Blackbird, Plate 76.4

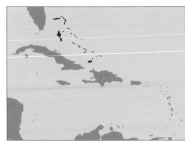

Brown-headed Cowbird, Plate 76.5

Shiny Cowbird, Plate 76.6

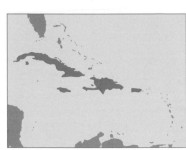

Greater Antillean Grackle, Plate 76.8

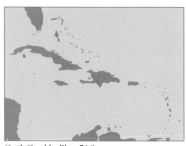

Carib Grackle, Plate 76.9

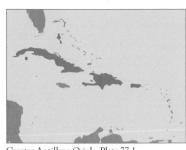

Greater Antillean Oriole, Plate 77.1

Jamaican Oriole, Plate 77.2

St Lucia Oriole, Plate 77.3

Montserrat Oriole, Plate 77.4

Martinique Oriole, Plate 77.5

Orchard Oriole, Plate 78.1

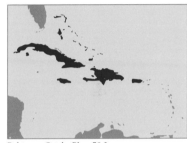

Baltimore Oriole, Plate 78.3

Troupial, Plate 78.4

Hispaniolan Crossbill, Plate 79.1

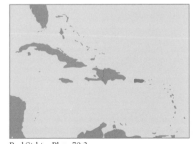

Red Siskin, Plate 79.3

Antillean Siskin, Plate 79.4

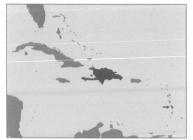

Village Weaver, Plate 79.7

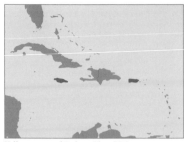

Yellow-crowned Bishop, Plate 79.8

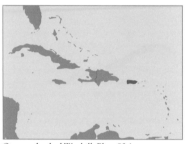

Orange-cheeked Waxbill, Plate 80.1

Black-rumped Waxbill, Plate 80.2

Red Avadavat, Plate 80.4

Indian Silverbill, Plate 80.5

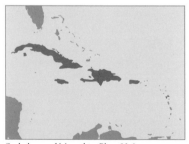

Scaly-breasted Mannikin, Plate 80.6

Chestnut Munia, Plate 80.7

232

FURTHER READING

Alström, P. & Mild, K. (2003) *Pipits and Wagtails of Europe, Asia and North America*. Helm.

Beaman, M. & Madge, S. (1998) *The Handbook of Bird Identification for Europe and the Western Palearctic*. Helm.

Bond, J. *Birds of the West Indies*. Collins.

Byers, C., Olsson, U. & Curson, J. (1995) *Buntings and Sparrows*. Helm.

Cramp, S., Simmons, K.E.L. & Perrins, C.M. (ed.) (1977–94) *The Birds of the Western Palearctic*, Vols 1–9. Oxford University Press.

Clement, P. & Hathway, R. (2000) *Thrushes*. Helm.

Clement, P., Harris, A. & Davis, J. (1993) *Finches and Sparrows*. Helm.

Curson, J., Quinn, D. & Beadle, D. (1994) *New World Warblers*. Helm.

Dickinson, E.C. (ed.) (2003) *The Howard and Moore Complete Checklist of the Birds of the World*. Helm.

Ffrench, R. (1980) *A Guide to the Birds of Trinidad and Tobago*. Harrowood.

Fry, C.H., Fry, K. & Harris, A. (1992) *Kingfishers, Bee-eaters and Rollers*. Helm.

Hancock, J. & Elliott, H. (1978) *Herons of the World*. London Editions.

Hancock, J., Kushlan, J.A. & Kahl, M.P. (1992) *Storks, Ibises and Spoonbills of the World*. Academic Press.

Harrison, P. (1983 & updates) *Seabirds: An Identification Guide*. Helm.

Hayman, P., Marchant, A.J. & Prater, A.H. (1986) *Shorebirds: An Identification Guide to the Waders of the World*. Helm.

del Hoyo, J., Elliott, A. & Sargatal, J. (eds) (1992–2009) *Handbook of the Birds of the World*, Vols 1–14. Lynx.

Jaramillo, A. & Burke, P. (1999) *New World Blackbirds*. Helm.

Madge, S. & Burn, H. (1988) *Wildfowl: An Identification Guide to the Ducks, Geese and Swans of the World*. Helm.

Madge, S. & Burn, H. (1991) *Crows and Jays*. Helm.

Madge, S. & McGowan, P. (2002) *Pheasants, Partridges and Grouse. Including Buttonquails, Sandgrouse and Allies*. Helm.

Mullarney, K., Svensson, L., Zetterström, D. & Grant, P.J. (1999) *Collins Bird Guide*. HarperCollins.

Olsen, K.M. & Larsson, H. (1995) *Terns of Europe and North America*. Helm.

Olsen, K.M. & Larsson, H. (1997) *Skuas and Jaegers: A Guide to Skuas and Jaegers of the World*. Pica Press.

Olsen, K.M. & Larsson, H. (2004) *Gulls of Europe, Asia and North America*. Helm.

Palmer, R.S. (ed.) (1962–88) *Handbook of North American Birds*, Vols 1–5. Yale University Press.

Peterson, R.T. (1980) *A Field Guide to the Birds*, 4th edn. Houghton & Mifflin.

Peterson, R.T. (1990) *A Field Guide to Western Birds*, 3rd edn. Houghton Mifflin.

Raffaele, H., Wiley, J., Garrido, O., Keith, A. & Raffaele, J. (1998) *Birds of the West Indies*. Helm.

Sibley, D. (2000) *The North American Bird Guide*. Helm.

Terres, J.K. *The Audubon Society Encyclopedia of North American Birds*. Alfred A. Knopf.

Turner, A. & Rose, C. (1989) *Swallows and Martins of the World*. Helm.

Winkler, H., Christie, D.A. & Nurney, D. (1995) *Woodpeckers: A Guide to the Woodpeckers, Piculets and Wrynecks of the World*. Pica Press.

INDEX

Accipiter gundlachi 40
  striatus 40
Actitis macularia 54
Agelaius assimilis 158
  humeralis 158
  icterocephalus 158
  phoeniceus 158
  xanthomus 158
Aix sponsa 30
Ajaia ajaja 22
Albatross, Black-browed
  10
Alle alle 70
Amandava amandava 168
Amazon, Black-billed 78
  Green-cheeked 80
  Hispaniolan 78
  Imperial 80
  Orange-winged 80
  Puerto Rican 78
  Red-crowned 80
  Red-necked 80
  Rose-throated 78
  St Lucia 80
  St Vincent 80
  Yellow-billed 78
  Yellow-headed 80
Amazona agilis 78
  amazonica 80
  arausiaca 80
  collaria 78
  guildingii 80
  imperialis 80
  leucocephala 78
  oratrix 80
  ventralis 78
  versicolor 80
  viridigenalis 80
  vittata 78
Ammodramus
  savannarum 154
Amphispiza bilineata 154
Anas acuta 30
  americana 32
  bahamensis 32
  carolinensis 30
  clypeata 32
  cyanoptera 30
  discors 30
  penelope 32
  platyrhynchos 30
  querquedula 32
  rubripes 30
  strepera 32
Anhinga 16, 172
Anhinga anhinga 16
Ani, Smooth-billed 82,
  195
Anous minutus 70
  stolidus 70

Anser albifrons 28
  caerulescens 28
Anthracothorax dominicus
  92
  mango 92
  prevostii 92
  viridis 92
Anthus rubescens 124
  spragueii 124
Apus melba 90
Aramus guarauna 24
Aratinga canicularis 76
  chloroptera 78
  euops 78
  mitrata 76
  nana 76
  pertinax 76
Archilochus colubris 94
Ardea alba 22
  cinerea 20
  herodias 20
Arenaria interpres 48
Asio flammeus 86
  otus 86
  stygius 86
Athene cunicularia 86
Auk, Little 70
Avadavat, Red 168,
  232
Avocet, American 50,
  183
Aythya affinis 34
  americana 32
  collaris 34
  marila 34
  valisineria 32

Baldpate 32
Bananaquit 144, 223
Bartramia longicauda 56
Becard, Jamaican 104,
  206
Bishop, Northern Red
  166
  Orange 166
  Yellow-crowned 166,
  232
Bittern, American 18,
  172
  Least 18, 172
  Little 18
  North American 18
Blackbird, Brewer's 160
  Cuban 160, 230
  Jamaican 160, 229
  Red-shouldered 158,
  229
  Red-winged 158, 229
  Rusty 160
  Tawny-shouldered
  158, 229
  Yellow-headed 158
  Yellow-hooded 158

  Yellow-shouldered
  158, 229
Bluebird, Eastern 116
Bobolink 156, 229
Bobwhite, Common 42
  Crested 42, 180
  Northern 42, 180
Bombycilla cedrorum 124
Bonxie 62
Booby, Blue-faced 14
  Brown 14, 171
  Masked 14, 172
  Red-footed 14, 172
  White 14
Botaurus lentiginosus 18
Brant 28
  Black 28
Branta bernicla 28
  canadensis 28
Brotogeris versicolurus 76
Bubulcus ibis 22
Bucephala albeola 34
  clangula 34
Budgerigar 76
Bufflehead 34, 177
Bullfinch, Barbados 152,
  227
  Cuban 152, 227
  Greater Antillean
  152, 227
  Lesser Antillean 152,
  227
  Puerto Rican 152, 227
Bulweria bulwerii 10
Bunting, Indigo 148, 225
  Lazuli 148
  Painted 148, 226
  Snow 156
Burhinus bistriatus 48
Buteo albicaudatus 38
  jamaicensis 38
  platypterus 38
  ridgwayi 38
  swainsoni 38
Buteogallus anthracinus
  38
Butorides striatus 18
  virescens 18

Cahow 10
Calidris alba 58
  alpina 60
  bairdii 60
  canutus 58
  ferruginea 60
  fuscicollis 60
  himantopus 60
  mauri 60
  melanotos 60
  minuta 60
  minutilla 60
  pusilla 60
Calliphlox evelynae 94

Calonectris diomedea 10
Calyptophilus frugivorus
  146
  tertius 146
Campephilus principalis
  100
Canary, Yellow-fronted
  166
Canvasback 32, 177
Caprimulgus cubanensis
  88
  carolinensis 88
  cayennensis 88
  ekmani 88
  noctitherus 88
  rufus 88
  vociferus 88
Caracara cheriway 36
Caracara, Crested 36,
  178
Cardinal, Northern 148
Cardinalis cardinalis 148
Carduelis cucullata 166
  dominicensis 166
  flammea 166
  tristis 166
Carib, Green-throated
  92, 200
  Purple-throated 92,
  200
Catbird, Grey 122, 213
Catharopeza bishopi 138
Cathartes aura 36
Catharus mustelina 118
  bicknelli 118
  fuscescens 118
  guttatus 118
  minimus 118
  ustulatus 118
Chachalaca, Rufous-
  vented 42, 181
Chaetura brachyura 90
  cinereiventris 90
  martinica 90
  pelagica 90
Charadrius alexandrinus
  52
  collaris 52
  hiaticula 52
  melodus 52
  semipalmatus 52
  vociferus 52
  wilsonia 52
Chat-tanager, Eastern
  146, 225
  Western 146, 225
Chat, Yellow-breasted
  142, 223
Chlidonias hybridus 70
  leucopterus 70
  niger 70
Chlorostilbon maugaeus
  94

ricordii 94
swainsonii 94
Chondestes grammacus 154
Chondrohierax uncinatus 38
wilsonii 38
Chordeiles gundlachii 88
minor 88
Chroicocephalus genei 64
philadelphia 64
ridibundus 64
Chrysolampis mosquitus 94
Cichlherminia lherminieri 120
Ciconia ciconia 24
Cinclocerthia gutturalis 124
ruficauda 124
Circus cyaneus 36
Cistothorus palustris 116
Coccyzus americanus 82
erythropthalmus 82
longirostris 84
melacoryphus 82
merlini 84
minor 82
pluvialis 84
rufigularis 84
vetula 84
vieilloti 84
Coereba flaveola 144
Colaptes auratus 100
fernandinae 100
Colinus cristatus 42
virginianus 42
Columba livia 72
Columbina passerina 74
Contopus blancoi 104
brunneicapillus 104
caribaeus 104
hispaniolensis 104
latirostris 104
pallidus 104
sordidulus 102
virens 102
Conure 76
Brown-throated 76
Cuban 78
Hispaniolan 78
Mitred 76
Olive-Throated 76
Orange-Fronted 76
Coot, American 46, 182
Caribbean 46, 182
Coragyps atratus 36
Cormorant, Double-crested 16, 172
Neotropic 16, 172
Olivaceous 16
Corvus jamaicensis 114
leucognaphalus 114

minutus 114
nasicus 114
ossifragus 114
palmarum 114
splendens 114
Coturnicops noveboracensis 46
Cowbird, Brown-headed 160, 230
Shiny 160, 230
Crake, Spotted 44
Yellow-breasted 44, 181
Crane, Sandhill 24, 175
Crossbill, Hispaniolan 166, 231
Crotophaga ani 82
Crow, House 114
Cuban 114, 210
Cuban Palm 114, 210
Fish 114
Hispaniolan Palm 114, 210
Indian House 114
Jamaican 114, 210
White-necked 114, 210
Cuckoo 82
Bay-breasted 84, 196
Black-billed 82, 195
Chestnut-bellied 84, 196
Common 82
Dark-billed 82
Eurasian 82
Mangrove 82, 195
Rufous-breasted 84
Yellow-billed 82, 195
Cuculus canorus 82
Curlew 56
Common 56
Eskimo 56
Eurasian 56
Long-billed 56
Cyanerpes cyaneus 144
Cyanolimnas cerverai 44
Cyanophaia bicolor 94
Cygnus columbianus 28
Cypseloides niger 90

Darter, American 16
Dendrocygna arborea 26
autumnalis 26
bicolor 26
viduata 26
Dendroica adelaidae 134
angelae 136
caerulescens 134
castanea 136
cerulea 136
chrysoparia 132
coronata 132
discolor 134

dominica 134
fusca 134
kirtlandii 134
magnolia 132
palmarum 136
pensylvanica 132
petechia 132
pharetra 136
pinus 134
pityophila 134
plumbea 136
striata 136
tigrina 132
townsendi 132
virens 134
vitellina 136
Diablotin 10
Dickcissel 150, 227
Diver, Great Northern 26, 175
Dives atroviolacea 160
Dolichonyx oryzivorus 156
Dove, American Mourning 74
Caribbean 74, 193
Collared 74, 192
Eared 74, 193
Eurasian Collared 74
European Collared 74
Grenada 74, 193
Mourning 74, 193
Necklace 74
Rock 72, 191
Spotted 74, 192
Violet-eared 74
White-winged 74, 192
Zenaida 74, 192
Dovekie 70
Dowitcher, Common 58
Long-billed 58, 186
Short-billed 58, 186
Duck, American Black 30
Bahama 30
Black-bellied Tree 26
Black-bellied Whistling 26
Black-billed Whistling 26
Cuban Whistling 26
Fulvous Tree 26
Fulvous Whistling 26, 175
Masked 34, 178
Red-billed Tree 26
Ring-necked 34, 177
Ruddy 34, 178
West Indian Tree 26
West Indian Whistling 26, 175
White-faced Tree 26

White-faced Whistling 26
Wood 30, 176
Dulus dominicus 124
Dumetella carolinensis 122
Dunlin 60, 187

Eagle, Bald 36
Egret, Cattle 22, 174
Great 22
Great White 22, 173
Little 22, 174
Reddish 20, 173
Snowy 22, 174
Western Reef 22, 174
Egretta caerulea 20
garzetta 22
gularis 22
rufescens 20
thula 22
tricolor 20
Elaenia fallax 102
flavogaster 102
martinica 102
Elaenia, Caribbean 102, 205
Greater Antillean 102, 205
Jamaican 104, 206
Yellow-bellied 102, 205
Elanoides forficatus 36
Emerald, Cuban 94, 201
Hispaniolan 94, 201
Puerto Rican 94, 201
Empidonax euleri 102
flaviventris 102
minimus 102
trailli 102
virescens 102
Estrilda melpoda 168
troglodytes 168
Eudocimus albus 24
ruber 24
Eulampis holosericeus 92
jugularis 92
Euneornis campestris 150
Euphagus carolinus 160
cyanocephalus 160
Euphonia jamaica 144
musica 144
Euphonia, Antillean 144, 223
Jamaican 144, 223
Euplectes afer 166
franciscanus 166

Falco columbarius 40
peregrinus 40
rufigularis 40
sparverius 40
tinnunculus 40

235

Falcon, Bat 40
  Peregrine 40, 180
Ferminia cerverai 116
Finch, Saffron 152, 228
  St Lucia Black 152,
    227
Flamingo, Greater 22,
    174
Flicker, Fernandina's
    100, 204
  Northern 100, 204
Florisuga mellivora 92
Flycatcher, Acadian 102,
    204
  Euler's 102, 205
  Fork-tailed 108, 208
  Great Crested 106,
    207
  Grenada 106, 207
  La Sagra's 106, 207
  Least 102
  Lesser Antillean 106,
    207
  Puerto Rican 106, 207
  Rufous-tailed 106,
    207
  Sad 106, 207
  Scissor-tailed 108
  Stolid 106, 207
  Willow 102, 204
  Yellow-bellied 102,
    205
Forpus passerinus 76
Fregata magnificens 14
Frigatebird, Magnificent
    14, 171
Fulica americana 46
  caribbaea 46
Fulmar 10
  Northern 10
Fulmarus glacialis 10

Gadwall 32, 177
Gallinago gallinago 48
Gallinula chloropus 46
Gallinule 46
  Purple 46, 182
Gallus gallus 42
Gannet 14
  Northern 14
Garganey 32
Gavia immer 26
Gelochelidon nilotica 70
Geothlypis rostrata 140
  trichas 140
Geotrygon caniceps 72
  chrysia 72
  montana 72
  mystacea 72
  versicolor 72
Glareola pratincola 48
Glaucidium siju 86
Glaucis hirsuta 92

Gnatcatcher, Blue-grey
    116, 211
  Cuban 116, 211
Godwit, Bar-tailed 58
  Black-tailed 58
  Hudsonian 58, 186
  Marbled 58, 186
Goldeneye 34
  Common 34
Goldfinch, American
    166
Goose, Blue 28
  Brent 28
  Canada 28
  Greater White-
    fronted 28
  Orinoco 28
  Snow 28, 176
  White-fronted 28
Grackle, Carib 160, 230
  Common 160
  Greater Antillean
    160, 230
Gracula religiosa 124
Grassquit, Black-faced
    150, 226
  Blue-black 150, 226
  Cuban 150, 226
  Yellow-faced 150,
    226
  Yellow-shouldered
    150, 227
Grebe, Least 26, 175
  Pied-billed 26, 175
  Red-necked 26
Greenshank 54
  Common 54
  Greater 54
Grosbeak, Blue 148, 225
  Rose-breasted 148,
    225
Ground-dove, Common
    74, 193
Grus canadensis 24
Guineafowl, Helmeted
    42, 180
Gull, American Herring
    66, 188
  Black-headed 64, 188
  Bonaparte's 64, 188
  Common Black-
    headed 64
  Franklin's 66
  Great Black-backed
    66, 189
  Laughing 66, 189
  Lesser Black-backed
    66, 189
  Little 64
  Ring-billed 66, 188
  Sabine's 64
  Slender-billed 64
Gymnoglaux lawrencii 86

Haematopus palliatus 50
Haliaeetus leucocephalus
    36
Harrier, Hen 36, 179
  Northern 36
Hawk, Broad-winged 38,
    179
  Common Black 38,
    179
  Crab 38
  Gundlach's 40, 180
  Red-tailed 38, 179
  Ridgway's 38, 179
  Sharp-shinned 40, 180
  Swainson's 38
  White-tailed 38
Helmitheros vermivorus
    138
Hermit, Hairy 92
  Rufous Breasted 92,
    200
Heron 20
  Great Blue 20, 173
  Green 18, 173
  Green-backed 18
  Grey 20
  Little Blue 20, 173
  Louisiana 20
  Night 18, 173
  Striated 18
  Tricoloured 20, 173
  Western Reef 22
Himantopus mexicanus
    50
Hirundo rustica 110
Honeycreeper, Red-
    legged 144, 223
Hummingbird,
    Antillean Crested
    92, 200
  Bee 94, 202
  Blue-headed 94, 201
  Ruby Topaz 94
  Ruby-throated 94, 201
  Rufous 94
  Vervain 94, 202
Hydrocoloeus minutus 64
Hydroprogne caspia 68
Hylocichla mustelina 118

Ibis, American White 24
  Glossy 24, 175
  Scarlet 24
  White 24, 174
Icteria virens 142
Icterus bonana 162
  cucullatus 164
  dominicensis 162
  galbula 164
  graduacauda 164
  icterus 164
  laudabilis 162
  leucopteryx 162

  mesomelas 164
  nigrogularis 164
  oberi 162
  spurius 164
Ixobrychus exilis 18
  minutus 18

Jabiru 24
Jabiru mycteria 24
Jacana spinosa 48
Jacana, Northern 48,
    182
Jacobin, White-Necked
    92
Jaeger, Long-tailed 62
  Parasitic 62
  Pomarine 62
Junco hyemalis 154
Junco, Dark-eyed 154
  Slate-coloured 154
Junglefowl, Red 42

Kestrel 40
  American 40, 180
  Common 40
  Eurasian 40
Killdeer 52, 184
Kingbird, Eastern 108,
    208
  Giant 108, 208
  Grey 108, 208
  Loggerhead 108, 208
  Tropical 108, 208
  Western 108, 208
Kingfisher, Belted 96,
    203
  Ringed 96, 203
Kinglet, Ruby-crowned
    116, 211
Kite, American
    Swallow-tailed 36
  Cuban 38, 179
  Hook-billed 38, 179
  Snail 38, 179
  Swallow-tailed 36,
    178
Kittiwake 64, 188
  Black-legged 64
Knot 58, 186
  Lesser 58
  Red 58

Lanius ludovicianus 124
Lapwing 50
  Northern 50
Larus argentatus 66
  atricilla 66
  delawarensis 66
  fuscus 66
  marinus 66
  pipixcan 66
  smithsonianus 66
Laterallus jamaicensis 46

Leptotila jamaicensis 74
   wellsi 74
Leucopeza semperi 142
Limnodromus griseus 58
   scolopaceus 58
Limnothlypis swainsonii 138
Limosa fedoa 58
   haemastica 58
   lapponica 58
   limosa 58
Limpkin 24, 175
Lizard-cuckoo, Cuban 84
   Great 84, 195
   Hispaniolan 84, 196
   Jamaican 84, 196
   Puerto Rican 84, 196
Lonchura cucullata 168
   malabarica 168
   malacca 168
   punctulata 168
Loon, Common 26
Lophodytes cucullatus 34
Loxia megaplaga 166
Loxigilla barbadensis 152
   noctis 152
   portoricensis 152
   violacea 152
Loxipasser anoxanthus 150
Lymnocryptes minimus 48

Mallard 30, 176
Mango, Antillean 92, 200
   Black 92
   Green 92, 200
   Green-breasted 92, 200
   Jamaican 92, 200
   Puerto Rican 92
Mannikin, Bronze 168
   Chestnut 168
   Nutmeg 168
   Scaly-breasted 232
Margarops fuscatus 122
   fuscus 122
Martin, Caribbean 112, 210
   Cuban 112, 210
   Purple 112, 209
   Sand 112, 209
Meadowlark, Eastern 158, 229
Megaceryle alcyon 96
   torquata 96
Melanerpes herminieri 98
   portoricensis 98
   radiolatus 98
   striatus 98
   superciliaris 98
Melanospiza richardsoni 152

Mellisuga helenae 94
   minima 94
Melopsittacus undulatus 76
Melopyrrha nigra 152
Melospiza georgiana 156
   lincolnii 156
   melodia 156
Merganser, Hooded 34, 178
   Red-breasted 34, 178
Mergus serrator 34
Merlin 40, 180
Microligea palustris 142
Mimus gilvus 122
   gundlachii 122
   polyglottos 122
Mniotilta varia 136
Mockingbird, Bahama 122, 214
   Northern 122, 213
   Tropical 122, 213
Mollymawk, Black-browed 10
Molothrus ater 160
   bonariensis 160
Moorhen 46, 182
   Common 46
Morus bassanus 14
Munia, Chestnut 168, 232
   Scaly-breasted 168
Myadestes elisabeth 118
   genibarbis 118
   sibilans 118
Mycteria americana 24
Myiarchus antillarum 106
   barbirostris 106
   crinitus 106
   nugator 106
   oberi 106
   sagrae 106
   stolidus 106
   validus 106
Myiopagis cotta 104
Myiopsitta monachus 76
Myna, Hill 124

Nandayus nenday 76
Neochen jubata 28
Nesoctites micromegas 98
Nesopsar nigerrimus 160
Nesospingus speculiferus 146
Night-heron, Black-crowned 18
   Yellow-crowned 18, 173
Nighthawk, Antillean 88, 198
   Common 88, 197
Nightjar, Cuban 88, 198
   Hispaniolan 88, 198

Puerto Rican 88, 198
   Rufous 88, 198
   White-tailed 88, 199
Noddy, Black 70
   Brown 70, 190
   Common 70
   White-capped 70
Nomonyx dominicus 34
Numenius americanus 56
   arquata 56
   borealis 56
   phaeopus 56
Numida meleagris 42
Nuthatch, Brown-headed 116
Nyctanassa violacea 18
Nyctibius jamaicensis 88
Nycticorax nycticorax 18

Oceanites oceanicus 12
Oceanodroma castro 12
   leucorhoa 12
Oenanthe oenanthe 116
Onychoprion anaethetus 70
   fuscata 70
Oporornis agilis 140
   formosus 140
   philadelphia 140
Orangequit 150, 226
Oriole, Audubon's 164
   Baltimore 164, 231
   Black-cowled 162
   Black-headed 164
   Greater Antillean 162, 230
   Hooded 164
   Jamaican 162, 230
   Martinique 162, 231
   Montserrat 162, 231
   Northern 164
   Orchard 164, 231
   St Lucia 162, 230
   Yellow 164
   Yellow-tailed 164
Ortalis ruficauda 42
Orthorhyncus cristatus 92
Oryzoborus angolensis 168
Osprey 36, 178
Otus nudipes 86
Ovenbird 138, 221
Owl, Ashy-faced 86, 196
   Bare-legged 86, 196
   Barn 86, 196
   Burrowing 86, 197
   Cuban Pygmy 86, 197
   Jamaican 86, 197
   Long-eared 86
   Short-eared 86, 197
   Stygian 86, 197
Oxyura jamaicensis 34
Oystercatcher, American 50, 183

Pachyramphus niger 104
Padda oryzivora 168
Palm-tanager, Black-crowned 146, 224
   Grey-crowned 146, 225
Palmchat 124, 215
Pandion haliaetus 36
Parakeet, Black-headed 76
   Brown-throated 76, 193
   Canary-winged 76
   Cuban 78, 194
   Hispaniolan 78, 194
   Mitred 76
   Monk 76
   Nanday 76
   Olive-throated 76, 193
   Orange-fronted 76
Pardirallus maculatus 46
Parrot, Black-billed 78, 194
   Hispaniolan 78, 194
   Imperial 80, 195
   Orange-winged 80
   Puerto Rican 78, 194
   Red-crowned 80
   Red-necked 80, 194
   Rose-throated 78, 194
   St Lucia 80, 195
   St Vincent 80, 195
   Yellow-billed 78, 194
   Yellow-headed 80
Parrotlet, Common 76
   Green-rumped 76, 193
   Guiana 76
Parula americana 130
Parula, Northern 130, 217
Passer domesticus 148
Passerculus sandwichensis 154
Passerina amoena 148
   caerulea 148
   ciris 148
   cyanea 148
Patagioenas caribaea 72
   inornata 72
   leucocephala 72
   squamosa 72
Pavo cristatus 42
Peacock 42
Peafowl, Common 42
Peewit 50
Pelecanus erythrorhynchos 16
   occidentalis 16
Pelican, American White 16
   Brown 16, 172

Petrel, Bermuda 10
    Black-capped 10, 170
    Bulwer's 10
    Capped 10
    Herald 10
    Jamaican 10, 170
    Leach's 12
    Trinidade 10
Petrochelidon pyrrhonota
    110
Pewee, Crescent-eyed
    104, 206
    Cuban 104
    Hispaniolan 104, 206
    Jamaican 104, 205
    Lesser Antillean 104,
    206
    Puerto Rican 104, 206
    St Lucia 104, 206
Phaenicophilus palmarum
    146
    poliocephalus 146
Phaethon aethereus 14
    lepturus 14
Phaetusa simplex 68
Phalacrocorax auritus 16
    brasilianus 16
Phalarope, Grey 48, 183
    Northern 48
    Red 48
    Red-necked 48, 183
    Wilson's 48, 183
Phalaropus fulicaria 48
    lobatus 48
    tricolor 48
Phasianus colchicus 42
Pheasant 42
    Common 42
    Ringed-necked 42
Pheucticus ludovicianus
    148
Philomachus pugnax 56
Phoebe, Eastern 104,
    206
Phoenicopterus ruber 22
Picoides villosus 100
Piculet, Antillean 98, 203
Pigeon, Blue 72
    Jamaican Ring-tailed
    72
    Plain 72, 191
    Red-necked 72
    Ring-tailed 72, 191
    Scaly-naped 72, 191
    White-crowned 72,
    191
Pintail 30, 176
    Bahama 30
    Northern 30
    White-cheeked 30,
    176
Pipilo chlorurus 152
Pipit, American 124

Buff-bellied 124, 214
    Sprague's 124
Piranga ludoviciana 146
    olivacea 146
    rubra 146
Plectrophenax nivalis 156
Plegadis falcinellus 24
Ploceus cucullatus 166
Plover, American
    Golden 50, 184
    Asian Golden 50
    Black-bellied 50
    Collared 52, 184
    Common Ringed 52
    Eastern Golden 50
    Great Ringed 52
    Green 50
    Grey 50, 183
    Kentish 52
    Lesser Golden 50
    Pacific Golden 50
    Piping 52, 184
    Ringed 52
    Semipalmated 52, 184
    Snowy 52, 184
    Thick-billed 52
    Wilson's 52, 184
Pluvialis dominica 50
    fulva 50
    squatarola 50
Podiceps dominicus 26
    grisegena 26
Podylymbus podiceps 26
Polioptila caerulea 116
    lembeyei 116
Pooecetes gramineus 154
Poorwill, Jamaican 88,
    198
    Least 88, 198
Porphyrio martinica 46
Porzana carolina 44
    flaviventer 44
    porzana 44
Potoo, Northern 88, 197
Pratincole, Collared 48
    Common 48
    Red-winged 48
Priotelus roseigaster 96
    temnurus 96
Progne cryptoleuca 112
    dominicensis 112
    subis 112
Protonotaria citrea 138
Pseudoscops grammicus
    86
Pterochelidon fulva 110
Pterodroma arminjoniana
    10
    cahow 10
    caribbaea 10
    hasitata 10
Puffinus baroli 12
    gravis 12

griseus 12
    lherminieri 12
    puffinus 12

Quail-dove, Blue-
    headed 72, 192
    Bridled 72, 191
    Crested 72, 192
    Grey-headed 72, 192
    Hispaniolan 72
    Jamaican 72
    Key West 72, 191
    Ruddy 72, 192
Quiscalus lugubris 160
    niger 160
    quiscula 160

Rail, Black 46, 181
    Clapper 44, 181
    King 44, 181
    Spotted 46, 182
    Virginia 44, 181
    Yellow 46
    Zapata 44, 181
Rallus elegans 44
    limicola 44
    longirostris 44
Ramphocinclus brachyurus
    122
Recurvirostra americana
    50
Redhead 32, 177
Redpoll 166
    Common 166
Redshank, Dusky 54
    Spotted 54
Redstart, American 138,
    221
Regulus calendula 116
Riparia riparia 112
Rissa tridactyla 64
Robin, American 120,
    213
    Bare-eyed 120
Rostrhamus sociabilis 38
Ruff 56, 185
Rynchops niger 70

Saltator albicollis 148
Saltator, Lesser
    Antillean 148, 225
Sanderling 58, 186
Sandpiper, Baird's 60,
    187
    Buff-breasted 50, 184
    Curlew 60
    Least 60, 187
    Pectoral 60, 187
    Red-backed 60
    Semipalmated 60, 186
    Solitary 54, 185
    Spotted 54, 185
    Stilt 60, 187

Upland 56, 185
    Western 60, 186
    White-rumped 60,
    187
    Wood 54
Sapsucker, Common 100
    Yellow-bellied 100,
    204
Sayornis phoebe 104
Scaup 34, 177
    Greater 34
    Lesser 34, 177
Screech-owl, Cuban 86
    Puerto Rican 86, 197
Seedeater, Yellow-
    bellied 150, 226
Seedfinch, Chestnut-
    bellied 168
Seiurus aurocapillus 138
    motacilla 138
    noveboracensis 138
Selasphorus rufus 92
Serinus mozambicus 166
Setophaga ruticilla 138
Shearwater, Audubon's
    12, 170
    Cory's 10, 170
    Great 12, 170
    Greater 12
    Manx 12, 170
    North Atlantic Little
    12
    Sooty 12, 171
Shoveler 32, 176
    European 32
    Northern 32
Shrike, Loggerhead 124
Sialia sialis 116
Sicalis flaveola 152
    luteola 152
Silverbill, Indian 168,
    232
    Warbling 168
Siphonorhis americanus
    88
    brewsteri 88
Siskin, Antillean 166,
    231
    Red 166, 231
Sitta pusilla 116
Skimmer, Black 70, 190
Skua, Arctic 62, 187
    Great 62, 188
    Long-tailed 62, 188
    MacCormick's 62
    Pomarine 62, 188
    South Polar 62, 188
Snipe 48, 182
    Common 48
    Jack 48
    Wilson's 48
Solitaire, Cuban 118,
    211

238

Rufous-throated 118, 211
St Vincent 118, 211
Sora 44, 181
Sparrow, Black-throated 154
  Chipping 154, 228
  Clay-coloured 154
  Grasshopper 154, 228
  House 148, 226
  Java 168
  Lark 154
  Lincoln's 156, 228
  Rufous-collared 156, 229
  Savannah 154, 228
  Song 156
  Swamp 156
  Vesper 154
  White-crowned 156, 228
  White-throated 156
  Zapata 152, 228
Sphyrapicus varius 100
Spindalis dominicensis 144
  nigricephalus 144
  portoricensis 144
  zena 144
Spindalis, Hispaniolan 144, 224
  Jamaican 144, 224
  Puerto Rican 144, 224
  Western 144, 224
Spiza americana 150
Spizella pallida 154
  passerina 154
Spoonbill, Roseate 22, 174
Sporophila nigricollis 150
Starling 124, 215
  European 124
Starnoenas cyanocephala 72
Stelgidopteryx serripennis 112
Stercorarius longicaudus 62
  maccormicki 62
  parasiticus 62
  pomarinus 62
  skua 62
Sterna antillarum 70
  dougallii 68
  forsteri 68
  hirundo 68
  maxima 68
  paradisaea 68
  sandvicensis 68
Stilt, Black-necked 50, 183
Stint, Little 60

Stork, European White 24
  White 24
  Wood 24, 174
Storm-petrel, Band-rumped 12
  Harcourt's 12
  Leach's 12, 171
  Madeiran 12, 171
  Wilson's 12, 171
Streamertail, Black-billed 94, 201
  Eastern 94
  Red-billed 94, 201
  Western 94
Streptopelia chinensis 74
  decaocto 74
Streptoprocne zonaris 90
Sturnella magna 158
Sturnus vulgaris 124
Sula dactylatra 14
  leucogaster 14
  sula 14
Swallow 110, 209
  American Cliff 110
  Bahama 110, 209
  Bank 112
  Barn 110
  Cave 110, 209
  Cliff 110, 209
  Golden 110, 209
  Northern Rough-winged 112, 209
  Tree 110, 208
  White-winged 110
Swan, Tundra 28
  Whistling 28
Swift, Alpine 90
  Antillean Palm 90, 199
  Black 90, 199
  Chimney 90, 199
  Collared 90
  Grey-rumped 90, 199
  Lesser Antillean 90, 199
  Short-tailed 90, 199
  White-collared 90, 199

Tachornis phoenicobia 90
Tachycineta albiventer 110
  bicolor 110
  cyaneoviridis 110
  euchrysea 110
Tanager, Green-tailed 142
  Hispaniolan Highland 142
  Hooded 144
  Lesser Antillean 144, 224

Puerto Rican 146, 225
  Scarlet 146, 224
  Summer 146, 224
  Swallow 146
  Western 146
Tangara cucullata 144
Teal, Blue-winged 30, 176
  Cinnamon 30
  Green-winged 30, 176
Teretistris fernandinae 140
  fornsi 140
Tern, American Little 70
  Arctic 68, 189
  Black 70, 190
  Bridled 70, 190
  Caspian 68, 189
  Common 68, 189
  Forster's 68, 189
  Gull-billed 70, 190
  Large-billed 68
  Least 70, 190
  Roseate 68, 190
  Royal 68, 189
  Sandwich 68, 190
  Sooty 70, 190
  Whiskered 70
  White-winged 70
  White-winged Black 70
Tersina viridis 146
Thalassarche melanophus 10
Thick-knee, Double-striped 48, 182
Thrasher, Brown 122
  Pearly-eyed 122, 214
  Scaly-breasted 122, 214
  White-breasted 122, 214
Thrush, Bare-eyed 120, 212
  Bicknell's 118, 212
  Cocoa 120, 212
  Forest 120, 213
  Grey-cheeked 118, 212
  Hermit 118, 212
  La Selle 120, 213
  Lesser Antillean 120
  Red-legged 120, 213
  Spectacled 120
  Swainson's 118, 212
  White-chinned 120, 213
  White-eyed 120, 212
  Wood 118, 212
  Yellow-eyed 120
Tiaris bicolor 150
  canora 150
  olivacea 150
Todus angustirostris 96

mexicanus 96
  multicolor 96
  subulatus 96
  todus 96
Tody, Broad-billed 96, 202
  Cuban 96, 202
  Jamaican 96, 202
  Narrow-billed 96, 202
  Puerto Rican 96, 203
Torreornis inexpectata 152
Towee, Green-tailed 152
Toxostoma rufum 122
Trembler, Brown 124, 214
  Grey 124, 214
Tringa erythropus 54
  flavipes 54
  glareola 54
  melanoleuca 54
  nebularia 54
  semipalmatus 54
  solitaria 54
Trochilus polytmus 94
  scitulus 94
Troglodytes musculus 116
Trogon, Cuban 96, 202
  Hispaniolan 96, 202
Tropicbird, Red-billed 14, 171
  White-tailed 14, 171
Troupial 164, 231
Tryngites subruficollis 50
Turdus aurantius 120
  fumigatus 120
  jamaicensis 120
  migratorius 120
  plumbeus 120
  swalesi 120
Turnstone 48, 183
  Ruddy 48
Tyrannus caudifasciatus 108
  cubensis 108
  dominicensis 108
  forficatus 108
  melancholicus 108
  savana 108
  tyrannus 108
  verticalis 108
Tyto alba 86
  glaucops 86

Vanellus vanellus 50
Veery 118, 211
Vermivora bachmanii 130
  celata 130
  chrysoptera 130
  peregrina 130
  pinus 130
  ruficapilla 130
  virginiae 130

Vidua macroura 168
Vireo altiloquus 128
  caribaeus 126
  crassirostris 126
  flavifrons 126
  flavoviridis 128
  gilvus 128
  griseus 126
  gundlachii 126
  latimeri 128
  magister 128
  modestus 126
  nanus 126
  olivaceus 128
  osburni 128
  pallens 126
  philadelphicus 128
  solitarius 128
Vireo, Black-whiskered
  128, 216
  Blue-headed 128, 216
  Blue-mountain 128,
  216
  Cuban 126, 215
  Flat-billed 126, 216
  Jamaican 126, 215
  Mangrove 126, 215
  Philadelphia 128, 216
  Puerto Rican 128, 216
  Red-eyed 128, 216
  St Andrew 126, 215
  Thick-billed 126, 215
  Warbling 128
  White-eyed 126, 215
  Yellow-green 128
  Yellow-throated 126,
  216
  Yucatan 128, 217
Volatinia jacarina 150
Vulture, American Black
  36
  Black 36
  Turkey 36, 178

Warbler, Adelaide's 134,
  219
  Arrow-headed 136,
  220
  Bachman's 130, 217
  Bay-breasted 136, 220
  Black-and-white 136,
  220
  Black-throated Blue
  134, 218
  Black-throated Green
  132, 218
  Blackburnian 134, 218
  Blackpoll 136, 220
  Blue-winged 130, 217
  Canada 142, 222
  Cape May 132, 218
  Cerulean 136, 220
  Chestnut-sided 132,
  218
  Connecticut 140, 222
  Elfin Woods 136, 220
  Golden-cheeked 132
  Golden-winged 130,
  217
  Green-tailed 142, 223
  Green-tailed Ground
  142
  Hooded 142, 222
  Kentucky 140, 221
  Kirtland's 134, 219
  Magnolia 132, 218
  Mourning 140
  Myrtle 132
  Nashville 130, 217
  Olive-capped 134, 219
  Orange-crowned 130,
  217
  Oriente 140, 222
  Palm 136, 219
  Pine 134, 219
  Plumbeous 136, 220
  Prairie 134, 219

  Prothonotary 138, 221
  Semper's 142, 223
  Swainson's 138, 221
  Tennessee 130, 217
  Townsend's 132
  Virginia's 130
  Vitelline 136, 219
  Whistling 138, 220
  White-winged 142,
  223
  Wilson's 142, 222
  Worm-eating 138, 221
  Yellow 132, 218
  Yellow-headed 140,
  222
  Yellow-rumped 132,
  218
  Yellow-throated 134,
  219
Waterthrush, Louisiana
  138, 221
  Northern 138, 221
Waxbill, Black-rumped
  168, 232
  Orange-cheeked 168,
  232
Waxwing, Cedar 124,
  214
Weaver, Village 166, 232
Wheatear 116
  Northern 116
Whimbrel 56, 185
Whip-poor-will 88
Whydah, Pin-tailed 168
Widow, Chuck-will's 88,
  198
Wigeon 32
  American 32, 177
  Eurasian 32
Willet 54, 185
Wilsonia canadensis 142
  citrina 142
  pusilla 142

  Wood-pewee, Eastern
  102, 205
  Western 102, 205
Woodpecker, Cuban
  Green 100, 204
  Guadeloupe 98, 203
  Hairy 100, 204
  Hispaniolan 98, 203
  Ivory-billed 100
  Jamaican 98, 204
  Puerto Rican 98, 203
  West Indian 98, 203
Woodstar, Bahama 94,
  201
Wren, House 116
  Long-billed Marsh 116
  Marsh 116
  Southern House 116,
  211
  Zapata 116, 210

Xanthocephalus
  xanthocephalus 158
Xema sabini 64
Xenoligea montana 142
Xiphidiopicus percussus 100

Yellow-finch, Grassland
  152, 228
Yellowlegs, Greater 54,
  185
  Lesser 54, 185
Yellowthroat, Bahama
  140, 222
  Common 140, 222

Zenaida asiatica 74
  auriculata 74
  aurita 74
  macroura 74
Zonotrichia albicollis 156
  capensis 156
  lecophrys 156